Gourdvine Black and White

Gourdvine Black and White

SLAVERY AND THE KILBY FAMILIES
OF THE VIRGINIA PIEDMONT

Timothy Kilby

Tree of Meaning Publications
Fairfax, Virginia

Copyright © 2021 by Timothy Kilby. All rights reserved worldwide. No part of this publication may be reproduced, distributed or transmitted in any form or by any means, including photocopying, recording, or other electronic or mechanical methods, without the prior written permission of the publisher, except in the case of brief quotations embodied in critical reviews and certain other noncommercial uses permitted by copyright law.

Published by Tree of Meaning Publications,
Fairfax, Virginia, USA
www.treeofmeaning.com

First edition: May 25, 2021

Book and cover design by the author

Publisher's Cataloging-in-Publication Data

Names: Kilby, Timothy, author.
Title: Gourdvine black and white : slavery and the Kilby families of the Virginia Piedmont / Timothy Kilby.
Description: Fairfax, VA : Tree of Meaning Publications, 2021. | Includes bibliographical references and index.
Identifiers: LCCN 2021900649 (print) | ISBN 978-1-7363748-0-1 (hardcover) | ISBN 978-1-7363748-1-8 (paperback) | ISBN 978-1-7363748-2-5 (ebook)
Subjects: LCSH: Kilby family—History. | Slavery—Virginia—History. | Slaves—Social conditions. | Race discrimination. | Virginia—History. | Genealogy. | BISAC: HISTORY / United States / State & Local / South (AL, AR, FL, GA, KY, LA, MS, NC, SC, TN, VA, WV)
Classification: LCC E445.V8 K55 2021 (print) | LCC E445.V830 (ebook) | DDC 975.5—dc23.

The way to right wrongs is to turn the light of truth upon them.
— Ida B. Wells

Contents

Map x
Principle Individuals xii
Timeline xiv
Preface xvii

Part One
SEEDS

The Promise of Light 3
"Masters, Mistresses, and Slaves" 8
The Land 20
Years of Tension, Years of Toil 27
Prelude to Freedom 36
Fractured Lives,
Indomitable Spirits 41
   Henry 42
   Sarah 43
   Juliet 48
What Name Shall We Use? 56
   Finding Juliet's Family After the War 59
   And Where is Juliet? 63
   A Question of Identity 65
   Using the Kilby Surname 68
   Simon Becomes Charles William 69
Transition to Freedom 71
Who Will Be Remembered? 77

Part Two
A TREE GROWS HERE

One Family, Separate Paths 83
Simon Kilby 86
Sarah Kilby 98
Bettie Kilby 101
John Kilby 104
James Kilby 113

Part Three
FACTS OF FAMILY

Genetic Ties 125
Conclusion 134

Appendix—
Sarah's Descendants: The First Two Generations 139

Notes 149
Bibliography 205
Index 211

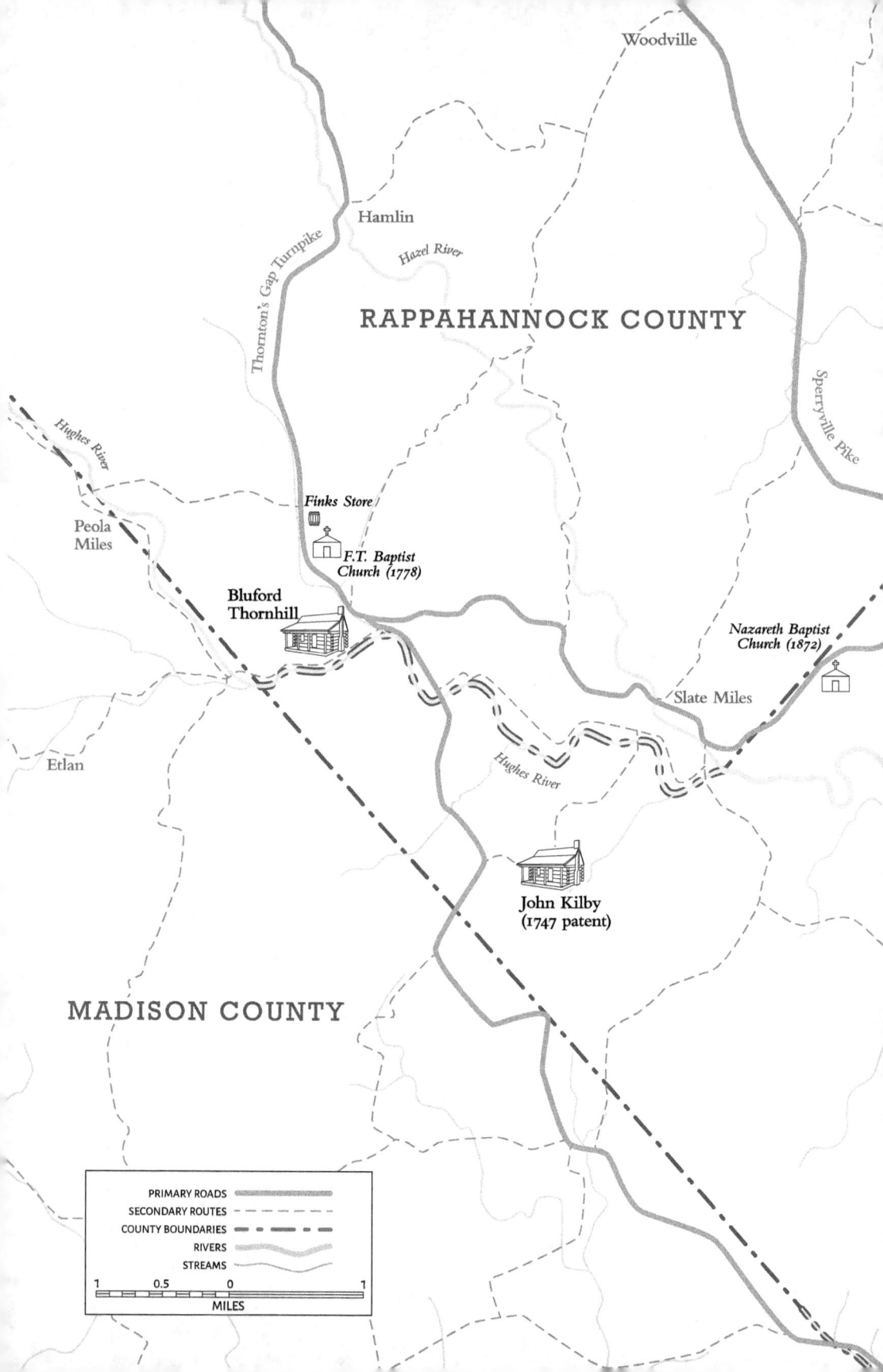

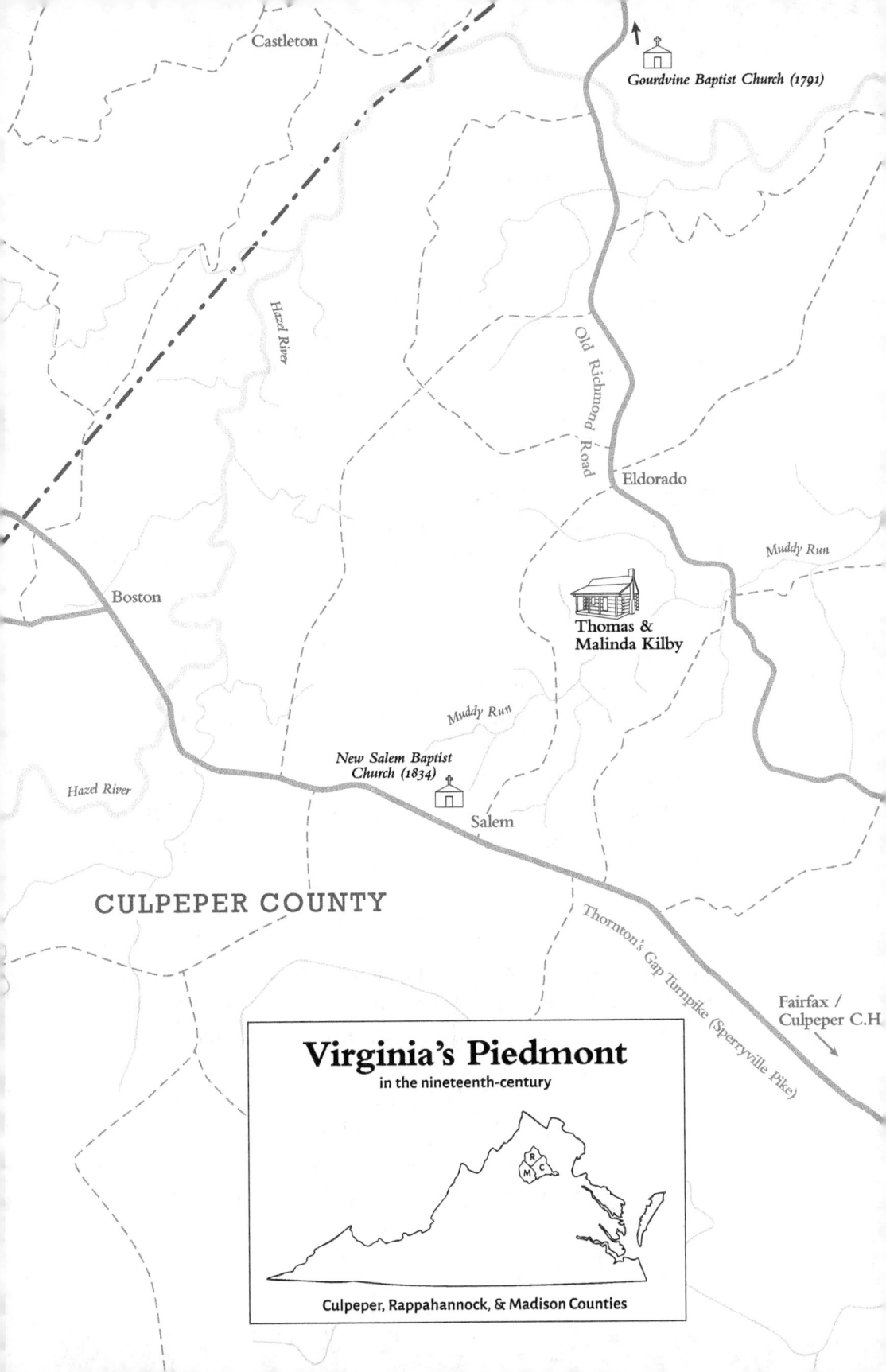

Principle Individuals

Malinda (Hawkins) Kilby Thornhill (1800–1874). The daughter of James Hawkins, wife of Thomas Kilby (widowed in 1834), and mother of their nine children. Malinda was an enslaver of Sarah, Juliet Ann, and Juliet's first four children. Malinda remarried in 1865, becoming the second wife of Bluford Thornhill.

Sarah (c. 1816–?). A woman enslaved first by James Hawkins and then Thomas and Malinda Kilby, mother of Juliet Ann. Sarah is thought to have been forcibly separated from Juliet Ann about 1839.

Juliet Ann (1834–1867). The daughter of Sarah, born enslaved by Thomas Kilby and after his death by Malinda Kilby, mother of five children, four of whom were also born legally enslaved.

Simon (a.k.a. Charles William) Kilby (1853–1924). The first child of Juliet Ann. Husband of Lucy Frances (Wallace) Kilby, father of nine children, farmer, landowner, and citizen of Madison County, Virginia.

John Kilby (1857–1932). The second child of Juliet Ann. As an adult, John migrated from Rappahannock County to Allegheny (Pittsburgh), Pennsylvania, where he married Virginia Frances Miles in 1890 and became the father of seven children.

James Kilby (1860–1949). The third child of Juliet Ann. James married Mary Eliza Richardson and migrated to Newport, Rhode Island, where they owned their home and reared their nine children. He was an employee of the city for over fifty years.

Sarah (Kilby) Reynolds (1861–1924). The fourth child of Juliet Ann, wife of James Reynolds, mother of two children. Lived in Winchester, Virginia, where she was a domestic and cook.

Elizabeth "Bettie" Kilby (1867–1921). The fifth child of Juliet, mother of two, early servant to Bluford Thornhill.

Thomas Kilby (1787–1834). A son of James and grandson of John Kilby, first husband of Malinda Hawkins, father of their nine children, planter and landowner in Culpeper County, Virginia, and enslaver.

Joseph Mortimer Kilby (1830–1888). A son of Thomas and Malinda Kilby, lead plaintiff in two legal suits against his mother, known mostly by his middle name.

James Franklin "Frank" Kilby (1820–1898). A son of Thomas and Malinda Kilby, landowner, planter, overseer. Known father of eighteen children by two wives.

Bluford Thornhill (1798–1882). A planter and landowner in Rappahannock County, Virginia, husband of Lucy (Hawkins) Thornhill, father of their ten children. After Lucy died, Bluford married Malinda (Hawkins) Kilby and became the last enslaver of Juliet Ann, Simon, John, James, and Sarah.

James Hawkins (1775–1833). The father of Malinda, father-in-law of Thomas Kilby, father-in-law of Bluford Thornhill, planter, landowner, enslaver of eight African Americans at his death.

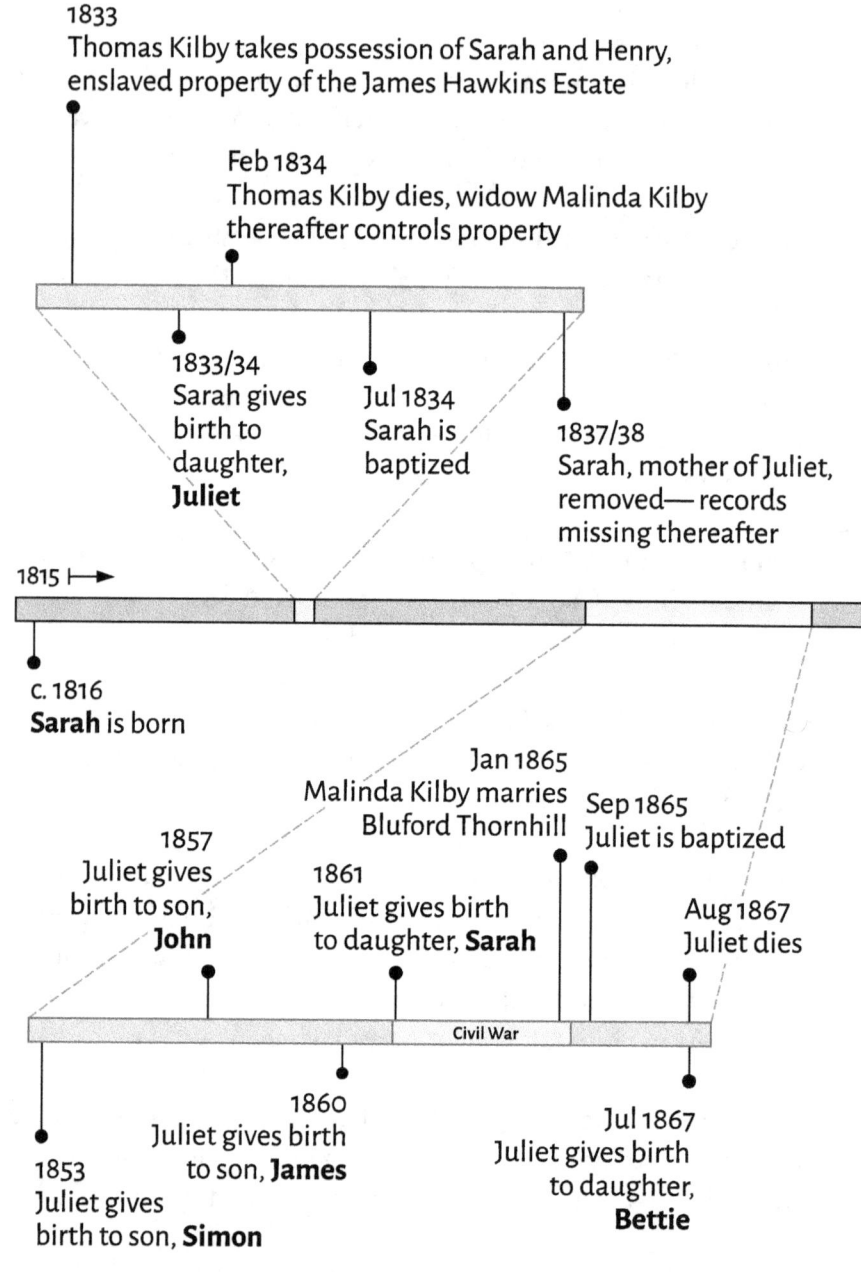

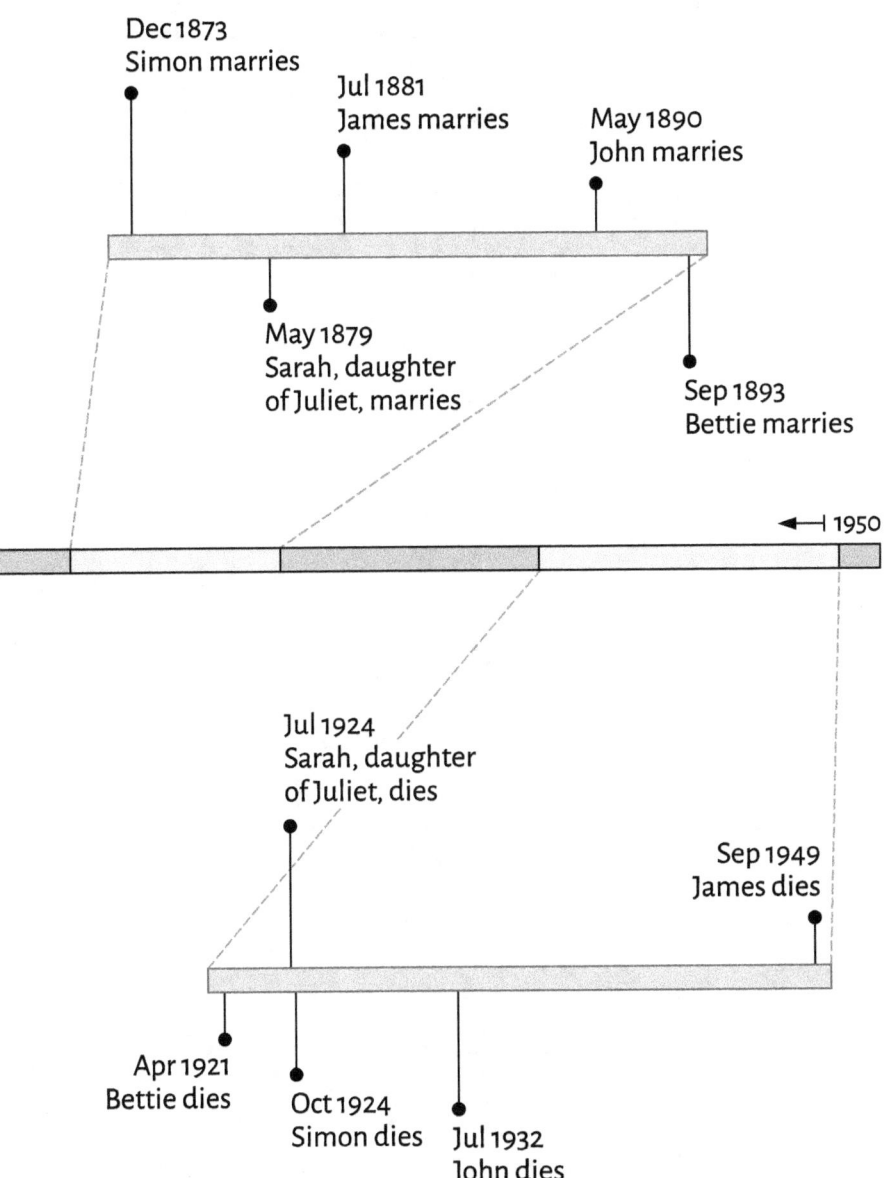

Preface

Of all human qualities, identity is most precious. To be unknown in our own time and to vanish from history's memory is not to be seen as human, not to be a person distinguishable from all others, not to be recognized for the love one receives and gives, not to be or have been. Identity connects us, one to another, and to be without identity is to be lost.

You are about to read the stories of three generations of African Americans enslaved in the Piedmont region of Virginia. You will discover their names and personalities, their relationships and events, and their stories hidden in the records. There is more than just facts to be learned. It is the existence of these individuals I wish to bring forward, for their full identities to live once again and take their place in our memories. They are present and want to be known.

Juliet Ann, born into slavery in 1834, is a central character in this true narrative. She was a mother of four children born before Emancipation and a fifth child born just as her life reached its end. Juliet's being was an inspiration to guide her children and grandchildren beyond self-doubt and the never-ending offenses born of racial prejudice. It is only through historical fragments that we can picture an existence filled with loss and abuse, an external identity denied in detail almost to life's end, but then revealed in all human qualities. Juliet survived, and she was loved by her children, who grew from her gift of endurance and of life itself.

Malinda Hawkins Kilby was Juliet's enslaver, a woman aware of her privilege to control human property as she saw fit, yet one who bore hardship and family turmoil of her own. You will see her character filled with contrasts of virtue and shortcoming, a product of her time and condition. Relatives and her encompassing White community would have sympathized with Malinda's struggles, not thinking of other sufferings that went on within her sphere of power. Malinda was playing out what she and others believed to be their birthright, perpetuating with no compunction the unending bondage of human "property" that most Virginians thought customary and morally justified. She was not unusual in this regard and is not singled out for atypical attitude and conduct. She was acting as circumstances would expect within her local social order and Southern White racial dominance.

Then there were the Kilby and Hawkins family members, some of earlier generations who set the examples for roles others would follow. There were Malinda's sons and daughters, neighbors and family associates, and a wide community that maintained beliefs and practices we now see as abhorrent and condemnable.

The Kilbys of those generations were the Kilbys of *my* ancestry, the Kilbys who left me a family name and a legacy of silence, a legacy of concealment of a disturbing reality, a legacy to open and acknowledge for its truths. My great-great-granduncle Thomas Kilby and his wife Malinda were doing no different than my great-great-grandfather Leroy, or their brothers, or their father, or his father before him—they all enslaved other human beings.

. . .

This narrative came from my extensive genealogical research of the Kilby family of Culpeper County. Genealogical research is a journey with no real end. There are only waypoints of discovery that link snapshot facts to the continuum of people's lives. You will find copious annotations and source citations in the Notes section of this book to support the facts presented herein. I encourage you to view the referenced records yourself. The age and power of the original documents found in archives and courthouses reach your soul with truth.

Beyond the written records, we can look to genetic genealogy to open doors to knowledge and reveal hidden truths. Substantial identity is carried in the DNA we unconsciously and unalterably bring forward from our progenitors. It is true in the Kilby family, just as it is true in any other family: DNA proves biological relationships and exposes secrets where records and ancestral voices were silent.

The ethos of our forebears is also a part of their legacy that becomes an inescapable influence on our own. We ask, where did our name come from? What is the powerful legacy it imposes? Hidden within the family name are the collective accomplishments and failings of our ancestors that build the cornerstones for our existence and influence the moral compass by which we live.

That which follows in this narrative attempts to relay facts thoroughly and objectively. I have gathered the thousand pieces of a jigsaw puzzle and assembled them into a complex picture. That picture is not always clear. New evidence may prove it wrong. There are pieces missing here and there for which you and I might construct different meanings. Some misinterpretation is inevitable, which may lead to disagreement but can also lead to clarity. The goal must be the truth. An authoritative nonfiction writer is not free to dismiss facts or blindly create an alternative history. The same goes for you, the reader. Seek the truth. Remember the forgotten. This is the credo that drove my research and this writing.

. . .

In this writing, I have attempted to avoid the familiar and yet demeaning language of the past, to use language that returns decency and dignity to those degraded in written and spoken content by dishonest labels. The term *slave* describes a status, not an identity or brand. I use the word *enslaved*, uncommon as this term may seem to some readers, as adjective and noun to describe a condition of servitude (or persons suffering such condition). *Slave owner* describes a legal status, but *enslaver* better characterizes the active role men—and women—took in controlling, oppressing, brutalizing, and terrorizing enslaved men, women, and children. These words are not meant to confuse a description, disguise the facts, soften meaning, or diminish sensitivities. Rather, they open the vocabulary for full, true meaning and return dignity and humanity where inhumanity prevailed.

I have chosen to capitalize *Black* as a matter of racial respect and recognition of a peoples' complex ethnicity and experience resulting from American slavery. My choice to capitalize *White* is not made for semantic symmetry. Rather, capitalizing *White* is meant to racialize and draw attention to the class of European-descended men and women who felt morally, intellectually, culturally, and even physically superior; who held power and privilege; and who used *any* means to advance their beliefs and status.

Where quoted material contained abnormal punctuation, spelling, capitalization, or phrasing in the original document, within the requirement of not changing meaning, I correct those errors.

Many citations for this research follow a structure and detail atypical for most academic writing. Sources of information useful to genealogy researchers can be quite diverse and unusual in their descriptions. Source documents can also be difficult to locate. I have followed the recommendations for documentation and citation format adopted by professional genealogists. These guidelines are adapted from those thoroughly described in the *Chicago Manual of Style*. Often, however, genealogists' citations have little resemblance to less detailed ones. With study, you will find the detailed descriptions and sources informative and useful for your own research.

. . .

I acknowledge with gratitude the staffs of the Library of Virginia, Virginia State Records Center, Rappahannock Historical Society, Hadley Library, Culpeper County Public Library, Madison County Public Library, and the Virginia Room of the Fairfax

County Public Library for their assistance in identifying, locating, and obtaining research material.

I also thank the staffs at the Clerks' offices of the Culpeper, Madison, and Rappahannock counties for directing me to rare records in the recesses of their archives. I thank the members of Fairfax Genealogical Society, Family History Writing Special Interest Group, who reviewed portions of this narrative and gave valuable criticism.

I gratefully acknowledge and give thanks to Char McCargo Bah and Tonya Singer, who read drafts, gave expert criticism and advice, and helped me grow in the understanding of perspectives beyond my own.

Special thanks are also due to the men and women who shared DNA test data in the search for genetic genealogy's truths. Protecting the privacy of these individuals requires that I not name names. Their gifts of information were essential to this story and are greatly appreciated.

Foremost, I acknowledge Janet "Phoebe" Kilby, Dr. Betty Kilby Baldwin, Rev. James M. Kilby, Roslyn Ella Lena Honesty, Barbara Corsey, and Virginia Haymon for their contributions and support for my research of *our* family's history.

PART ONE

SEEDS

As nations and as people, we cannot choose the history that we inherit, but we can choose what lessons to draw from it, and use those lessons to chart our own futures.
— United States President Barack Obama,
Address, Pearl Harbor, Hawaii,
December 27, 2016

CHAPTER ONE

The Promise of Light

1865

The coming of spring was as it had always been in the Gourdvine Neck. Dawn's last shadows faded into history as the pallid sun imperceptibly melted the last morning frost. An awakening sky filled with dancing swallows; birdsong heralded the day. Chilled breezes swirled off Ragged Mountain down the streambeds and across the rolling hills. Smoke trickled from chimneys as kitchen fires warmed pots and hands. Accustomed activities were well underway. The smell of burning oak mixed with the musty aroma of old ham. Sounds were gentle: creaks from cabin doors, footsteps on squeaking floors, muffled voices unnoticed. Mindless routine attended the homes. Outside, farm animals awaited attention. Buds on the sycamore were beginning to open. Preparations were underway for a new season of planting. The land was tranquil, beautiful, reassuring. Patterns were set, customs would prevail, order would not be disrupted—or so White Southern society demanded. But this year, in particular, marked momentous changes to come for those accustomed to privilege—and changes, too, for those with hopes for freedom.

Not far away, war's battles tested men and White Southern conviction. The clock's tick-tock amplified the weariness and despair that built up over too many years. A social institution with the permanence of stone was at risk of crumbling. The calendar had turned to '65. A time of reckoning was fast approaching.

The Gourdvine was no longer the wilderness the early settlers found more than a century earlier. Virginia had grown from its colonial past. The area was populated and thriving. In this narrow geographic appendage of Culpeper County, a rifle report could be heard in neighboring Madison County to the west and Rappahannock County to the north. For those with privilege, travel was easy by road or by trail. A trip to Culpeper Court House would take two hours by ambling horse. Woodville, Sperryville, and Little Washington to the north and Madison Court House to the south—these were just place names where goods might be traded, news and gossip shared. Jurisdictional borderlines controlled governmental affairs, where officials levied taxes and judges held court. But on the ground and in daily lives, those county boundaries were invisible and mostly meaningless. For those bound to place, there was no *there*—there was only *here*.

Gourdvine Neck lay at the intersection of the three jurisdictions, where the Hughes River flowed in curves around wooded hills, merging into the Hazel River and downstream currents.[1] Early cartographers did not need an aerial perspective to liken the twisting river course to the familiar garden vine, and thus they would create the sectional name. Maps showed the roadways and the mountain tops and the river mills. Commerce followed the flow of the streams. Mill wheels turned slowly, capturing nature's power to saw the timber or grind the harvested grain. The land was bountiful, though life's labor was arduous and unending. Economic, political, and social structures were in place, giving a sense of stability and security—at least up to the last decade. Now, the future was in question.

As on any day, Juliet attended to the wants of her aged enslaver,

Malinda.[2] Commands required immediate obedience. There would have been little time left over from her many duties to look after her own four children. Simon, the oldest at age twelve, probably had been given his defined duties: splitting kindling and bringing in firewood before feeding the animals.[3] Milch cows and hogs, guineas and dogs; they would need tending and take priority over his morning hunger. He likely also had to keep reign over his siblings: John and James, ages eight[4] and five[5], and his sister Sarah, age three.[6] They, too, were learning the life of toil. Juliet had recently turned thirty-one; any appearances of youth had long since passed. New labors followed completed ones—little respite, no change. Still, her thoughts were her own, surely resistance among them. Escape, she may have thought, but what of the consequences and how with four children to consider? News of the war—what Juliet could overhear in White conversations and piece together from incomplete details, facts and guesses filtered by time and the telling—was as stale as the previous day's bread that remained for her children. Neither souls nor bodies would be nourished by military reports not relevant to their immediate situations. Would liberty ever come? Was freedom possible?

Malinda was settling into marriage with her new husband, Bluford Thornhill.[7] They were married just days into the new year, widow and widower, each now beyond their years, each having known the other since youth. The circumstance of the marriage may have appeared unseemly to many and suspicious to her grown children, sudden as it was and to a degree threatening.

Malinda's first husband, Thomas Kilby, had accumulated land and the necessities to operate a farm decades earlier.[8] His ambition surely had been to advance his wealth as a typical planter, and like so many of his neighbors, owning human property fit his plan. Then, his sudden death in 1834, when husband and wife were carefree and prospering, left Malinda ill-prepared to support and tend to their nine children.[9] No will, no plan, no solace to ease the family and guide them forward. The years that followed were tough on widow and progeny. Malinda's debts and, some might say, a misguided determination would take their toll. Yet, some had suffered far more than she. Juliet, across the chasm of racial identity, bearing a different perspective on what freedom meant and survival required, watched it all unfold.

Decades had passed, and Malinda, as administratrix of Thomas's estate, had ignored settlement of the property.[10] The division had dragged on far too long. The children had reached maturity and could receive their divisions outright. But she minded her own judgment, maintaining control and possession of the real and personal property that Thomas once held and what it all had grown to be.

Malinda's son Mortimer, a middle child in the Kilby brood, took the lead in filing suits for the division and transfer of his inheritance.[11] Malinda, now Mrs. Thornhill, still held the Kilby enslaved property under her control.[12] Was Mortimer upset by his mother's late marriage, or was he motivated by greed to grab something of value before a scorned step-father claimed possession? We will never know. Legal disagreements followed. Whatever the reason, Mortimer's second chancery suit against his mother, filed soon after her second marriage, left the written record of unsettled grievances in the family, just as it provided given-name identities for the human chattel in contention: Juliet and her children. Here was the document, the evidence, the confirmation—names for delving into the past and following a forgotten family forward.

The facts were these: Juliet and her four children were born enslaved, bound in labor and body to their Kilby enslavers. They were the property that Malinda could use—and did—as collateral for debts, to manipulate as she saw fit.[13] They were unwitting pawns in family disputes, without a say in their destinies. They were also human beings who would eventually be among the freed persons struggling to make lives anew in a locale filled with White anger, hate, and hostility.

However, on this day in 1865, the future lived in dreams; only the past was clear and certain. The tasks for the day had to be completed, commands obeyed. How Juliet and her children bore the indignities of position and deprived humanity, how they overcame hardships and the injustice of stolen labor, and how they built new lives is a story of resilience, perseverance, and hard work. The starting point for their story began many years earlier.

CHAPTER TWO

"Masters, Mistresses, and Slaves"

1833–1834

Born around 1800 to well-to-do parents James and Sarah Hawkins, Malinda Hawkins and her three brothers and two sisters grew up in relative comfort.[1] Enslaved house servants cooked their meals and cleaned their clothes. Field hands tilled the land, harvested the crops, and tended the livestock that created the profits. When James Hawkins died in 1833, he left a considerable estate: 440 acres of land among four parcels, nine horses, forty sheep, twenty-four cows, thirty-two hogs, great quantities of farming implements, home furnishings, crops and stores, and eight enslaved human beings.[2] Malinda's father was a wealthy man.

Like all such women of her class, Malinda grew to understand her predestined role in a male-dominated White household served by enslaved women, men, and children.[3] Malinda's father was literate and had books in his house, which might have given Malinda an early start in her own abilities to read and write, a general expectation of someone in a leading family.[4] Cooking, sewing, and keeping house would not have been something she would have been taught—there were always servants forced to do those chores. Also, there was no need to understand the details of handling money, operating a farm, or managing the enslaved property. Those were men's responsibilities. The ladies of the house only needed to show a degree of gentility to foster a family's reputation.

Was this an accurate portrait of Malinda as a young woman? If the grit Malinda would find later in life is any indication, she did not fit the stereotypical dainty, helpless Southern belle. The years as wife and bearer of nine children were otherwise unremarkable—that is, until family burdens fell to her shoulders following her husband's sudden death. Through observation, she had learned from father and brothers and husband the role of farm manager, though she never expected to have to put that knowledge into practice. Her tests of skill, fortitude, and survival would come to dominate her life for the next forty years.

Malinda's father was a prominent landowner in his own right and a son of Matthew Hawkins, patriarch of a large family with great land ownings.[5] As a family of some wealth, Matthew Hawkins's children could each look forward to a worthy inheritance, a view lacking consideration for the impact on those who actually created the wealth. Matthew prepared an explicit will, and when he died in 1820, he left to his wife and progeny sixteen enslaved men, women, and children.[6] Distributions always meant that enslaved families might be broken apart. Matthew's son James—he was an enslaver on his own for many years—inherited real estate that added land holdings to that which he already owned.[7] The James Hawkins lands, comprised of a number of tracts, stretched across the Gourdvine Neck of Culpeper County from the Hughes River to the Madison County border and beyond.[8] Any suitor of James's daughters would have known that marrying into the Hawkins family would be financially advantageous. Out of mind would have been the suffering that the enslaved would endure.

Living close to the Hawkins family were the Kilbys, early settlers and planters like the Hawkinses. Common religious beliefs led members of the two families to the same church, where they could socialize and gossip after hearing admonishing messages from zealous Baptist ministers.[9] It was also a place where young men could meet potential mates.

. . .

Malinda Hawkins might have first met the man she would marry at church. Thomas Kilby, born in 1787, was the fifth son of James and Lucy (Sparks) Kilby.[10] His grandfather, John Kilby, patriarch of the Kilby family, died fifteen years earlier.[11] Thomas would have heard the story of how John came in 1747 to the Blue Ridge foothills of Virginia to settle on land he obtained from the vast Northern Neck Proprietary of Thomas Lord Fairfax.[12]

As a landowning planter far from centers of commerce, John Kilby would have found self-sufficiency essential. He raised some livestock—horses, cattle, hogs, and sheep—and grew crops for personal consumption and trade.[13] John is thought to have built and lived in a log house, probably with an outbuilding or two. In the vernacular of the time, he and others would refer to a farmable tract with a house and outbuildings as a plantation, though a grand interpretation of that term would not be fitting. If it were not for the fact that at least one enslaved person was forced to labor there, John would have been considered a yeoman, an independent planter reaping the benefit of ones' own labor. For the standards of that time and place, his family enjoyed a comfortable life, rewarded as one could expect to be as White citizens with class privilege.

Probate records indicate that John, who died in 1772, had prospered and was able to leave certain real and personal property of value to family members.[14] Evidence that John was an enslaver appears in his estate's inventory.[15] Among the listing of farm tools, livestock, furniture, and cooking utensils, there is another item: one "servant man" valued at twenty pounds currency. Nothing else is known about John's enslaved man, not his name, whence he came, for how long he was held in bondage, nor how he was used on the plantation, though one might assume he was a forced field laborer.

Perhaps the virtue of work, the prosperity and self-respect coming from one's own labor, had not abandoned John Kilby as he aged, but this attitude would change within his descendants as evident in their increased reliance on forced labor from enslaved servants.

James Kilby, fourth of John and Elizabeth Kilby's six sons, inherited a portion of his father's land and continued the tradition of farming. James and his first and second wives together produced three daughters and seven sons.[16] Culpeper County Personal Property Tax records for years 1782 to 1864, combined with United States censuses and slave schedules show that James Kilby and all of his sons—Joseph, John, Henry, Leroy, Thomas, St. Clair, and Thompson Albert—were enslavers at various times.[17]

In the eighteenth and nineteenth centuries, Virginia counties levied a capitation tax (at times known as a head tax or poll tax) each year on White males aged sixteen and older to be paid by the head of the house. Heads were usually men but sometimes women, unmarried adults or widows. They also had to pay a tax on their enslaved property sixteen years of age or older (in a few years as young as twelve), both male and female. That portion of the levy was for *property* the person owned. The enslaved persons were property, along with the livestock, wagons and other wheeled vehicles, watches, and clocks that identified one's wealth to be taxed. The tax collectors opened their ledgers, penned the facts, collected the monies, and maintained the books as a matter of public record.

These tax books hold counts of persons sixteen and over whom the county's White citizens enslaved. What about all the children held in bondage? Enslaved children as young as four were required to begin work as field hands or house servants, but children up to the age of sixteen were not considered to be taxable property and not included in counts of slaves for the poll tax. Not until 1862 were counts of slaves of *all* ages recorded in the tax books. Because of inconsistencies in who would be included for purposes of taxing, an accurate count of all enslaved persons from year to year is not possible. Nonetheless, records show that James Kilby and sons enslaved numbers of men, women, and children through the years.[18] With only a few exceptions, as will be told, the identities and fates of these human beings remain unknown.

The tradition of working the land and prospering through ownership motivated White settlers and their aspiring offspring. James Kilby and wife Lucy had started their family at the time of the American Revolution, and after briefly serving the patriot cause, James resumed his life as a planter.[19] James's sons, including son Thomas, learned from their father and the community of surrounding landowners the value of owning enslaved human property to ease an owner's burden and increase one's wealth and standing among the White master class.

. . .

Thomas Kilby would follow the models before him—those of his father, uncles and aunts, and grandfather before them, and those of neighbors and family associates—of increasing his land holdings and buying human property for their labor.[20] Thomas's brother Leroy provided a start by selling him 139 acres of land downslope from Stonehouse Mountain and along the upper reaches of Muddy Run, seven miles east of John Kilby's original landholdings.[21] On this hilly tract, Thomas built his house, harvested timber, grazed livestock, cultivated fields, and commanded the labor of enslaved Blacks. The mythic image of the large Southern plantation with a multi-roomed manor house at its center and multitudes of enslaved laborers indoors and out in the fields is not accurate for Thomas's modest enterprise. He never had the acreage or numbers of enslaved people to compare with the wealthy gentry, though his ambitions certainly leaned that way. His status was somewhere between planter and farmer. Yet calling his operation a farm, which evokes contemporary visions of peaceful, virtuous, self-reliant agricultural activity, distorts the dark reality of the time. No, *plantation* is closer to the truth.

Marrying well and rearing a large family would increase Thomas's prospects, and that was undoubtedly his plan. Thomas Kilby and Malinda Hawkins married on the second day of January 1817.[22] Malinda was only seventeen when she married, and Thomas was thirty. He was likely anxious to start a family, and Malinda obliged with the birth of a girl, Martha Ann.[23] In 1820, a son was born. They named him James Franklin.[24] Frank, as he would later be known, was followed in birth by Louisa, Missouri, Adeline, Chesterfield, Mortimer, Thomas L. (only his middle initial is known), and Burgess, the last of their children, born in 1833.[25] These are the names that you will hear over and over as the story unfolds.

There it was, a large family like many others of the time, but one that would endure tragedy, turmoil, and dysfunction in years to come. Drawn in as unfortunate victims of this White family's troubles were the enslaved people they held: Sarah and her daughter Juliet, and Juliet's children as their young lives unfolded. Whites and Blacks, haves and have-nots—the roles were fixed, and the hierarchy was clear to all.

The U.S. census offers once-a-decade snapshots of the household makeup of the Thomas Kilby family in the early years and beyond. Without separately recorded evidence, in-between years hold mystery. The local personal property and land tax rolls, produced annually at the county level, help fill the gaps. The 1820 U.S. federal census, for example, shows that Thomas Kilby enslaved one unnamed, middle-aged woman that year.[26] Ten years later, the personal property tax ledger for Culpeper County indicated he enslaved an individual above age sixteen, sex and name unknown.[27]

Tax ledgers are an important source of information about the enslavers of Virginia and the human property they held in bondage. Enslaved men and women as young as age sixteen, and in some years as young as age twelve, were counted as taxable property.

Except in rare instances in the later eighteenth century, names of slaves in Culpeper County were not recorded in the ledgers. The counts for tax purposes are useful in gauging the extent of enslavement in a local area and the enslaver's other holdings. However, the pictures are incomplete. Enslaved children under age twelve were not counted nor taxable.[28] The yearly tax lists never provided counts of *all* slave holdings, and thus the picture of slavery on any one plantation often was much worse. For whatever reason—absent individuals, hired-out slaves, purposeful misinformation, inaccurate recording—and in spite of substantial penalties for misleading or fraudulent information, there were occasional errors and gaps in information in both censuses and tax lists.

If researchers are to believe the county tax records as complete and accurate, Thomas did not own working-age slaves continuously during his adult years. In some years, yes. No records identify by name the two slaves counted for years 1820 and 1830. The number of enslaved children he held is unknown. Not until 1833, and from a different source, do we learn singular descriptions and named identities of Thomas's and Malinda's newly acquired human property.[29]

. . .

In May 1833, Malinda's father, James Hawkins, died.[30] He had a considerable estate but had prepared no will. Since his wife had died earlier, James's six children were left to inherit the real and personal property.[31] For James's three daughters, their inheritance would become the legal property of their husbands, who would make decisions on their wives' behalf. The heirs agreed to sell Hawkins's land holdings and split the proceeds equally, which they quickly did.[32] A public estate auction was a common solution for disposing of tangible personal property, with the heirs buying items at the sale and having the prices deducted from their share of an inheritance.

But when it came to Hawkins's enslaved people, individuals whom some heirs wanted to retain for themselves, an equitable division was problematic. A private sale among the heirs was needed, and to that solution they agreed.[33] In effect, they conducted an auction at which only family members were allowed to bid. Thus, the slave property was divided, and each heir received an equal share in either cash or human chattel.

The probated inventory ordered by the court itemized James Hawkins's personal property and affixed dollar values to each owned asset.[34] Once the property was sold, an account of the proceeds became part of the public record.[35] Here, along with the names of the purchasing heirs, were the names of eight individuals: men named Isaac, Andrew, and Ben; a "woman" named Betty with "child" Mary; a "girl" named Rachel; a "boy" named Henry; and a "girl" named Sarah.

Son and estate heir Augustine Hawkins purchased Isaac. Brother Thomas J. Hawkins bought Andrew, Betty, and Mary. A son-in-law,

Record of the sale of enslaved persons from the James Hawkins estate, 1833.

Jacob Rudasilla, bought the man named Ben. Bluford Thornhill, the husband to James's daughter Lucy—and a man who will be prominent as this story unfolds—bought Rachel. That left the two most valuable persons: Henry, for whom Thomas Kilby paid the estate $510, and Sarah, for whom he paid $365, the values as debits on Malinda's inherited share.[36] The agreed prices for the enslaved human property were such that some heirs ended with debits and others ended with credits, all to be sorted out by the estate's administrator in the final accounting.[37] Augustine Hawkins, the administrator for his father's estate, failed somewhat in bookkeeping and disbursements, a situation that caused Malinda to file suit six years later to correct neglected distributions.[38] Details of the estate's distributions are revealed within the suit records.

The 1830 census shows that among the nine unnamed enslaved people James Hawkins owned that year, five were males aged from ten to twenty-four. Four were female: one under ten years old, two from ten to twenty-four years, and one between thirty-six and fifty-five.[39] Could these be age range descriptors for Mary, Rachel, Sarah, and Betty, respectively? While only one biological relationship is evident, that of Betty and her child Mary, other kinships are possible, if not probable. Given that in 1834 Henry was described as a "boy," in 1830 he was likely in the youngest end of the ten to twenty-four age category of the census. The facts and descriptions, few as they are, create the possibility that Betty was the mother of two of the three younger female slaves, maybe all three. She may also have been the mother of one or more of the males. It is not beyond the possibility that Sarah and Henry were brother and sister. But a possibility is not evidence, and no evidence constitutes proof of biological kinships. Nonetheless, there were certainly "created kinships," strong social and emotional bonds among the enslaved people on the James Hawkins plantation, family-like connections that would be cruelly broken once the heirs dived up their Hawkins's property.

The death of an enslaver and the division of his property thereafter too frequently resulted in the separation of Black families. No question can be raised that bonds of love and affection existed among some or all of the Hawkins enslaved people. The tragedy deepens with the thought that 1833 may have been the last time man and wife, mother and child, brother and sister, persons in this enslaved group, fictive families or true kin, were able to see and comfort each other.

. . .

Thomas and Malinda Kilby were fulfilling their dream. They had nine children, and they had property: land, livestock, and human property. Debts Thomas accrued along the way would be paid, they thought, without concern. Their plan was being fulfilled.

Then in February 1834, the unforeseen happened—Thomas Kilby died.[40]

He was only forty-seven, the cause of his death unknown. Was it an accidental death? Many perils accompanied those working the land. Or perhaps a sudden illness? Ailments considered trivial today were serious and often fatal in the early nineteenth century. Whatever took Thomas to his Maker, his death remains a mystery. One imagines it was sudden and quite unanticipated, for he had not prepared a will.

The reality of Malinda's situation as head of household, provider, manager, and debt holder quickly set in. Her children, the oldest age fifteen and the youngest an infant not yet one, needed all the same care as before. Genteel dependency on a husband and father was over. She was instantly forced into new roles for which she was ill prepared.

The county court appointed Malinda administratrix, and an inventory of Thomas's personal property was ordered and submitted to record.[41] Distribution of the real and personal property would not be completed for decades and would become contentious. But in 1834, all of Malinda's children were still young. Whereas in some cases a male, relative or otherwise, would be

The 1834 inventory of the Thomas Kilby estate that includes three enslaved persons.

appointed by the court to act as guardian of the children until their respective ages of maturity, Malinda's role was not contested and no court involvement was necessary to stipulate the relationship and responsibilities.[42] Malinda took control of all the assets.[43]

Among the probated inventory of personal property—the livestock, the wheat and rye crops, the tools and farm equipment, and the household furniture—the list included the most significant and most valuable items: "Negro Boy, Henry – $400.00" and "Negro woman, Sarah & her child, Juliett Ann – $300.00."[44] The enslaved persons who had numbered two less than five months before now numbered three—a new name and a new life. What would their futures hold?

CHAPTER THREE

The Land

1822–Today

"Beginning at a forked pine gum and white oak sapling corner to Charles M Tutt thence with his line N 67¼ W thirty-two poles to three white oaks standing on each side of the road . . ." Thus begins a metes and bounds description, the compass directions and distances, the straight lines and meanders that comprise a legal description of "a certain tract or parcel of land" amounting to 139 acres. The 1822 deed's description, recorded in Culpeper County's official books for posterity and all to see, was sufficient in the transfer of land title from Leroy Kilby to brother Thomas.[1] What Thomas bought, though, was not lines and angles and compass directions; it was the fields where crops could be planted, the forests from which lumber could be cut, the creeks and a stream where water could be drawn; it was where a cabin site could be chosen and building stones could be gathered; it was a cradle for sky-view breezes and life-giving rains; it was game for the taking; it was protection and security, a home and a future. And it was a place where he and his family could prosper from the stolen labor of others.

Many features of this location have changed very little since Thomas and Malinda's first years. The land was mostly forested—majestic oaks of many types, chestnut, hickory, red cedar, poplar, cherry, and black walnut, and below the canopy, dogwood, chinquapin, sassafras, pawpaw, and persimmon. This was not the virgin land as seen by the earliest settlers; patches had been cleared for crops and livestock grazing. Thomas planted crops of corn for feeding livestock and wheat and rye for cash.[2] Trails and rudimentary wagon roads provided access in and out. A short distance to the north was the Richmond Road and to the south the Thornton's Gap Road, well-traveled arteries for journeys to families and friends, church, and markets in the county seat of Culpeper (or Fairfax, as it was called in those days).

Two hundred and fifty yards down from the highest point of the property, protected from the harshest winds, the slope eased to a flattop knoll before easing further to a streamlet and one of Muddy Run's tributaries. It was a good site for a cabin, and this

Site where the Thomas and Malinda Kilby plantation house once stood. (Photo by author)

was where Thomas and Malinda built. Likely the unassuming house was of timber-frame construction sitting on a foundation of local stone, with a rock chimney at one side and lined with handmade bricks. A giant sycamore stands sentinel today over

Old sycamore tree still standing near the foundation of the plantation house. (Photo by author)

younger trees, it perhaps old enough to have shaded Thomas and Malinda's homestead and all who lived and worked there.

Down from the flat of the cabin site are two island piles of smaller stones, perhaps waste from shaping larger ones. Or they could be the remains of some structure, now collapsed and melting into the hillside. Could these be the locations of outbuildings or slave quarters? No evidence provides an answer.

In 1823 Culpeper County levied a tax of $0.78 on Thomas's land, purchased the previous year and valued at $973.[3] No value was placed on buildings, if any had stood at the time. That land value did not change year to year until 1840 when the 139 acres was assessed at $695, a reduction in proportion to other tracts in the records. One year later, 1841, the land tax rolls show a fifty-dollar value for buildings on Thomas's (now Malinda's) land, the apparent minimum assessment for building improvements across all County records, an indication of very modest structures. Not until 1847 were building improvements assessed at double the prior amount, and not until 1851 did the land value exclusive of structures increase slightly. But is the 1841 assessment for improvements, the first time taxing a structure on this tract, an indication of the date when the plantation house was constructed? Many plausible explanations make it unclear exactly when before 1841 the family's cabin was constructed and first inhabited.[4]

The 139-acre tract is not the only one Thomas Kilby owned. In September 1833, at the same time the Hawkins' estate was being divvied up and Thomas got Henry and Sarah as enslaved property, he bought more land.[5] Of two parcels included in the purchase, one he quickly resold.[6] The other, a tract of 115 acres, was later set apart as Malinda's dower land, but the tract eventually fell to a tenant who provided Malinda some desperately needed financial relief.[7]

All of the cabin on the original tract is gone today except for the half-buried stone rubble from the presumed foundation and chimney, fallen remnants on their way to being reclaimed by the earth, gracefully blending with grasses and scrub trees, hiding secrets that cannot be told. No outline is visible to indicate size or shape or exact location. Two other rock piles some distance away mark locations where outbuildings may have stood, where the enslaved may have slept, where whatever history any buildings once held vanished in the dust and rains. Where the main cabin once stood, no walls or floors or wooden materials of any kind remain, having either rotted away or been carried off long ago. No artifacts survive to clarify the story of the White Kilby family that once lived here and the other people they bound to work the surrounding land—that is, except for one found object.

...

It was a late September day in 2019. The landowner pointed to a hill in the distance and offered a ride on his four-wheeler to save a long walk. I was set free to roam at my leisure. A few cirrus clouds sought no attention. The soft blue sky framed a brilliant noon sun, a perfect day to walk silently and explore where ancestors once lived. Under a cluster of trees, I was told, I would find the remains where a house once stood. Alone to take it all in, to contemplate what I would have seen if I had been here two centuries earlier, I surveyed the ground under the giant sycamore, looking for something to reveal the story of this place. The voices of my thoughts rushed forward. *Just there, were those stones once a wall?* I thought. I shuffled a withered branch aside to see what was underneath—nothing but more dirt and corners of stones half-buried. Over here, more stones, surfaces smooth, corners recognizable, seemingly shaped for a purpose. I could make no sense, but I looked for more clues. I wandered to the left, looking down at tufts of field grass, moldering animal dung, some bare patches catching dried and curled leaves, tidbits of moss, light and shadows patterned by the leafy canopy. The corner of something reddish and hard caught my eye. I brushed aside some blades with my foot to see if it was worth investigating. *What's this?* Squatting down, I pulled a brick from the ground,

Brick from the Thomas and Malinda Kilby plantation site. (Photo by author)

lifted it to shake off loose debris, and picked away at caked dirt stuck to its back and sides. My pulse quickened as I realized there was something more, something out of the ordinary, something unusual, something special, very special. What this brick's surface *should* look like—its texture, its color, its general uniformity with all others—was different here in one significant way. I recognized what may be the imprint of fingertips, and then a palm. *Yes, it is a handprint!* I placed my hand in comparison and judged the imprint to be smaller, not of a young child but of a woman or a young man. I recalled the names of those known to have been here. My mind raced. *Could this be . . . ? Is it . . . ?* I processed what I was seeing with what I knew of history and how bricks were made and who made them and how this brick may have come into being and whether it was coincidence or luck or fate that brought me to this exact spot and what mysteries were working to make sure I found it and it found me. *Henry? Sarah? Juliet?*

. . .

The very earliest images created by ancient humans were of their hands, signatures as such on cave walls and cliff faces, not accidents but intentional expressions to tell others known and unknown, "I existed." Was this nineteenth-century brick's maker consciously creating something similar, made and separated out in hopes someone in time near or far would find it and remember? Was it a symbol of resistance like spit in the water bucket? Or was it an accidental blemish, to its maker unworthy of correction or further notice, likely to be covered with mortar and hidden forever? Were there awareness and motivation in its making? Does it tell a story for and about the enslaved of this property?

As if finding me, rather than the other way around, a single brick from the site reveals its maker in the form of a handprint captured and hardened through firing, an imperfection finding greatest value through time and the circumstances of its creator, an unsure identity but likely of one I know bound to this land, an imprint that speaks directly to me of one and for many.

CHAPTER FOUR

Years of Tension, Years of Toil

1834–1865

Hard times were with Malinda from the day her husband died. The burden of responsibility, the power of control, was now hers alone. She was in charge, and the fate of others—and her own—was from then on dependent on her decisions.

The realities of supporting the family through the vagaries of farming created great stress, all in a time when the oldest children were about to leave home and the others were asserting their independence. Finding the means to survive was Malinda's first concern. Her assets became her security: the land, the crops she could grow, and the estate property she controlled, including chattels.

The debts that Thomas incurred, with no forethought as to how they would be repaid should he die, soon came due. Thomas had borrowed against his land holdings and his estate, meaning Malinda as administratrix and the only adult heir-at-law was legally responsible for paying the debts.

The first shock came in June 1836 when a creditor took Malinda to court for a debt of $751.50 plus interest and costs.[1] In addition to the 139 acres of land Thomas Kilby had purchased from his brother in 1822, he bought another nearby tract only five months before his death, and it appears he had not rendered the full purchase price at the time of sale.[2] The circuit court issued a judgment against Malinda, inheritor of the debt, to be paid "in money &^{c} to be levied of the goods & chattels of the defendants intestate in the hands to be administered if so much thereof she hath."[3] That meant that Malinda had to come up with cash or the equivalent in crops, livestock, and human property. The obligation had to be paid.

Then, in November the same year, a second judgment for a different debt Thomas had incurred fell to Malinda to pay. It was for $200.00 plus interest and suit costs, again to be paid in money or goods and chattel property.[4]

This was 1836, and Malinda had to find some way to pay the debts. Could Malinda have bargained away Henry and Sarah to get enough money? Crops and livestock would have been insufficient to pay the lofty amounts. Selling some land was an option, but no land sales were recorded. The two tracts in Thomas's name remained in her possession. Malinda may have borrowed from family or friends this time. Somehow, she managed this crisis. And yet, new debts would plague her.

Over the next few years, Malinda continued to struggle financially. Her children were old enough to begin helping with income-producing activities, but there were many mouths to feed and bodies to clothe. She needed cash.

In July 1839, six years after her father's death, Malinda brought suit against her brother Augustine Hawkins, administrator of the James Hawkins estate, to recover an amount she felt due to her deceased husband's estate but never distributed.[5] Her claim for "upwards of one hundred dollars" likely caused family tensions and a rebuke from Augustine, who had thought he had fulfilled his legal duties. Malinda needed the money regardless of potential damage to family relations. The amount she ultimately recovered a year later was $60.28, a substantive sum for sure, but not enough to allay her persistent indebtedness and insecurity.[6] Could relief be found by using her slaves' labor and property value to cover some debts?

. . .

The year 1840 brought another national census. The day a census enumerator appeared, Malinda reported two enslaved persons living in her household. The enumerator noted one female under the age of ten and one male between thirty-six and fifty-four.[7] The young girl was surely Juliet, but who was the adult man? Was he owned property or hired? Given the age discrepancy, it is unlikely this adult male was Henry, the "boy" listed on the inventory of Thomas Kilby's estate six years earlier. The absence of other records indicates that the enslaved man's presence was short-lived and his identity unknown.

The census of 1840 counted persons of all ages and status, free and enslaved. On the other hand, the yearly Personal Property Tax assessment levied a tax on White males and enslaved persons, both male and female, age sixteen and over. Juliet had just turned six years old. Thus, in 1840, only one of the two enslaved persons counted in the national census was included in the local count for purposes of taxing.[8] The facts did not change in 1841 for local taxing, but starting a year later, Malinda reported no slave property subject to taxes.[9] Juliet was still too young to cause Malinda to be taxed for her. However, the adult enslaved male who was counted as Malinda's property for two years was not around when her life circumstances deteriorated further.

. . .

By February 1843, Malinda's debts had accumulated to just under six-hundred dollars, and she entered into a deed of trust with a willing lender, a local landowner.[10] Malinda pledged everything she held of value: land, livestock, a wagon and all farming equipment, household property, a growing crop, and "one negro girl named Juliet Ann." The stresses of debt had come to a head, and she was going for broke with this agreement to consolidate and pay off obligations. Note that neither Sarah nor Henry were among the human property guaranteed in the trust—another indication that they were no longer her property.

In the following years, Malinda twice renegotiated the 1843 trust agreement, each an attempt to forestall foreclosure and buy time for crops of wheat and corn to generate ready cash.[11] The conditions for crop growing and available labor favored Malinda, for she was able to retain her property. A disaster was avoided. Yet, her children, now adults, were fully aware of their as-yet-undivided inheritance of their father's estate. Pressures on Malinda would not abate.

At his death, Thomas Kilby owned two land parcels. The first and earliest was a tract of 139 acres, and the second was a nearby tract of 115 acres. Malinda tried to manage both to produce the income she desperately needed. Obvious to her were the profits she needed to extract from free labor, initially from Henry and Sarah, and in later years from Juliet and her children. They would have known the place of their bondage well—the cabin on a knoll that sheltered Malinda and her children; the tall hill that locals called Stonehouse Mountain; the stream known as Muddy Run that ran through the properties; the timbered portions where they harvested logs, fence rails, and firewood; and the scattered fields where plantings meant grueling labor under a hot sun.

. . .

Chesterfield Kilby, Malinda and Thomas's second-born son, died in 1855 at a young age of twenty-eight.[12] He was unmarried and had accumulated nothing in the way of wealth except for what others considered of value, namely, his share of his father's inheritance and several siblings' interests in that inheritance. Their interests included a share in the chattel property, meaning Juliet and her issue. Mortimer, Chesterfield's younger brother, became the legal administrator of Chesterfield's estate.[13]

Four years later, seeking legal remedy through the chancery

court (the means for achieving equity in civil disputes), Mortimer initiated a lawsuit against his mother on behalf of himself and as the administrator of Chesterfield's estate.[14] His petition asked for a resolution in the distribution of real property left in his father's estate. His brothers and sisters then living, heirs-at-law, were brought into the suit. The case would drag on for nearly four decades, relevant papers of various sorts accumulating in the court files, documents that revealed many family facts. Mortimer's suit had profound implications for Juliet and any children she might have had by that time.

The suit principally argued for an equitable division of lands of his deceased father, Thomas Kilby. A lawyer prepared the bill, which was handwritten in ink on blue paper and entered into the court in 1859. A penned footnote explained that Mortimer had administered the personal property of Chesterfield's estate "except an interest of one 8th in a negro woman and her two children which [sic] have not been divided and are in the possession of the s^d [said] Malinda his mother."[15] The footnote appears to have been written in a different hand, which could indicate it was added at a later date as a matter of clarification. Regardless, this is the earliest indication that Juliet had born two children by that year.

Under normal circumstances, owing to the absence of a wife and children to whom to leave an inheritance, the nearest living relatives would agree amicably to a division of Chesterfield's estate. However, these were not normal circumstances, and Malinda and children were not a normal family. In the years and decades that followed, the plaintiff in two Kilby family lawsuits would be none other than son and brother, Mortimer Kilby, a man not shy about seeking a legal remedy.[16]

As the administrator, Mortimer legally had to act in the best interest of the heirs-at-law of Chesterfield's estate. The court had to determine who in the family was entitled to what. There is no indication Mortimer ever sought a peaceful settlement among family members. His motivation in aggressively seeking legal remedy may have been more self-serving and spiteful than just fulfilling a fiduciary responsibility. One can imagine the disagreements among Malinda's children as each apparently wanted a division of their father's estate, real and personal property, to which they believed they were entitled. The succession of documents reveals the manipulations brother Frank took to ultimately gain title to his father's land, the homeplace and farm where in earlier times enslaved persons were born and toiled.

The time had come to use Chesterfield's death as a reason to force the long-sought distribution of undivided property through court action. Some of the heirs may have been indifferent, and others may have felt the pull of greed and entitlement. History could have forgotten it all except that this time, the fate of human beings kept in bondage, powerless and alone, was held in the balance.

Brother against brother, with a mother and three sisters drawn into the entanglements, ownership of Thomas Kilby's land would bother the chancery court for decades, to be settled only after deaths of many parties and to the satisfaction of none.[17] Over the years, trees were felled and lumber hauled to buyers, seeds were sown and crops were harvested, and whatever was needed to produce income and make the land productive and valuable was done. Juliet Ann and her children, even the youngest, had helped support Malinda by their involuntary, unpaid labor. Yet they would receive no consideration or say in daily decisions or legal decrees that might affect their futures.

...

By 1860, five of Malinda Kilby's children were married or making a living at other locations. Malinda's unmarried daughter Adeline, aged thirty-three, remained on the plantation to aid her sexagenarian mother. They both watched as Juliet's young children advanced in age.[18]

The name of Malinda's son Mortimer, a recent widower, appeared twice on the census of 1860 of Culpeper County—once in the household of his mother and once in the household of his mother-in-law.[19] His deceased wife's family, the Humes, was apparently caring for his four-year-old son.[20] His occupation, captured in the appropriate column of the census form and duplicated in both instances, was teacher.

There could be little doubt that Malinda appreciated what help Mortimer might have given. In less than a year that followed, the realities of the coming conflict between soldiers of North and South added new perils to Malinda's tenuous way of life. Stresses were always with her, and now they were rising.

All hope of reconciliation of grievances with the North was abandoned when on April 17, 1861, Virginia followed other Southern slave states in seceding from the United States. In Culpeper County, the White citizens prepared for war.[21] Initial exuberance waned as the realities of casualties set in. A year later, 1862, a Richmond newspaper reported the massing of 40,000 Federal troops in Rappahannock County, where they were "treating the inhabitants of Madison and Culpeper outrageously," and "They steal horses, cattle, and sheep, induce the negroes to run away, and commit all sorts of depredations upon private property."[22]

In a 1940 WPA interview, Annie Wallace, a formerly enslaved Black woman born about the same year as Simon and only miles from where he was held in bondage, described the "patterolls" who ranged the area looking for runaways and the Federal troops that came around searching for "Johnnies."[23] Had Annie Wallace known Juliet Ann or her children? Likely, but it cannot be known for sure. Wallace's experience during this time might also describe those of Juliet and her family.

The Kilby men, sons of Thomas and Malinda Kilby and their kin—whether through a sense of duty, honor, or self-righteous zeal—began to enlist in local military units or provide provisions for the armies.

Were their loyalties to the Confederacy, to old Virginia, or to their community and families? Were their convictions fervent or merely lukewarm? And, as a woman and an enslaver, did Malinda stand firm in her beliefs, or did she have public or private doubts? No letter or journal exists to provide answers to such weighty questions.

Mortimer Kilby enlisted in the Seventh Virginia Infantry in the fall of 1862.[24] If he was no longer a teacher as in years before, then Mortimer was not exempt from the conscription law enacted in April that same year. Perhaps he enlisted so he could be in the same unit with two of his Kilby cousins and a nephew.[25] Regardless, the four would fight together on July 3, 1863, as Pickett ordered his division in a charge across the fields at Gettysburg, and all would survive the day to return to Virginia. Mortimer was later wounded and taken prisoner at the Battle of Five Forks on April 1, 1865, and released upon taking the Oath of Allegiance on June 28, 1865.[26]

A year after Mortimer enlisted, his brother Burgess joined the Fourth Battalion, Virginia Infantry, Local Defense, a unit stationed along the James River in Richmond.[27]

Frank, the other of Malinda's living sons, who was over forty at war's outset and somehow escaped conscription, never entered military service, but he did provide badly needed livestock feed for the Confederate Army.[28] The same was true for Malinda's brother-in-law, Bluford Thornhill, who received Confederate States receipts for the beef, hay, oats, and corn he provided.[29] There is no doubt Malinda was sharing her worries with her sister Lucy and brother-in-law Bluford as the related family's young men went off to war and they were left at home to cope.

Malinda Kilby and her neighbors skirting Stonehouse Mountain and along the Muddy Run must have felt that they were at the epicenter of the war. Nestled between the Thornton's Gap Turnpike (known today as Sperryville Pike) and the Richmond Road (now Eggbornsville Road), Confederate troops and Federal troops would crisscross the area, ever ready for a skirmish, always in search of intelligence, and quick to take whatever property they pleased.³⁰ Either side could be the enemy of the moment. Malinda probably worried for her safety and loss of her property—cut timber, fencing, livestock, grain, foodstuffs, and personal valuables.

She might have also been worried that Juliet and her children would run away or be lured away by the soldiers in blue. War and the institution of slavery that was at its core trapped man and woman, young and old, those with freedom and those with none.

Threats to body and property were high, and Malinda was defenseless. She needed refuge. And as the war dragged on, she found it—and emotional comfort, as well—in the home of her sister and brother-in-law, Lucy and Bluford Thornhill. It was here that the events of late 1864 and the following months changed Malinda's life, which in turn altered the lives of those souls she still commanded in bondage.

CHAPTER FIVE

Prelude to Freedom

1864–1865

Despite the lingering war and frequent incursions of passing troops, both United States Army and Confederate, in the closing week of 1864, the inhabitants of the Gourdvine Neck were attempting to maintain the traditions of Christmas. Whites would attend family gatherings, Blacks would receive small tokens—perhaps a piece of cloth, some tobacco, or extra rations—passed out by paternalistic enslavers, all contemplating with apprehension the coming new year.

A storm of hail and snow had passed through the hills the week earlier, as described in a report of the unopposed movement of United States Army Cavalry through Rappahannock County and past the Bluford Thornhill plantation.[1] The intense cold spread gloom and misery, promoting minor ailments into concerning illnesses. Two stories can be told, but only one can be true.

First is a death record collected according to law, penned for posterity in the county's official register book of citizen mortality and purported to be accurate. On the list of those who had died in 1864 is the name Lucy Thornhill, Bluford's wife of forty-three years, the former Lucy Hawkins, sister of Malinda (Hawkins) Kilby.[2] She had died, according to the record, on December 28, 1864, of pneumonia, or in those days, what was known as "winter fever." There would be nothing unusual about this death other than the date, which, if accurate, would have shocking implications for what followed.

Rappahannock County's Register of Deaths was the only source of information about Lucy Thornhill's end of life to be found—no tombstone, no family Bible, no newspaper obituary or death notice—until the discovery of an inconspicuous notation in a church record book:

Lucy Thornhill   Deceased Dec. 30th 1863.[3]

From these two sources, a county register and a church record book, note two days difference in the month—perhaps the date of the funeral service rather than death date—but more importantly, a year earlier. Had the church scribe made an error? Had Lucy, in fact, died on December 28, 1864? Or had she actually died in 1863, leaving Bluford a widower for a year by the winter of 1864?

The year of Lucy's death is significant, for on this precise day, the twenty-eighth day of December 1864, Malinda Kilby and Bluford Thornhill appeared before the Culpeper County clerk of court and applied for a marriage license.[4] Had Bluford's wife passed to eternity earlier the same day, as the "official" county record would indicate? Or had Bluford completed twelve months of mourning before taking this step toward remarriage? It is enticing to believe the former case, to imagine secrets withheld and scandal in the making at such hasty action. However, it is more likely that the county's record was wrong; that is, the widower and widow had waited a respectable time before obtaining a license to marry. Whichever story you believe, Bluford and Malinda were married six days later,

January 3, 1865, with Aldridge Grimsley, pastor of the F.T. Baptist Church, officiating.[5]

The reactions of friends and the religious community to this union are unknown, but the sudden remarriage of Malinda, and the transfer of property rights that went with the marriage, apparently irritated Mortimer Kilby enough to file a new lawsuit against his mother.[6] Juliet and children must have followed as Malinda moved to her new husband's plantation barely over into Rappahannock County in the Gourdvine Neck. Malinda's children, or at least Mortimer, who was the instigator and plaintiff, must have wanted the remaining personal property—human property—that he or they thought should have been theirs by right. With the war going badly, apparently, Mortimer thought that time was drawing short for obtaining cash for something of value while the opportunity still existed. Animosity may have played a role. However, the true motivation for this suit must be left to speculation.

Kilby v. Thornhill was filed with the Rappahannock County chancery court in late March 1865.[7] Mortimer's timing puts into question his motivation—and his sense of reality regarding the war! Nonetheless, the suit was filed in hopes of an immediate court action. The existent documents present the clearest evidence of Malinda's slave holdings at the time and names of Juliet's children.

> *To the county court of Rappahannock County in Chancery*
> *Your complainant Mortimer Kilby respectfully represents that [Thomas] Kilby departed this life sometime since in the county of Culpeper intestate possessing of a small amount of personal estate and a servant woman named Juliet. Whatever there was of his personal property has been long since disposed of and applied according to law.*
> *His widow Melinda [Malinda] Kilby now Melinda Thornhill has had possession of the said slave Juliet who has given birth to several children to wit Simon, John, James and Sarah. These slaves have been*

raised by the same Melinda until the oldest has got to be a boy that could render some service. They are all valuable.

Some few years since the same Melinda married Bluford Thornhill of Rappahannock County and it has become a matter of some importance that said slaves should be divided between those entitled thereto according to their respective rights.[8]

The ink on the suit documents was barely dry when Mortimer was back in uniform. By the end of April, the war was over, the Confederate Army having surrendered, the Southern cause lost, the Emancipation Proclamation at last enforceable in Virginia. Regardless of the legal merits presumed by the plaintiffs in the chancery suit, the "matter of some importance" was no longer so, and counsel for Mortimer dropped the suit.

Up to this time, Juliet no doubt lived in fear that her children might be taken from her, removed to another farm, or quickly sold to slave-labor plantations of the deep South. She must have been haunted by memories of separation as a child from her own mother. This fear would have compounded the brutalization of forced labor, deprivations, and physical assault. Opportunities to escape to nearby United States Army lines in preceding years had passed. Freedom must have seemed far away, unreachable, an earthly promise unfulfilled.

How and when Juliet, Simon, John, James, and Sarah received the news of their freedom from bondage was never recorded. The atmosphere on the Thornhill plantation and the relationships between Bluford and Malinda and those they previously enslaved may have changed little in the following months. It took time to sink in what the new order might look like. If Juliet had celebrated—and surely she must have—she likely gave no external expression, at least not in front of the Whites still in power.

At war's end, Mortimer returned to Culpeper County to join his brother Frank and their sisters in adjusting their lives to a new reality, part of which was knowing they no longer had a claim to their father's former human property. At age thirty-one, Juliet must have felt bewilderment at what her future would hold. She also must have felt great pain for the years of stolen service and denied humanity. Most of all, Juliet must have thought about her children and what would become of them. They were young and would need care and guidance, which was not assured from a dispirited and angry White society bent on maintaining a tradition of privileged superiority. Juliet and her children would have to find their own ways.

Freedom and the healing of spirit would come slowly. The stranglehold of racial prejudice exhibited by Whites would not yield to open opportunity for the newly freed. Their drawn-out emancipation began with a declaration of family identity.

CHAPTER SIX

Fractured Lives, Indomitable Spirits

1834–1865

Juliet Ann. It was a beautiful name, especially so as a double name, but even more greatly cherished if chosen by her mother. Only in the Thomas Kilby estate inventory and one deed of trust do I find Juliet's second name, Ann, a fragment of identity so precious to those with little other claim to self.[1] All subsequent records, few as they are, record her only as Juliet, without her middle name, and by the first name alone would her children remember her.

As Sarah was enslaved, so were any children born to her. That was the law of the land.[2] Juliet was the newborn property of the Thomas Kilby estate and subject to any decision made by Malinda.

The legal ownership of the enslaved property of the estate became an issue of dispute in a later lawsuit, but until Malinda, as administratrix, settled the estate, she had complete command of Thomas's property. There is no evidence that the circuit court ordered or approved a trust to be established to formally hold estate assets for Malinda's child heirs until they each reached the legal age of adulthood.[3]

After Thomas Kilby's death, Malinda held his enslaved property, then three in number, in her possession. To care for her nine children, to manage the plantation and provide needed income, to plan for a future while grieving the loss of a husband and provider, to just survive—these exigencies created strains for which solutions had to be found.

Brothers, sisters, in-laws, and family associates surely provided advice and perhaps some assistance, but the ultimate responsibilities and the decisions fell to Malinda. What would she do? Sell immediately? Or would she try to complete Thomas's and her dream of a successful farming enterprise? There were options, choices others in a similar situation might take. Likely Malinda thought only of the welfare of herself and her children. Whatever happened to Henry and Sarah and infant Juliet Ann—their well-being, their happiness—was of little concern to Malinda, except for how their labor benefited her family.

There is little doubt that some in the family must have advised Malinda to use her chattel property as a bargaining currency when needed. Sometimes by necessity, always by choice, Malinda did indeed use their labor and value to further her interests.

It was 1834, and Juliet's future had just begun. And for Henry and Sarah, a reset, a new start with a new enslaver was their fate. Each would be forced into differing courses in life, as the facts and their stories will reveal.

Henry

Neither character of legend nor subject of any narrative, he existed only in the documented reference to "boy" and "Henry" and his monetary value for the lifetime of forced labor he could produce for his enslaver. To the dominating caste, his place in the world, his relationships to those who may have been kin, whom he loved and who loved him, his identity and his humanity, these were irrelevant to the reality that he was chattel property that could be transferred from one owner to another, from James Hawkins and through his estate to Thomas Kilby and subsequently to Malinda.

All I know—all that the few existent probate records reveal—is that Henry was one of eight members of the James Hawkins enslaved community in early 1833, soon to be split apart and sent to plantations of new owners.[4] By years' end, he would leave kith and kin and, along with Sarah and her soon-to-be-born child, begin laboring for the Thomas Kilby family.

The whereabouts of the enslaved Henry in years after Thomas's death is a deep mystery. As a young Black man bringing $550 at the sale to Thomas Kilby, the highest price of all the human property sold to the James Hawkins heirs, Malinda surely understood his great monetary and labor value.

The property tax rolls for Culpeper County, through counts of taxable slave property, suggest that Malinda lost Henry sometime before March 1837.[5] Thomas's debts fell to Malinda, and perhaps she had to sell Henry to avoid foreclosure. Without records regarding Henry's fate, we are left to wonder about this man, the contributions he made, and the possibility he had descendants.

Sarah

Described as a "girl" on the James Hawkins estate property inventory and then as "woman" on the Kilby inventory, it is likely that Sarah was a maturing teen at the time of her sale to Thomas Kilby.[6] The dollar amounts ascribed by estate appraisers and later recorded upon sale—$292 and $365, respectively—indicate that Sarah was valued highly for her labor and child-bearing potential.[7] Combining these descriptive facts, I can estimate her year of birth to be around 1816. She was likely born in Virginia.[8]

As a general rule, enslavers encouraged—absolutely counted on as a matter of course—the "increase" of their female property. And the sooner they began bearing children, the better. Reproductive rights were not their own. Thomas and Malinda must have wanted Sarah to bear children early on as her responsibility and to their favor.

Sarah was one of eight enslaved persons listed on the deceased James Hawkins property list, and it is reasonable to assume she was a member of a connected group, a member of a social family, if not blood-related. As suggested before, Betty, known to be the mother of Mary and sold together to another Hawkins heir, may have been the mother of Sarah as well.[9] Was Betty, in fact, the mother of Sarah? Was Sarah born on the James Hawkins plantation? Was Sarah's father one of Matthew Hawkins's male slaves, or was her father one of Matthew's sons, James or another? The possibilities are several. As to Sarah's mother, there are some tantalizing clues, inconclusive as they are. But as to her father, there are none. Beyond the written record of Sarah's sale to Thomas Kilby and the age ranges of the enslaved females reported in the census, determining Sarah's origin and parentage is conjecture. What is known is that Sarah was taken from the larger, connected community on the Hawkins plantation, perhaps even from her mother and other blood family members.

Just as with Sarah's unknown parentage, the question of who fathered Juliet remains unanswered. The timing of Juliet's birth, thought to be sometime in the first month of 1834, suggests Sarah was impregnated around the time of James Hawkins's death around March 1833 or soon thereafter.[10] One might speculate that the most closely associated possibilities, James Hawkins's sons Thomas, Albert, and Augustine, those with the greatest unrestrained power and locational opportunity, are suspects as Juliet's father.[11] One could perhaps add more names to the list of possibilities: sons-in-law—Thomas Kilby and Bluford Thornhill were two such kin—and other men who would "come a' calling." White men had power, and they used it to rape enslaved women and girls who were expected to bear children and increase the owner's holdings and wealth. But then, human reproduction was surely not first in mind when Sarah was impregnated, only fulfilling a man's carnal appetite. The degradation of all-too-common sexual assault on enslaved women by White men in power cannot be overlooked and must be assumed in this case. As you might guess, documented evidence of paternity simply does not exist.

. . .

The Culpeper County Personal Property Tax records from 1834 to 1864, where counts of slaves subject to the head tax by their enslavers are shown, provide traces of information about those Malinda Kilby held in bondage. In the first two years after Thomas's death, 1834 and 1835, the count of Malinda's taxable property was for two enslaved persons over age sixteen. They are not named, though one might reasonably presume these individuals are Henry and Sarah. As a baby, Juliet would not have been property to be taxed, and thus she was not included in the count of slaves. The 1836 personal property tax records indicate that Malinda owned only one slave for whom the county levied a tax, and one year later, the tax records show no taxable slave property under her name. After that, numbers in the county tax rolls present only questions. Had Juliet been separated from her mother? Did Malinda hire out Sarah and Henry? Were they sold to cover Malinda's mounting debts? Church records offer some clues.

The one place Black people were allowed to gather was in church, but for regular, White-approved religious instruction only. Thomas and Malinda had been members of the Gourdvine Baptist Church before his death.[12] There is no evidence that any of Thomas's enslaved persons were members of or even attended services at that church.[13] The meeting house was five miles distance from Thomas's homestead, north on the meandering Richmond Road. It was so far that attendance would require some conveyance other than walking: buggy, cart, wagon, or horseback.[14] Walking, however, would have been the only option for the enslaved. The New Salem Baptist Church, formally constituted in January 1834, was much closer, a little over two miles to the south, and this became Malinda's spiritual home after Thomas's death. It was here that she could commune with friends, relatives, and neighbors such as James and Susannah Glasscock, John Scott, John Connor, and Mary Stringfellow.

"Received for baptism . . . Sister Kilby's Sarah"—this entry is found in the New Salem Baptist Church Minute Book for July 6, 1834.[15] Who was Sister Kilby? Was she Malinda? Other than Malinda—and her given name does not appear in the church records until later—there was only one other Kilby woman noted among members during 1834. Virenda Kilby was a twenty-four-year-old unmarried woman, distantly related through marriage, and unlikely to have enslaved someone herself. The Sarah mentioned here is certainly the woman of the same name enslaved by Malinda. If true, then another mention of her in the Minute Book reveals important facts.

The minutes of November 1839 read, "Brother [James] Glasscock presented a charge against Sarah (a colored member the property of Sister M[ary] Stringfellow) that she concealed stolen goods."[16] Sarah was ordered to appear before the church leaders to answer the charge. After several months of postponements, she did appear to testify at what must have been a very intimidating moment. The minutes provide the outcome:

> *After investigation of the evidence On Motion, it was resolved that she be admonished by the pastor of the impropriety of such conduct as she had been guilty of and be retained in the fellowship of the church. The pastor gave her wholesome and faithful admonishment.*[17]

Not recorded are any details of the accused infraction and the motivation. In the era of slavery, concealing stolen goods could have meant something as simple as pocketing a leftover biscuit or picking up a dropped handkerchief.

We cannot be sure, but the evidence suggests that this Sarah, "Sister Kilby's Sarah," and the Thomas Kilby estate's Sarah are the same and that Malinda sold or bargained away Sarah to Mary Stringfellow, she becoming Sarah's new owner. Stringfellow was a close neighbor to Malinda, and she is recorded in the same church as a member.[18] She was a single woman who had two children out of wedlock and close in age to Malinda's younger ones.[19] As they both were raising children without husbands to run their respective farms, they may have commiserated each other's plight.

As property tax records show, Malinda held one enslaved person for whom tax was due in 1836 and no taxable slaves the years 1837–38. Malinda may have sold Sarah sometime during these years.[20] No bill of sale is part of the public record. Private transactions were the custom, and papers, if any ever existed, were likely held by Stringfellow, not Malinda. Sarah's name disappears from records and any association with Malinda Kilby after 1834. On the other hand, the property tax record for Mary Stringfellow shows for the first time in 1838 that she held in her control one slave above age sixteen.[21] For the next twelve years, Mary Stringfellow's human property, as counted in the property tax ledgers, remains at one.[22] These facts and the mention of Mary Stringfellow's Sarah suggests a clue to the fate of Sarah, previously the chattel property of Malinda Kilby.

Can I prove that Sarah, the mother of Juliet Ann, is the same Sarah described in the church minutes in 1839? No. However, the circumstances of only one African American woman named Sarah on church membership lists, property tax records for the two property-owning White women with other ties as friends and neighbors, and no negative evidence to suggest otherwise, I am left to believe Juliet's mother, Sarah, became the property of Mary Stringfellow. Sarah's trail ends there — or does it?

In 1850, the U.S. federal census included, for the first time, a separate enumeration of enslaved people. Rather than capturing names of the enslaved, the slave schedules recorded the names of "slave owners" and the age, sex, and race of each person that enslaver held. Mary Stringfellow is prominent on the schedule for Culpeper County.[23] The record shows that Stringfellow held six Black children varying in age from nine months to eleven years. Also, she held one Black woman, age thirty-two. Could this woman be Sarah, whom I believe to have been one or two years older? Without birth records, ages of enslaved persons were only estimates. Though highly speculative, with no evidence yet found to either confirm or refute the suggestion that this person was Sarah, this record from 1850 seeds hope of her rediscovery and geographic location near daughter Juliet. The slave schedule of 1860 includes no woman of appropriate age to be associated with Stringfellow. Thus, all traces of Sarah vanish. Future research may uncover Sarah's fate, but genealogy demands we follow the preponderance of the evidence, and that takes me no further than the church record of 1839.

Beyond the other horrors of Sarah's bondage, which should never be forgotten, the sorrowful implication here is the probable separation of mother Sarah and young daughter Juliet. Malinda Kilby did not set a precedent in separating mother from child. It was an act of cruelty common among enslavers who considered property rights above humanity, an act that caused everlasting pain to its victims while creating no moral disquiet in the perpetrators.

Juliet

The exact whereabouts of Juliet in her early childhood years is an open question. One hopes that Malinda allowed Sarah to keep her daughter close while she was very young. But, if Sarah was the property of Mary Stringfellow, where was Juliet, and who would have been responsible for her care? Profound questions remain unanswered, yet records show that as the administratrix of her deceased husband's estate, Malinda retained possession and legal control of Juliet in later years.

According to the 1840 census, living in Malinda Kilby's household were two young boys (her children Thomas and Burgess), two boys between ten and fifteen (Mortimer and Chesterfield), and the three still-living girls spread across the age range (Adeline, Missouri, and Louisa).[24] Martha Ann, the oldest daughter, died a year earlier.²⁵ Also living on the plantation, as counted in the census, were one enslaved female under age ten (Juliet) and one middle-aged enslaved male (identity unknown).²⁶

Malinda's income in succeeding years did not meet her expenses. In each of the years 1843, 1844, and 1845, Malinda pledged crops, land, and personal property in three separate deeds of trust as security for her debts.²⁷ The trust document signed and recorded in 1843 listed specific collateral, including Juliet Ann by name, providing evidence that Malinda had possession and assumed authority.²⁸ Apparently, Malinda ultimately paid her debt and did not lose her guarantee.

Whether during her formative years young Juliet served Malinda at home, was hired out, or was lent to a Kilby son starting an independent life, no record has been found.

By the time of the next federal census in 1850, Malinda's household composition had dwindled. Daughters Louisa and Missouri had married.²⁹ Sons Franklin, Chesterfield, Mortimer, and Thomas had moved away from the homestead to start independent lives. Only son Burgess and daughter Adeline were left to help Malinda keep going.³⁰ Year by year, those closest to Malinda were leaving her.

In that same year (1850), the federal census included a separate enumeration of enslaved persons among the populace, commonly known as the "slave schedule." Malinda does not appear on this companion census as a "slave owner."³¹ Juliet was sixteen in 1850, the age when she would have become the countable taxable property of her owner in her residence county. However, Malinda's record on the county property tax list for that year shows no taxable enslaved property.³² One possibility is that Malinda hired out Juliet to someone else, which would account for the absence of a record on the census or tax list that year. Hiring out Juliet could have been the case, but there is no direct evidence.

The following year, the count of enslaved property of Malinda in the Culpeper County Personal Property Tax ledger suddenly goes from zero to one, and that remains the count in years 1851–1854, 1856, and 1857.[33] Was this one enslaved person, the property of Malinda, now over age sixteen, in fact, Sarah's daughter Juliet? What had happened in the years 1855 and 1858–1864? The idea that Malinda may have hired Juliet away periodically could account for sporadic counts on yearly tax lists. Hiring out Juliet would also mean detaching her from her young children born starting in 1853. If this was the case, as Juliet had been separated from her mother many years earlier, the cruelty was once again perpetrated by an enslaver with only financial considerations at heart.

. . .

The year-to-year whereabouts of Juliet during her early years remains unknown, but as events in Malinda's family would reveal, Juliet remained the enslaved property of the Thomas Kilby's estate, and Malinda had control.

By analyzing records and their revealed event dates, I deduce that Juliet was nineteen years old when she gave birth to her first child, a son.[34] His name would be a question to be revealed through subsequent records.

The first mention of Juliet with a child appeared in a deed of sale dated March 30, 1858, and recorded March 16, 1859, at the Culpeper County Courthouse.[35] In this deed, James Franklin Kilby "doth grant, bargain, sell, and convey . . . two negroes, the one called Julet [sic] and the other Charles William, and the future increase of the said Julet" to his brother Burgess for the sum of one hundred dollars.[36]

The circumstances of this deed raise many questions for which satisfactory answers have not been found. First, there is no evidence that Frank had legal ownership of Juliet and Charles William. The laws of Virginia at the time regarding dower rights stated:

Fourth. If the intestate leaves a widow, and issue [children] by her, the widow shall be entitled to one-third of the said surplus [of personal estate], but she shall have only the use for her life of such slaves as may be in her share.[37]

Applying this rule of law, Malinda had no ownership, but she had the use of Juliet and Charles William "for her life," and Frank had only a small ownership share and questionable right to their labor.

About this time, Frank's occupation was overseer—likely for his mother—and he may have thought that he had an ownership right to his father's chattel property.[38] There is no evidence that Burgess ever took possession of this human property. Seven years later, Juliet and her children were still in Malinda's possession.

Regarding this recorded deed, it is more likely that Frank intended to sell his *interest* in the estate's human property, not the actual persons, and that there was a wording error. The low sum of monetary consideration would support this as the case.

A separate question arises from this deed. Was Charles William the son born of Juliet in 1853 and known at other times as Simon? Most likely, the answer is yes, for other evidence shows that Simon used the forenames Charles William late in life, a name he must have remembered from childhood.[39]

Several facts from the 1860 federal census are relevant. This record shows the occupations of both Frank Kilby and brother Thomas L. Kilby as overseer.[40] Frank's character is revealed in the Hudson family history collected by the genealogist Craig M. Kilby in which he stated, "He [Frank Kilby] was an overseer. Stories are his first wife, Margaret Hudson, used to cry when he whipped the slaves."[41] Family historian Joyce Colleen Libes carried the story further:

> Bessie Belle Hawkins Evans remembered hearing her mother, Frank's daughter Lucretia, tell about how frightened she was seeing her father whip a slave for some infraction of rules. She thought her father Frank Kilby was a very hot-tempered man

and she feared him! She said it also bothered her mother to see him whip the slaves. Although Frank may have whipped some of the slaves, it's said by some in the family that he liked one female slave—at least well enough to have had some children by her.[42]

Perhaps Frank was, in part, working for his mother on the family's marginal plantation. While he may have wandered about looking for jobs in the preceding years, his connection to the local area and to the New Salem Baptist Church, his and Malinda's church, is confirmed in the recorded minutes of 1851. In that year he was charged and then excluded from the membership for "irregularities" and "improper conduct."[43] The specifics of

James Franklin Kilby. (Photo courtesy of Joyce Colleen Libes)

the infraction are not known, but the severe penalty indicates something quite serious in Frank's misconduct.

Census records show that in 1860 he was also the hirer of an eight-year-old enslaved girl.[44] A married man with seven children, he may have wanted a servant to look after his wife. This may show his willingness to separate Black families for his own benefit.

Thomas L. Kilby was known to have been employed as overseer by a landowner in Orange County in 1850 and 1857.[45] Among his brothers, Mortimer's listed occupation in 1860 was teacher, and Burgess was a carpenter boarding in the village of Fairfax (the original name for the town known today as Culpeper) with another carpenter, a free man of color, and his family.[46] Chesterfield was not enumerated in 1860 as he had died five years earlier.[47] These facts, by themselves, may hold little relevance. Yet location and occupation, when combined with details found in chancery suit documents, become pertinent to the lives of Juliet and her children.

The United States federal government population census of 1860, as was the case in 1850[48], included a special slave schedule to enumerate the slave population. Malinda Kilby's name—phonetically entered as Molinda—appears on the schedule as owner of three enslaved persons: a female age twenty-five, a male age seven, and another male age four.[49] By design, census takers were instructed to record only a number for each enslaved person, not a name.[50] Thus, the names of the three individuals Malinda held were not recorded, but the ages and sex provide clues.

On this schedule, the twenty-five-year-old female was surely Juliet; the seven-year-old, Simon; and the four-year-old, John. The count in the column labeled "No. of Slave houses" is one. This suggests that Juliet and her children were housed in a building separate from Malinda's abode.

Also, on the 1860 slave schedule, on a different page, is a curious entry for William C. Apperson. Apperson, who had a distant family connection to Malinda, married in 1857 and may have

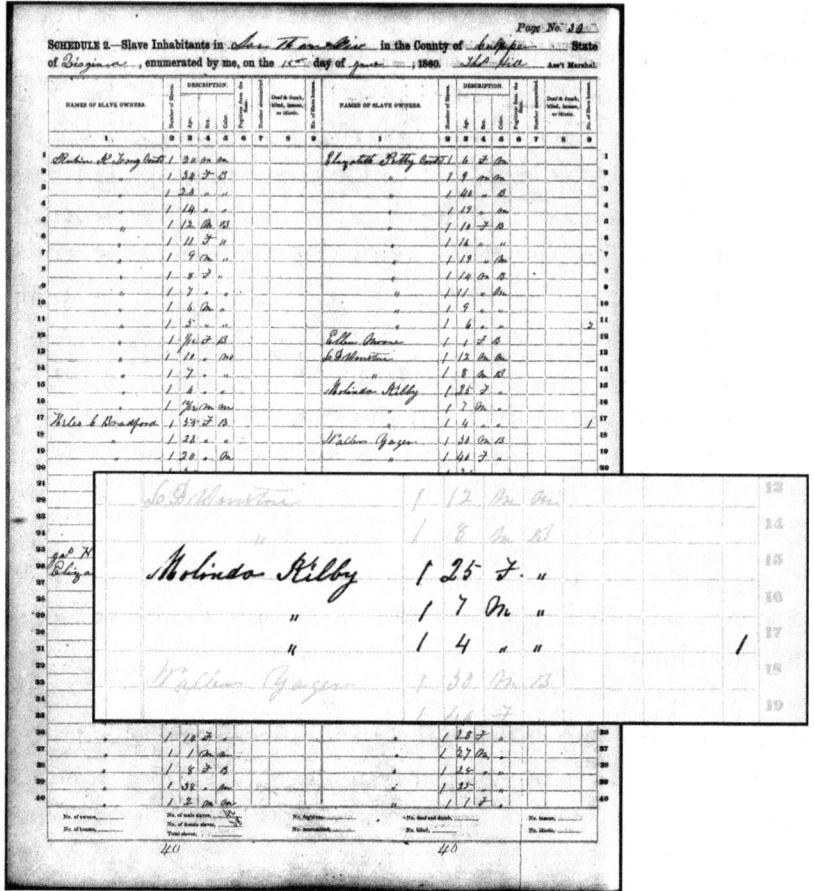

The 1860 U.S. census slave schedule for Culpeper County
showing Malinda Kilby as the enslaver
of one female and two males.

sought a servant or cook for his household soon afterward.[51] Following Apperson's name is the letter "E," which was used to indicate that he was the employer. Below Apperson's name is the inscription, "Mrs Kilby own[er]."[52] This record for Apperson may indicate that Malinda Kilby hired out Juliet for a period of time. As the properties were not far apart, Juliet still may have been able to provide some care for her children who remained in Malinda's custody.

In 1862, for the first time, the Culpeper County Commissioner of Revenue charged his subordinates to record not only the numbers of slaves held by County citizens but their total value, as well. The purpose of this was for taxing personal property and, for the first time, all slaves of all ages. For Malinda, the record shows she held four enslaved persons valued at a total of $1,000.[53] Later records prove that Juliet had born four children by this time. Nothing shows for Malinda in the column for slaves over the age of sixteen. Why the record shows four enslaved persons and not five, I can only speculate. If Malinda had hired out Juliet, as previously suggested, then that could account for the discrepancy.

The only other taxable property Malinda declared was a clock valued at five dollars—no horse or cows or other livestock, and no household possessions of even modest value. She was taxed $6.03 that year. Sons Frank and Mortimer, who may have lived with or close by, added only six cows and one horse to the aggregate.[54] The numbers did not change substantially the following tax year, except Malinda's tax levy during wartime rose to $10.55.[55]

By 1863, Malinda's sons who might help on the plantation were either already dead (Chesterfield and Thomas L.) or away fighting for the Confederacy (Burgess and Mortimer). Only Frank remained close by to look in on Malinda. Her income must have been meager and impoverishment her concern.

As Malinda's clock slowly marked the passing hours and days, its pendulum scythe cutting away slices of time, as the next year came and stretched on, as the war would not end, as clashes as close as sounds of gunfire would carry threatened her safety, Malinda had time to think of past travails and fading fortune. Yet there was her late husband's land and the Black infant who grew into a woman, now with children of her own, all destined by slavery to serve and obey Malinda's commands. Juliet and her children had survived. Their lives were still unfolding.

CHAPTER SEVEN

What Name Shall We Use?

1865–1870

Juliet Ann lived thirty-one years without a sanctioned family surname. No doubt Simon, upon gaining freedom at age twelve, had previously asked his mother about his name. Did he have a full name, a family name, like White people had? If Juliet had adopted a family name before emancipation, it was her secret—oral tradition is silent about this. Enslavers, for their purposes, saw no reason to allow any personal identity beyond a single given name. If any reference to Juliet was made beyond the Thornhill household, it would have been "Bluford Thornhill's Juliet" or in earlier times "Juliet, who belongs to Malinda Kilby." That would have been sufficient in the minds of the domineering class. Few Whites would need more than a given name to identify a slave. No record lists surnames for any person of African descent held in bondage by any Kilby, Hawkins, or Thornhill family member of the Gourdvine Neck region.

With freedom came the necessity for African Americans to adopt surnames as part of a personal and public identity, names to relate one family member to another, a common name to be passed on to future generations. In the eyes of those in authority, they needed a public identity provided by a two-part personal name. For Blacks, they viewed a chosen surname as their "entitles," a family identifier to which they were inherently deserving.[1] The addition of a surname would offer a personal element of identity, a step in the direction of developing independence and beginning a new life. Choosing a family surname was an obligation, but it was also a right of freedom they had earned. In addition to the perception of dignity and respectability a particular surname might bestow, the practicalities of engaging with officials required a surname choice. Orders from the Bureau of Refugees, Freedmen, and Abandoned Lands, commonly known as the Freedmen's Bureau, a federal agency with military authority, became the law of the land. Among the orders issued in August 1865 was this:

> Every freedman having only one name is required to assume a "title" or family name. It may be the name of a former owner, or of any other person. When once assumed it must always thereafter be used, and no other.[2]

The newly freed understood the power of a surname in binding together members of a family group and in granting status, just as they had observed in White families. Each freedman, man or woman, for themselves and their family group, gave careful consideration in selecting and publicly acknowledging a surname. Leon Litwack, historian, teacher, and author, explains that freed people did not always choose the surname of their former enslaver.[3] By analyzing records of the F.T. Baptist Church, members of which included Bluford Thornhill and Juliet Ann, I discovered that the majority of African American members did *not* choose public surnames of their presumedly last former enslavers.[4] For this group of men and women, at least, new lives started with new names, the first opportunity for a personal choice to be honored and to have everlasting importance.

A freedman who wanted to disassociate with a recent cruel owner might choose the name of an earlier owner. But this was not always the case, as Litwack points out:

> The freedman who took the name of an earlier owner, perhaps the first owner he could recall, often made that choice out of a sense of historical identity, continuity, and family pride—the reputation of the particular master notwithstanding. The idea was not to honor the previous master but to sustain some identification with the freedman's family of origin.[5]

The historian Herbert Gufson wrote that "A surname often symbolized the close tie between an immediate slave family and its family of origin and the social identity separate from that of an owner. Slaves often retained surnames identified with earlier owners."[6] Juliet and her children's last owner was Bluford Thornhill, but Juliet was born under the ownership of Thomas Kilby and subsequently of his widow Malinda, which means Juliet's family of origin was Kilby. The same was true for Juliet's children. Their family of origin was Kilby, too. And in addition, their father—genetically proven for four of her five children, as I will show later—was a Kilby. They were *entitled* to the Kilby family name, though the choice was theirs to make.

There was no formal process for surname selection, no official document specifically for declaring the selected name. Only in records that would follow—censuses and tax records, deeds and agreements, marriage and death records—do we know their choice of Kilby as a permanent surname. In his book, *Shadow and Act*, Ralph Ellison offered this reasoning:

> Perhaps, taken in aggregate, these European names which (sometimes with irony, sometimes with pride, but always with personal investment) represent a certain triumph of the spirit, speaking to us of those who rallied, reassembled and transformed themselves and who under dismembering pressures refused to die.[7]

Finding Juliet's Family After the War

In 1870, for the first time, the previously enslaved were recorded in the U.S. census with both given names and surnames. The logical first place to look for records of Juliet and her children is in the household of their prior owner, Bluford Thornhill.[8] There one finds the names of Bluford and Malinda; Alice Kilby, a granddaughter of Malinda; and five biracial children ranging in age from three to eighteen. As the first record of these freed children by full name, this census record is important. A transcription of the original handwritten record is shown in Table 1.

Table 1. 1870 U.S. census, Rappahannock County, Bluford Thornhill household.

The name of every person whose place of abode on the first day of June, 1870, was in this family.	Description			Profession, Occupation, or Trade of each person male or female.
	Age at last birthday. If under 1 year, give months in fractions, thus 3/12	Sex—Male (M.), Female (F.)	Color—White (W.), Black (B.), Mulatto (M.), Chinese, (C.), Indian, (I.)	
Thornhill, Bluford	71	M	W	Farmer
_____ Malinda	68	F	W	Keeping House
Kilby, Alice	22	F	W	At Home
Walker, James	18	M	M	Farm Laborer
_____ John	13	M	M	" "
_____ James	10	M	M	" "
_____ Sarah	7	F	M	
_____ Elizabeth	3	F	M	

The first names recorded are Bluford and Malinda Thornhill. They are followed by Malinda's granddaughter Alice, who was living there at the time. Five biracial children are included in this household unit having a common address but presumably not under a common roof. The children are named James Walker, age eighteen; John, age thirteen; James, age ten; Sarah, age seven; and Elizabeth, age three. The descriptions for John, James, and Sarah correlate well with known facts of Juliet's children. If these are Juliet's children, where is Simon, and what of the surname Walker? Two children in the household, both named James Walker, is a sign there may have been a recording error. The surname Walker for the Black children in the Thornhill household becomes an obstacle to presumed identity if the record is accurate. The results of a thorough search for individuals with these forenames and the surname Walker, living in Rappahannock or neighboring counties separately or as a group and having the approximate same ages, came up empty.

One possible explanation as to the confusing census entries, though far from conclusive, is the local presence of an older family of formerly enslaved persons headed by Lewis Walker and wife Jane. Records show that in 1866, only one year after the Civil War ended, Walker was living on the lands of John Strother Buckner.[9] Buckner's land was further north by a few miles from that of Bluford Thornhill. In 1867, Walker was living on the property of John Walden[10], and in 1868 and 1869, he was living on Augustine Walden's land.[11] John and Augustine were brothers, sons of William Walden, a former enslaver and owner of vast landholdings in southernmost Rappahannock County, some of which neighbored those of Bluford Thornhill. Lewis and Jane Walker are recorded on the 1870 census as nearby residents to Malinda and Bluford, meaning they were in close proximity to Juliet's children living in Thornhill's household.[12] The Walkers were parents to ten children, some of whom were about the same age as Juliet's children.[13] One Walker son, Lindsay, would play a pivotal role in James Kilby's life as an adult, as will be explained later. In the early years of Reconstruction, Lewis Walker apparently worked for wages. He must have been saving, for he would become an early African American landowner, neighbor to the parents of Simon's future wife, and seller of land parcels to Simon in 1898 and 1901.[14] The later association with Walker could have had roots in or before 1870. It is reasonable to think that Lewis and Jane Walker were watching over Juliet's children, casually or directly, as they grew into young adults.

The surname confusion for the African American children in the 1870 Bluford Thornhill household, when their surnames were recorded as Walker, presents an unanswered puzzle and still a plausible explanation in a Lewis Walker association.[15]

Selecting permanent surnames was a process, not an event. The timing for selecting a family name was not always immediate. Until a freedman or freedwoman had an encounter with an authority who required a complete name—for example, entering into a contract, obtaining a license, or registering to vote—he or she had time to think about, to "try on" as it were, a family name. Juliet's children, young as they were, probably had no contact with an official demanding a second name. Disregarding the Lewis Walker association, unsubstantiated as it is, there are other possible explanations for the census entries.

Census takers, officially known as "enumerators," had the duty to visit each village and farm or plantation, each place of residence, and gather data required for that census. Word may have gotten around that the enumerator was in the neighborhood or might show up on a particular day. However, no appointments were made, the time the enumerator would arrive was not known, and the head of the household might have been away or too busy. Family daily activities went on as usual. All household members need not be present to provide their own information. If the head of household—and that typically was the male landowner—was not available, then his wife or any other adult present could provide the requested information. A census taker never visited twice, never returning later if it happened that a male head of household was not at home upon the first visit.

If Malinda's granddaughter Alice provided the information, she likely was ignorant of servants' last names. Then again, any one of the adults may have willfully provided false information in an attempt to protect a White family name and disassociate from those they thought inferior and undeserving of family identity. Genealogical lecturer and writer John Philip Colletta described the problem with census accuracy this way:

> Census information was transmitted verbally by whomever was at home or near at hand when the census taker came calling. It can constitute either primary or secondary information, depending on the situation of the informant. This is unknowable to the researcher, but a high frequency of discrepancies between censuses and other sources suggests that much census information is secondhand and vulnerable to error.[16]

All other information in the census about ages, genders, race, inclusion in the household of their former enslavers, and given names—at least for three—makes a strong case that these were, in fact, Juliet's children. A reasonable conclusion is that the surname the census taker entered is erroneous. As for the eighteen-year-old Black child, the description, other than the name, matches Simon and would complement a known family group.

A third explanation for the census record must be considered. Maybe the surname of Walker for the children believed to be Juliet's was accurately recorded this day, just not the surname they would ultimately choose. Perhaps Sarah, James, John, and Simon had not "fixed" a permanent surname, and in the absence of their mother to offer a response, and through association with Lewis Walker, they had chosen in this instance to identify with that surname. They were also young and unlikely to be present to have responded for themselves.

The accuracy of last names in the census record is suspect. Separate evidence strongly suggests that these children were Juliet's offspring. Accepting that these were Juliet's children, young people who would thereafter adopt Kilby as their surname, places them in a time and location of great importance for testing freedom. The record suggests they likely had support and guidance from the Walkers and other role models to emulate as they matured.

The fifth child in this household is Elizabeth, a Black female age three. It is easy to think that she was a sister to the other African American children in this family group. Yet, in the 1880 U.S. census, I find "Betsy Kilby," now ten years older at age thirteen, in the same household performing duties as a cook—and likely all home and personal care—for Bluford.[17] With age, household, and name, Betsy certainly is the Elizabeth of ten years earlier, now taking the surname Kilby. However strong the circumstantial evidence, to date there is no *direct* evidence that Elizabeth is the fifth child of Juliet.

And Where is Juliet?

After analyzing other clues and reconciling what appears at first take as contradicting evidence, the 1870 census record provides a snapshot of the family of Juliet's children and their ties to their former enslavers. However, Juliet's name is conspicuously absent. Where was she? What happened to Juliet at war's end? The records of the F.T. Baptist Church, Bluford and Malinda Thornhill's place of worship, provide some clues.

The Baptist Church of Jesus Christ at F.T., commonly known as F.T. Baptist Church in the late nineteenth century and today, was the spiritual home to many Kilbys, Thornhills, and related families.[18] The initials F.T. in the church's name came from the early eighteenth-century landowner of the area, Francis Thornton, and from whom the names F.T. Valley and F.T. Village are derived.

Until other congregations formed and built new churches, F.T. was the prominent congregation that drew parishioners from miles around. Among its members were a substantial number of free and enslaved "colored."[19]

The F.T. Baptist Church minute books are a written record of meeting notes, baptisms, excommunications, dismissals, deaths, and membership lists. There one finds that Lucy, Bluford Thornhill's first wife, was baptized in 1832.[20] One could assume that Bluford attended services with her. After Lucy died in late 1863 — or was it 1864? — and after Bluford and Malinda were married, the new couple attended this church as their spiritual home. There is no indication that they were ardent churchgoers or devout Christians, perhaps attending to keep up appearances. Malinda waited until 1869 to transfer her membership from New Salem Baptist Church, and Bluford hesitated to join the church fellowship through baptism until 1875.[21]

In the church's membership list of the time, one baptismal record stands out:

B. Thornhill's — Juliet   Sept 17 – 1865[22]

Though an insignificant notation to the casual reader, this simple entry reveals a date of high significance in Juliet's life. Sunday, the seventeenth of September 1865, creates visions in my imagination of a small congregation of the F.T. Baptist Church meeting on the banks of the nearby Hughes River as Blacks and Whites made their confessions and the pastor dipped them below the waters.

The phrasing of this entry reflects the attitudes of the time, whether of Bluford's own words or those of the church scribe; Juliet was still the property of Bluford and Malinda. To Whites, she had no independent identity. The simple respect of a self-chosen surname was not yet hers, at least not one acknowledged by her former owner and recorded by the church clerk. Yet, internally, Juliet must have started to build an identity never before experienced, the self-realization that freedom would afford.

A Question of Identity

Like a jigsaw puzzle with pieces scattered about, we orient and test, piece by piece, to find where fragments fit and to expand the picture. So it is with the scattered bits of information found in the F.T. Church 1855–1878 minute book.

To be a member of the congregation of F.T. Baptist Church during the nineteenth century, one was expected to scrupulously follow its rules of conduct. Any member could be called to account for a reported infraction. In his book about this church's history, Rev. A. Paul Thompson described church discipline this way:

> In early days, Baptist congregations often disciplined their members for violating codes of conduct and statements of doctrine as prescribed by the congregation for its members. F.T. was not an exception. . . . F.T., as other Baptist congregations, being self-governed, decided the ethical, moral, and doctrinal standards by which her member[s] governed their lives.
>
> The disciplining procedure followed this pattern. A charge against a member was brought to the attention of the church sitting in congregational meeting on a Saturday "after divine worship." When the charge was heard . . . a [White] member, or a committee of [White] men (rarely, if ever, a woman) was appointed to visit the supposedly erring member.[23]

The appointee determined if the charge had substance and, if so, "invited" the accused to answer the charge at the next monthly meeting. If the accused's explanation was unsatisfactory to the church—White members were the only ones allowed to vote—the offending member was excluded from the congregation. This was strict punishment, though not always permanent, for one could ask to be restored to membership after so much time and professed repentance.[24]

Some of what we see in the minute book appears to form an identifiable picture, but we must not force ill-fitting pieces into a false picture of reality. Some intriguing entries may create an informative image of Juliet—or they may be a trap leading the historian to spurious conclusions. Here is what the church recorded:

> F.T. Church meeting Saturday July 13 – 1867 . . .
> Charges brought against Juliet Milton, Louisa Stailing, Henrietta _____ and Juliet Wiginton for having committed fornication, whereupon the church directed that they be invited to attend our next meeting and answer to the charge brought against them.

> F.T. Church meeting Saturday August 10 – 1867
> After divine worship by brother A M Grimsl[e]y, Then convening for business, when Juliet Milton, Louisa Stailing, Henrietta _____ and Juliet Wiginton were called under a former charge for fornication. Juliet Milton had previously confessed great concern and professed to have been forgiven. She was retained. The other three Viz. Louisa Stailing Henrietta _____ and Juliet Wiginton failing to attend and answer to the charge brought against them, were excluded from the fellowship of the church.[25]

The four charged women—Juliet Milton, Louisa Stailing, Henrietta (with no last name), and Juliet Wiginton—were each included in the recognized list of "colored" members of F.T. Baptist Church.[26] The minute book shows that Milton and Stailing had each been baptized the September 17, 1865.[27] We see from another entry that "B. Thornhill's Juliet" was baptized that same day, as was "Allen Yowell's Louisa."[28] Juliet and Louisa, Juliet Milton and Louisa Stailing; puzzle pieces seem to fit. Wiginton was restored to the church in 1876, long after the time of Simon's marriage and report that his mother was deceased, thus excluding Juliet Wiginton as Juliet Ann.[29] The record here suggests that the woman identified as Juliet Milton was the same as Bluford's Juliet, who was the same as Juliet Ann, known mother of Simon, John, James, and Sarah. There are no other Miltons as members of this church or inhabitants in the immediate area to provide contradictory evidence. The surname Milton would never be used in connection to Juliet Ann by family members and public records. If Juliet Ann took the name Milton as her new identity, if only for a short time, we may never know the reason for this choice and why next generations only knew her as a Kilby.[30]

The charges brought against the four women by the White church leaders should be considered in the proper context. Sexual relations outside marriage were forbidden and condemned as a grave sin in the religious institutions of the day.[31] Fornication was a term that applied to any illicit sexual activity, whether consensual or not. A woman having a child out of wedlock, for example, was guilty of fornication, even if the pregnancy was the result of rape.

By reading through minute books of the region's Baptist churches, one can see that charges of fornication and bearing children out of wedlock were all too common, the preponderance directed toward African American women as bearing sole blame in each case.[32] Taking this into consideration, in this instance concerning Juliet Milton, no conclusion of impropriety on her part should be drawn.

The entries for January 13, 1866, listing the "Names of Colored Members for New Book" includes Juliet Milton, baptized "Sept 17, 1865."[33] Penned to the right of her name is the addition:

Deceased – August 9 – 1867.

If this is Juliet Ann, then this notation is the only record of her day of death. Had Juliet "confessed great concern and professed to have been forgiven" on her death bed? Had her statement of contrition been presented by someone else at the church meeting a day later, and sorrow and forgiveness been granted there?

Next, I can correlate two other points of information. First, there is a statement made in 1873 regarding his mother when Simon wanted to marry. The document stated that she was dead.[34]

Second, and perhaps of greater significance, was the fifth child in the 1870 Thornhill household, Elizabeth, age three and thus born in 1867. In 1880, the census included in the household of Bluford Thornhill a thirteen-year-old Black cook named Betsy Kilby.[35] Certainly, Elizabeth and Betsy were just different names for the same child. The birth year of one person and the death year of another suggests a connection. Had Juliet Ann died after giving birth to Elizabeth?

The preceding presents a mystery that may not be fully answered. Conjecture does not constitute genealogical proof, but until conclusive evidence is uncovered, these notes from history may picture the close of Juliet's life.

Juliet Ann's identification is more than a surname that she may have used. She was born, grew to adulthood, bore children, and died. Any other description is unneeded to honor and respect her as a human being. I remember and venerate Juliet's personhood, and that was her true, inalienable identity.

Using the Kilby Surname

No direct evidence has been found to indicate that Juliet ever used the surname Kilby. Not until the marriage of her oldest son on December 30, 1873, and the subsequent official records do we first find the name "Juliet Kilby," mother of the groom, in an official document.[36] Simon provided the Kilby surname for his mother and himself in applying for and obtaining a license to marry.

A written marriage consent signed by a parent, normally needed only for a bride of young age, was penned by Paschal Finks for Simon to show he was of legal age to marry, that being twenty-one. Finks was a well-to-do White merchant, a Thornhill in-law and adjacent landowner, a likely employer of Simon, and a man well known to county officials. On that consent document, Finks made the statement, "His father & mother are both dead."[37] Had Juliet been alive to see her firstborn marry, she would have been age forty, but her life beyond slavery and to mother her growing children had ended too soon. On a death certificate and in newspaper obituaries many years later, "Julia Kilby" is named as the mother of the deceased.[38] So, we have Juliet's son using the Kilby surname for himself and on behalf of his mother. We have no *direct* evidence Juliet ever used the Kilby surname for her own identity.

Simon Becomes Charles William

As Juliet's children grew to maturity and took wives and husbands, vital records, tax records, and censuses show that each used Kilby as their surname. The marriage records for Simon and his bride, Lucy Frances Wallace, are the first public records of one of Juliet's children using the Kilby surname.

The question must be asked, was "Simon" the name Juliet gave to her first child at his birth? That was the name of one of the children given in Mortimer Kilby's 1865 chancery lawsuit while Juliet and children were still enslaved.[39] Multiple official records up until 1901 show Simon to be known by that given name.

Then suddenly, the name Simon Kilby disappears from public records, and we see a new name where Simon should appear, the name Charles W. Kilby. The family unit was intact, but the head of household was now going by a different given name. Was this, in fact, the same person? The answer is found in a land deed recorded in 1945 wherein Simon and Fannie's children and grandchildren, the heirs-at-law to their parent's estate, sold three tracts of family lands. The deed reads in part, "Whereas, Charles W. Kilby, who was also known as Simon Kilby, and is the same person as Simon Kilby . . ." and goes on to emphasize that Charles W. and Simon were one and the same person.[40] In a 1933 published death notice for Fannie Kilby, her husband's full name as he used it later in life is revealed as Charles *William* Kilby.[41] "Charles William" are the same forenames that appear in the 1858 deed of sale between James Franklin Kilby and Burgess Kilby, sons of Malinda.[42]

Why did a forty-eight-year-old man decide to use a different forename? When he was only a child, could his enslavers have forced one name upon him, dismissing his mother's chosen name entirely? With which name did Juliet bless him at his birth? The records are silent, but this man, known by two different forenames and maybe conflicted over their origins, likely knew the history of both and exercised his freedom to redefine his identity.

CHAPTER EIGHT

Transition to Freedom

1865–1870

The one thing that both planters and freed people shared in the first months following the Civil War was widespread uncertainty. What had changed and what remained the same? What would it take to move forward, or for some, to survive the day? The economic, political, and social landscape was disorienting for all Virginians, Whites and Blacks. From the perspective of those released from bondage, dreams of freedom's paradise clashed with a reality of obstinate White domination. Planters, feeling the loss of free labor, were angry and resentful, yet they had to have workers or risk ruin of their farming enterprises.

While other freed persons were leaving their former owners' farms and plantations, searching for displaced family, realizing employment options, gathering together in community, and generally testing the bounds of freedom, formerly enslaved children, and the adults who cared for them, did not have the necessary means in knowledge, skills, and maturity to become self-sufficient.

Newly freed people needed food, clothing, and shelter, as always. However, for the first time, they were responsible for obtaining their own subsistence. First-year freedom had its limits. Agreements needed to be reached if freed people were not to be thrown out of their homes. White planters, exercising their position of power, used coercive tactics to force work agreements in their favor. The United States Army maintained a sparse yet forceful presence in the region to maintain peace and initiate the federal government's attempts at Reconstruction. Local offices of the Bureau of Refugees, Freedmen, and Abandoned Lands, more commonly known as the Freedmen's Bureau, were established at Culpeper, Madison, and "Little Washington" in Rappahannock County.[1] The local assistant commissioners/assistant superintendents—one for each location and each a military officer—had the responsibility to hear claims and complaints, to issue rations, and to provide medical relief to freed persons. They also had the authority to bring offenses to judgment in the Freedmen's Court, witness and supervise labor contracts, and create apprenticeships for Black orphan children.[2]

No evidence has been found of a work contract between Juliet and the Thornhills, no documentation of any contact recorded with the Freedmen's Bureau.[3] Traveling the distance to see the agent for assistance or to file a grievance would have been difficult and risky. With four children to care for, it is likely she saw no other option than to continue serving Bluford and Malinda under conditions they set.

Had Juliet been absent or dead, the Freedmen's Bureau superintendent would surely have apprenticed Simon, John, James, and Sarah to Bluford for many years, virtual enslavement enforceable through legal contract.[4] Historian Mary Niall Mitchell described these lopsided covenants this way: "An apprenticeship contract would have placed a child . . . in service to a master usually until the age of 18 (or 15, if the child were a girl) with stipulations that the child learn a trade or skill, be fed and clothed, and receive some schooling."[5] In Virginia, the law stipulated apprenticeships to the ages of twenty-one for boys and eighteen for girls.[6] The emphasis was always on the labor the child was forced to provide with total obedience. "Schooling" was subject to the master's judgment and will, and education was most often neglected. Conditions may not have been as harsh as they could have been before emancipation, but until they became of age, Juliet's children had to take direction from their former owners.

Malinda and Bluford Thornhill, like so many other Whites, exploited Blacks before they could take a foothold in their own self-determination. Juliet's children's presence in the Thornhill household in 1870 gives evidence of their continued servitude.[7] Wages for farm laborers in the area ranged between $6.00 and $10.00 per month, according to one report from the Freedmen's Bureau.[8] There is no evidence that Simon initially made even that. If Simon was held under an apprentice agreement, formal and written or not, he most likely received far less or no more than minimal ration and a place to sleep at night.

. . .

Many African Americans were members of the F.T. Baptist Church before and immediately after the Civil War. In January 1866, the church minute book included ninety-eight "Names of Colored Members." Juliet became a member by being baptized there in September 1865. Attending services at F.T. may have been the first opportunity for Simon and his brothers to hear sermons from the pulpit. It may have been here that their spiritual foundations first lay. Even though Simon was not listed as a member, nor Lucy Wallace, his bride-to-be, Rev. Aldridge Grimsley, the White pastor of F.T., married the couple in 1873.[9]

F.T. Baptist Church minutes reveal that slowly at first and then increasing in numbers as the 1870s ended, Black members requested letters of dismission to formally leave the church for another. The movement of African Americans leaving primarily White congregations to organize their own churches accelerated during the years of Reconstruction. F.T. maintained separate lists of its Black membership, denoting baptisms, dismissions, and exclusions. The minutes also reveal Black participation in delivering sermons. Wesley Gillison and Joshua Brown were African American members of the congregation who "came forward" and were "granted license to exercise his gift and to preach . . . as long as he shall remain a consistent member of this church." Leaving F.T. in 1881, they likely went on to minister to newly organized Black congregations.

One such church was the Nazareth Baptist Church, organized in 1879 to minister to African Americans living in the Gourdvine Neck region. Simon, his wife, and his family became devout members of this church community. One hundred forty years later, Nazareth Baptist Church counts at least four generations of Kilby descendants who followed Simon's example by becoming active members.[10]

. . .

In the years and decades following the Civil War, newspapers that served Virginia's Piedmont readership fanned the flames of White animosity toward freed people and their families, encouraging the spread of racial bigotry and violence. Local publishers of small-town papers, who were often also the writers and editors, were not hesitant about reprinting northern newspapers' reporting and putting their own biased spin on the story. George Bagby, co-publisher of *The Native Virginia* in Orange, Virginia, wrote several articles in 1868 and 1869 about what he described as "a strange and mysterious organization," the Ku Klux Klan.[11] More than an unbiased reporter, he was an advocate, a provocateur, a purveyor of hate, and most likely a secret Ku Kluxer himself.

Bagby was not alone among writers and publishers in expressing harsh racial intolerance, perpetuating crude stereotypes, and even suggesting retaliation for perceived assaults on White political, economic, and social dominance. His loyal readership apparently appreciated his thinking. Were the readers of Culpeper, Madison, and Rappahannock counties so different than their neighbors in Orange? As newspaper accounts in succeeding decades would tell,

> † K . † K . † K . †
> WE HAVE COME!
> WE ARE HERE!!
> † † † ↓ † † † † † † † † †
> BEWARE!!
>
> [CIRCLE] TAKE HEED!
>
> When the *black cat* is gliding under the shadows of darkness and the death watch ticks at the lone hour of midnight, then we, the pale riders, are abroad. † †
>
> ☞ Speak in whispers and we hear you. † †
>
> ☞ Dream as you sleep in the inmost recesses of your houses, and hovering over your beds we gather your sleeping thoughts while our daggers are at your throats. † †
>
> Ravishers of the liberties of the people for whom we died and yet live be gone ere it be too late. † †
>
> ☞ *Unholy Blacks, cursed of God take warning and fly.* †
>
> ☞ TWICE HATH THE SACRED
> ☞ SERPENT HISSED
>
> When again his voice is heard your doom is sealed!!
>
> ☞ BEWARE!! TAKE HEED!
>
> Given under our hand in the DEN OF THE SACRED SERPENT on the Mystical Day of the Bloody Moon!!!
>
> B. K. N. & L. G. Q.
> Grand Cyclops of the Ku Klux Klan,
> For the Tenth Divi-ion.
> To be executed by the Grand White Death and the Rattling Skeleton.

Ku Klux Klan article in an 1868 Orange County newspaper.[12]

elements of racial intimidation continued to terrorize Blacks of these rural counties.

And it was more than rancorous talk. Threatening talk and physical violence against African Americans—whether by avowed members of the Ku Klux Klan or mere "concerned citizens"— tended to cast blame upon the victim and more broadly his race, justify extra-judicial punishment, and exonerate the perpetrators (if and when they could be identified). Sentiments never favored racial harmony. White-controlled media—newspapers, periodicals, books, and the new medium of movies—openly used racist language and imagery to fan prejudices. Touted in the local paper as "the one great picture of all time," *Birth of a Nation* glorified the Lost Cause and demonized Blacks. It played only one night at the Criglersville High School in northern Madison County in September 1923.[13] Simon Kilby, his wife and children, and other African Americans may have felt the heat of racial prejudice heightened by the movie's local showing.

The *Alexandria Gazette* ran a column titled "Letters from Rappahannock" periodically in the 1880s and 1890s. The folksy but racist writing catered to White readers and revealed facts and attitudes of White dominance. "The negroes . . . are as a rule well-behaved, industrious and polite in their manners, but now and then they forget themselves, and the result is they have come to repent," opened one article.[14] This temperate wording hid the reality of vigilante retribution for offenses like "attempted assault on a young married [White] lady." Such an allegation was made against John Fitzhugh, a Black man lynched in Rappahannock County in August 1884.[15]

The messages to African Americans were clear—accept your position, know who is in control, do not get out of line. In the immediate aftermath of the Civil War and for the years and decades that followed, these were times of peril for African Americans who tried to rise beyond a slave's existence. It took great courage to not succumb to fear, to persevere under the storm clouds of White intolerance and oppression.

For Simon and his new wife, for James and his recent bride, for Sarah and her young husband, and for independent and still youthful John, navigating the limited choices of freedom required understanding of their oppressive environment and deep courage and determination to overcome the obstacles that lay ahead.

CHAPTER NINE

Who Will Be Remembered?

1870–1898

The war was over. Its battles had claimed the dead. Weariness replaced anguish, and anger and hostility set in. As freed persons united in purpose and struggled toward the clear air of freedom, Southern Whites seethed in bitterness and resentment, unable to accept racial equality. The old order of White superiority remained in their hearts and guided their behaviors. Divisions festered. Families were broken.

Malinda Hawkins Kilby Thornhill, the woman who had started adult life with ambition and promise, who had born many children and quickly lost a husband, who perpetuated a tradition of racial superiority through practice and belief, who withstood legal claim and family discord, who endured war's threat to body and land, who abandoned her past and found refuge in a widowed brother-in-law and his home's protection, who thereafter settled for obscurity and rest, died on April 29, 1874.[1] Surely there was a funeral service, quiet and solemn, attended by family and loyal friends, words from the Bible spoken as her casket was lowered into the earth. But there was no published account, no newspaper notices or poems in memorial, no family notes to offer words of remembrance or even a date of passing—all details are lost from history.[2] Only the church minute book recorded her death, and that with a perfunctory notation. The location of her final resting remains unknown, a memory erased for a wife, mother, matriarch, and former owner of human property.

Bluford Thornhill, widower of Malinda, defender of the South, enslaver of Juliet Ann and her children until forced emancipation tempered but did not end that cruelty, died on May 19, 1882.[3] Like Malinda, his body lies in a grave lost to time and memory.

Thomas and Malinda Kilby's children met unsought fates. Martha Ann died a few years after her father.[4] Chesterfield was the next to die in 1855, then Thomas L. in 1861.[5] Burgess disappeared, last known to be in Richmond as the Civil War came to its end, his fate thereafter unknown.[6] In the mid-1880s, Mortimer moved with his wife and daughters to Dakota Territory (now North Dakota) and died there in the winter of 1888, just two weeks after and perhaps as a result of the deadly Schoolhouse Blizzard.[7] Malinda's daughters Louisa, Missouri, and Adeline survived their parents but sold all their interest in the Thomas Kilby estate early on.[8] Only Frank, the oldest son and the last of Malinda's family to die (1898), remained in Culpeper County to witness his birth family's dissolution.[9]

Rights to the lands Thomas Kilby had bought nearly a half century earlier, property his children thought they would one day inherit, had changed control many times as some heirs would sell their share to others and later inherit shares from passing siblings. Court proceedings would finally settle ownership issues so that titles could be cleared. Only Frank was left to retain ownership of the land where he and his siblings grew up, the place where Juliet and four of her children were born.[10]

By 1833, Thomas Kilby was living the dream of a prosperous landowner: the prototypical small-scale plantation owner with crops, livestock, and human property to increase his wealth, and the family man with children to carry forward his legacy and memory. His family's future seemed assured. Destiny would have it otherwise. Malinda had the will to move forward, though she struggled with inherited debt and brewing disharmony with and among her children. Prosperity and notable achievement—far more important, happiness—eluded them all. And caught in the flow of time were the African-descent humans held in disregard of the moral imperative of humane behavior. One family was headed for obscurity while another was rising to the light of a new era.

PART TWO

A TREE GROWS HERE

As you will soon see, finding freedom is only the first part. Living free is a whole other.
 — TA-NEHISI COATES, *THE WATER DANCER*

Juliet's Cry

You took my body,
and you tortured my spirit.
You worked me so.
You demanded I be mute,
but my voice will be heard
through my children
and their children
and their children.

CHAPTER TEN

One Family, Separate Paths

Though they were not slaves, they were not yet quite free.
— FREDERICK DOUGLASS,
LIFE AND TIMES OF FREDERICK DOUGLASS

They had crossed Freedom's river, but what did they expect to find on the other side? It was a time to own the air they breathed, to contemplate the unthinkable, and then to accept a reality of individual responsibilities and self-directed possibilities. Some paths led away from the painful past and toward fertile opportunities in a distant location, toward a new start and expectations of happiness. Other paths came with the security of the known, yet required accepting familiar and accommodative roles, where a change to independence came too slowly for some and reluctantly for those still holding power. Choices were limited by one's skills; social, familial, health, and economic circumstances; knowledge and familiarity with an outside world; and a White populous making way. Could Juliet look after herself and her four children by taking the path toward the unknown? Simon, the oldest, was twelve, and the youngest, Sarah, was only four. Juliet had no strong influences to pull her away from the Thornhills. She knew no other choice; she had to take the path that meant virtual captivity. And that path defined the futures of her children as well—at least until they were able to break away in distance and accomplishment.

After emancipation, Juliet's four known children, and her fifth child born soon thereafter, would find their ways beyond the confines of life centered on the land of their former enslavers. After Juliet's passing, the children remained together as their own family unit within the Thornhill household.[1] History is silent as to whether Malinda and Bluford provided even basic nurturing and guidance that the children deserved, and there is no record that Simon or his siblings received any schooling. Many Whites were bitter over the loss of ownership and authority over their human property, blaming the formerly enslaved for all their woes. Perhaps, like so many other White landowners who needed field laborers and house servants, the Thornhills exploited these children for their labor, providing only food, clothing, and shelter, only as much as they would have received if still enslaved. They may have thought their responsibilities ended there. There were African American adults close by to offer support and guidance as Simon, John, James, Sarah, and Bettie came of age and needed help in making life's decisions. The historian Leon Litwack generalized in saying, "If some absorbed the cultural ethos of the white family from constant contact with it, the vast majority of black children formed their view of the world in the quarters and usually within their own family groupings. . . . In the absence of parents, the child was still more likely to obtain the love and learning he needed from other blacks than from his 'white folks.'"[2] There were other Blacks living close by who in later times are known to have been associates, if not fictive kin. A connection with the Lewis Walker family may have begun during this period.

Each child grew into adulthood to find a chosen path of life. The sibling bonds of early years would gradually be broken as each found a marriage partner and started a family of his or her own, whether near their historical roots in southern Rappahannock County or in more promising, distant locales. The 1880 U.S.

census is silent on the whereabouts of James, Sarah, John, and Simon, but we can trace their paths through other records. The widower Bluford Thornhill was living alone except for Betsy Kilby, who, at age thirteen, remained in his household as a cook.

On May 19, 1882, Bluford Thornhill died.[3] The last of those who once claimed ownership of Juliet and her progeny was gone. But the onset of Jim Crow would prove that racial discrimination and oppression were not buried with the former enslavers.

The decades that followed would present harsh social and economic realities to test the souls of those struggling for a footing in freedom. Each of Juliet's children in his or her way would prevail. Here are the stories of each of Juliet's children, as much as the records so far reveal.

CHAPTER ELEVEN

Simon Kilby

1853–1924

On the third day of October 1924, a cloudless, crisp autumn Friday, the prominent townsfolk of Madison, Virginia, took time to remember and bask in the county's past and proclaim the righteousness of the present by reserving a full day for public celebration.[1] The Madison Gala Day started with a grand parade that wound through the village. A brass band led the procession of thirty-three floats and marching groups. An old stagecoach driven by "Uncles" Kirtley and Strother, passengered by antebellum-period costumed ladies, and accompanied by Confederate costumed horsemen riding alongside, brought "memories of the Old South" to life.[2]

Joining in the citizens' parade was a car decorated with the slogan, "A safe and clean Madison." The car escorted a company of marchers wearing "white robes and hoods," members of the "Madison kaunty klan," which contributed six dollars to the celebration's sponsor, the town's "Community League." Schoolchildren of the several (White) county schools paraded in union with the adults. The day's events continued with demonstrations, sport games, plays, and hobnobbing. The League served dinner, and the band played "Dixie" as a townsman "waved the dear old Southern flag and cheered loudly." For the White citizens of Madison County, it was a day to reminisce over a glorified past and revel in their sense of achievement. Among the other news of the following week—comings and goings of the people, notable deaths, business ads, legal notices, and farm product prices—the *Madison County Eagle* printed articles detailing and praising the Gala Day activities.[3] But some news never made it into the paper.

Neither in this issue nor in issues to follow would there appear a notice of the passing of one of their county's citizens, a long-time resident, a hard-working man who had saved money and bought his own land, a taxpayer, a dedicated churchgoer, a loving husband and father—and a man who as a child had been enslaved. The day after others had celebrated their progress and the advantages of unlimited opportunity, out of their sight and minds, Simon Kilby, the first child of Juliet Ann, quietly passed from life.[4]

For the privileged inhabitants of the villages and farms of northern Madison County and southern Rappahannock, this death was no cause for reflection, no questions, no concerns. Their disregard was just another opportunity to cleanse history and bury the past with the other dead. Few of them would know of Simon's history, and few would keep the memory of his life alive for the cherished kin who would follow.

. . .

The twenty-first day of May 1853 was known by one of his daughters as Simon Kilby's day of birth, recorded for the first time with specificity on his official certificate of death seventy-one years later.[5] Simon never knew with accuracy or authority the day when he was born. Maybe Juliet had told him he came to life on a warm spring day when the laurels were in full bloom. That might have been the best she could do, not having the advantage of calendar knowledge. Malinda Thornhill would have found it impertinent had a young Simon made such an inquiry. She made no record for her own purposes.

Frederick Douglass wrote in his 1845 autobiography, "By far the larger part of the slaves know as little of their ages as horses know of theirs, and it is the wish of most masters within my knowledge to keep their slaves thus ignorant. I do not remember to have ever met a slave who could tell of his birthday. . . . A want of information concerning my own was a source of unhappiness to me even during childhood. The White children could tell their ages. I could not tell why I ought to be deprived of the same privilege."[6] This fact of identity, a precise date of birth that any White child would know and possess of his own, was an unknown Simon had to endure. His actual date of birth and his real age remained a painful mystery. Like Douglass, who never knew the day, month, and even year of his birth, Simon may have distressed at the loss of this essential fact throughout his life. With no actual birth certificate and no other record providing both day and month of Simon's birth, any degree of certainty cannot be established. The synthesis of other recorded information suggests that 1853 was likely the correct year of birth, initially celebrated quietly by his mother and no other.[7]

Edward Ball wrote about being introduced to the term "step-asides." As he was told by an African American family member, "That means that the White father does not acknowledge his black children, He has them, and he 'steps aside.'"[8] Simon was the first of the "step-aside" children born of Juliet. If Simon ever knew his father, ever received any acknowledgment, all today is silent.

It appears that Simon remained with his mother and three siblings, all under the control of Malinda and Bluford Thornhill at war's end. He legally could have left after the Civil War, but where would a boy of age twelve go? The 1870 census gives credence that Simon remained in service to Bluford at least until that year.

Young men in particular were desperately needed after the war to work Virginia's farms. Free slave labor disappeared almost instantly. According to law, ex-enslaved workers had to be paid for their labor going forward. Former enslavers had to negotiate, though, in this skill they had the upper hand and easily took advantage of freed persons. In some cases, the Freedmen's Bureau intervened to negotiate and enforce written work contracts. After a complete search, no contract document for Simon—or Juliet or Simon's siblings—has been discovered. Yet, the Freedmen's Bureau, when they were aware and focused on individual cases, enforced required care, minimal though it was, for vulnerable and dependent African American children. Like it or not, Simon and his younger brothers and sister needed the shelter and sustenance Bluford and Malinda provided. Perhaps they felt—or maybe it was reality—there were no alternatives but to stay and do as they were told.

For the freedmen, male and female, of Virginia's Piedmont, the decade after war's end was marked by unleashed ambition, tempered by an atmosphere of resurgent racial prejudice, dashed hopes, and tremendous hardship. The emancipated Blacks saw land ownership as a key to self-determination and prosperity. Bartering their labor for shelter and provisions and saving what pittance of money they could earn through wages or sharecropping, some were able to progress toward realizing their land-owning dream. For freedmen of both genders, the experience and skills of working crops, raising livestock, and tending a house were already familiar, just not for their own benefit. While some would leave for more hospitable regions, the unknowns of leaving were too great. Simon might have thought about leaving for more hospitable regions, but two things kept him in his home: younger siblings who needed his watch and paying work that was oppressive but tolerable.

Paschal Finks was Bluford Thornhill's son-in-law, a merchant operating a country store, and a large landowner.[9] Finks's store and farm and Thornhill's farm were adjacent, only separated by the small lot where the F.T. Baptist Church sat.[10] Linked White families, adjacent farming operations, and a community church at the center were facts that prefigured Simon's future. Simon may have worked for both men in his early years, tending toward Finks (and then his son) as years passed and as Malinda and Bluford, in turn, died.

Maybe it was at F.T. Baptist Church, where Blacks could socialize a bit after Sunday services that Simon must have noticed Fannie Wallace as a young lady who could capture the hearts of many young men. She might have seen him as a strong and handsome man, a good candidate for a mate and family provider.

Lucy Frances Wallace, "Fannie" as she was familiarly called, was the daughter of Walker and Martha (Parks) Wallace.[11] Walker Wallace, a long-standing church member, had been appointed sexton of F.T. Baptist Church in 1872.[12] He also may have been working for Paschal Finks as a "farmhand."[13] Fannie may have been living with her parents on the Finks farm in 1873.[14] The Finks and Wallace families knew each other by acquaintance but certainly not socially. Whether Simon first met Fannie at Sunday church services or through some other chance encounter, fate took its course. Lucy Frances and Simon decided to marry.

To get married, under state law each couple first needed to obtain a license from county officials. For young people, that required documentary evidence of age and, if underage, parental permission. Implicit in this step was a degree of literacy these parties did not have. Though alternatives were possible to persuade officials, Simon and Fannie, for the sake of expedience or, more likely, a sense of obligation, got help from Paschal Finks. A newspaper of the time described Finks thus: "As administrator, he represented more estates than perhaps any other person in the county. . . . He was at one time supervisor from his district, and held other places of public trust."[15] As a prominent White landowner and merchant in southern Rappahannock County, and a man who handled many legal documents, Finks would have been recognized by court officials as an unquestioned voucher.[16]

Four days after Christmas, 1873, Lucy Frances Wallace appeared with her mother, Martha, to ask Finks to pen a statement. Martha Wallace was illiterate; she could not create the document herself. So, Paschal took out a slip of paper and wrote out Martha's statement.

In the document, Finks wrote—in Martha's voice but his wording—that she gave her consent for Lucy Frances to be married to Simon Kilby. Martha signed with her mark, and Paschal Finks certified the document with his signature.[17] Simon must have been there, too, as Paschal prepared a second paper to state that in his belief, Simon was "over twenty one," the legal age for men to be married.[18] In addressing the paper to the county clerk, he gave his assurance to the fact that "his [Simon's] Mother & Father are both dead" and thus unable to vouch for Simon's age, or at least what Paschal thought to be a correct age. In reality, Simon was twenty, not twenty-one, but perhaps neither Paschal nor Simon knew differently.

The law of the time stipulated that "The consent of the father or guardian, or if there be none, of the mother, is necessary to the marriage of a person under twenty-one years."[19] Such a consent document was typically necessary for young women to marry but not so common for a prospective groom. The law was not specific regarding gender. Of course, Simon's biological father would not come forward to admit paternity and offer consent. His secret was intact—he was "dead." Assuming Finks had known the truth, he knew better than to create a document that might embarrass a White man, and more particularly not defame an in-law.[20] Simon could neither deliver a parent to the clerk's office nor produce proof of his age. He needed Fink's statement and signature to persuade the county clerk to issue a license.

Certainly, Paschal Finks helped by using his knowledge and writing skills toward preparing necessary documentation. Nonetheless, there remains the impression of interference by a condescending, paternalistic, controlling overseer who still wielded power over the young couple looking for a new start in life. Did Finks "allow" Simon and Fannie to marry only if they agreed to continued service to him? Altruism was not in Finks's character.

The clerk issued the license, and a day later, Tuesday, December 30, 1873, Simon and Fannie were married.[21] According to the marriage return, Rev. A.M. (Aldridge Madison) Grimsley, pastor of the F.T. Baptist Church, married the couple at the "residence of the bride."[22]

. . .

What is known about Simon and Fannie's first years together? Unfortunately, very little. Possibly the young couple was living with Fannie's parents, Walker and Martha Wallace. African Americans were struggling to find employment at fair wages, to structure lives as they saw fit, to benefit from options previously unavailable: mobility, education, enfranchisement, and legal protections. The White planters—the landowners—some of whom were former enslavers, were not inclined to assist freed persons in their push toward autonomy and better lives. Contrary to helping, sentiment among many Whites was shaped by their sense of divine superiority and a right to dominate economic and social conditions. Attitudes seemed to harden as the plight of the freedmen and their families increased. No doubt, Simon faced limited opportunity as he and Fannie began life together. Paschal Finks may have provided Simon with wage-earning employment during the years of Reconstruction. If so, it was likely through coercive demand, not benevolence. Later associations suggest this early relationship. Finks's descendants had oppressive influence over a son and grandson of Simon into the twentieth century, so a continuous association between White Finkses and Black Kilbys is believed to have existed.[23]

Fannie and Simon began their family with the birth of a daughter, Bertie, on May 15, 1876.[24] The fact that Bertie was born in Rappahannock County suggests that Simon and Fannie were living in this district at that time. They probably moved across the county border into Madison County shortly thereafter, for Simon appears on that county's personal property tax rolls in 1880 for the first time. More children would follow: Hubert Reid (1881),[25] James Oscar (1882),[26] and John Henry (1884).[27] Martha Ann, known as Mattie, was born in 1888, and then followed Thomas (1890) and Ophelia (1892).[28] The names of two other male children appear on censuses as the couple's sons: Simon Jr. (1894) and Robert E. (1896).[29] The inconsistency in the number of children born and the number still living as claimed in 1900 and 1910 has not been reconciled.[30]

Simon Kilby, c. 1917. (Photo courtesy of Karin Bivins)[31]

One can imagine the hard work and sacrifices Simon and Fannie endured to provide for their family. Farming provided precious little income, and working as a farm laborer, even less.[32]

The record shows that Simon was a renter of his home while raising a family.[33] It is all the more remarkable that he was able to save small amounts through the decades to become a landowner himself in 1898: eight acres adjacent to his father-in-law's land in Madison County for which he paid fifty-one dollars.[34] Walker Wallace had purchased land from Lewis Walker, who would later sell to Simon a small parcel that bordered his (Simon's) father-in-law.[35] Before the year was out, Simon bought a sliver of adjoining land and a right-of-way from Lewis Walker for six dollars and thirty cents.[36] Lewis Walker, Walker Wallace, and Simon formed a supportive, family-like association. Once more, in 1901, Simon purchased another one-acre parcel, again from Lewis Walker, for the sum of ten dollars.[37] Though perseverance, personal sacrifice, and determination, Simon and Fannie were able to earn landowner rights and self-sufficiency while modeling admirable family life. It was a long time coming, yet in his post-emancipation, second life, Simon was able to achieve the autonomy and independence of a landowner that so few other African Americans achieved.

Simon and Fannie became members of the Nazareth Baptist Church, perhaps as early as its founding in 1879. They remained in fellowship there for the remainder of their lives. The recorded history of the church mentions that Simon and a son-in-law provided lumber for expanding a portion of the church building, most likely wood cut from Simon's own land.[38]

As the 1900s took hold, Simon and Fannie's adult children married and started independent lives. Bertie Kilby married Oscar Albert Hill on December 2, 1899.[39] The couple had five children.[40] Bertie died the year the family moved to upstate New York. Mattie Kilby married Sim Wright on March 25, 1905.[41] Sim and Mattie Wright had six children.[42] Mattie's sister Ophelia Kilby married Major Washington on March 8, 1922.[43] Ophelia and Major Washington had four daughters and one son.[44]

Hubert Reid was the next, marrying eighteen-year-old Malinda Green Frye in 1904.[45] Malinda was the daughter of Oliver Frye and M. Green.[46] Hubert was a farmer in Madison County from the time of his marriage until his death in 1949.[47] The couple had eleven children, the first child born in 1905 and the last in 1930.[48] A large number of Hubert and Malinda's descendants live today in Madison and nearby counties. Following the lead of his mother and father, Hubert and Malinda were members of the Nazareth Baptist Church, and they rest together in the church cemetery.[49]

James Oscar Kilby and sisters Bertie, Martha Ann, and Ophelia.
(Photo courtesy of Cecelia Johnson-Dunlap)

James Oscar Kilby remained a single man until he was thirty-nine.[50] Like his father and older brother, James Oscar was a farmer, initially working as a farmhand for another landowner and on land he would eventually buy for himself.[51] He also learned carpentry, his second and primary profession later in life. It was 1909 when he bought his first properties from an aunt—two parcels of about twenty-three acres—historically, land of Lewis Walker.[52]

In 1911, James Oscar applied for and was granted membership in Lodge 2121 of the Grand United Order of Odd Fellows, the benevolent society separated by segregation from the Whites-only Independent Order of Odd Fellows in the same county (Madison).[53] In 1918, James Oscar registered to vote in his local jurisdiction, courageously overcoming White society's restrictions designed to suppress Blacks from voting.[54] A photographic portrait made sometime later shows him as a handsome man dressed in a fashionable suit and tie, erect, chin up, eyes looking up and outward, and ready to take on the world with dignity and determination. These were qualities any woman would have found attractive in a mate.

Catherline Thomas and James Oscar Kilby were married on February 1, 1922.[55] The couple's first child was born two years later. They had four sons and three daughters.[56]

As a teenager in 1900, John Henry Kilby lived with brothers and sisters in the house Simon rented for the family in Madison County.[57] The 1910 census showed that John Henry was working for Andrew Finks, son of Paschal Finks.[58] Andrew was running the family farm inherited from his father and maintaining the legacy of property and racist beliefs of the Finks family.[59]

In 1913, John Henry married Mary Ella Smith.[60] Their union produced seven children, four sons and three daughters.[61] Mary Ella died in 1945, and John Henry passed in 1958.[62] Side-by-side granite headstones mark the graves of John Henry and Mary Ella Kilby in the Nazareth Baptist Church Cemetery.[63]

. . .

Simon/Charles William Kilby died quietly at home on the fourth day of October 1924.[64] He was the first of his family to be buried in the Nazareth Baptist Church Cemetery, across the road from the church that was a part of his life for so many years. His grave is unmarked.[65]

Lucy Frances Kilby died nine years after her husband.[66] The death notice published in the *Madison County Eagle* said that Charles William (Simon) and Fannie "lived a happy life together."[67] It went on to say that she was a longstanding member of Nazareth Baptist Church and "she was a good Christian and always attended church." Lucy Frances "Fannie" Kilby was buried in an unmarked grave in the church cemetery where she could be with Simon.[68]

How much, if any, of his youth in slavery did Simon share with his children, we do not know. They knew some facts of Juliet, but likely not the details of her life in bondage.[69] Perhaps Simon did not know about his grandmother Sarah, when she was taken away from his mother, and what her fate was afterward. With reason, it may also have been too painful to tell whatever he knew of his father. Simon had survived by many decades all of the sons of Thomas and Malinda Kilby, one of whom was his biological father. Maybe he had forgotten him—or chose to do so. When his children asked, he may have eased their curiosity with stories of a made-up person who loved and cared for his family. After his passing, one of his daughters, acting as informant for the death certificate, told officials only what she wanted to tell or thought she knew about Simon's parentage.[70] The certificate's name for a father, inaccurate as it is, has unfortunately misled researchers doing insufficient investigation and validation of information. Due to a daughter's lack of knowledge or desire to bury the past, a history of injustice, hardship, and final triumph—and the name of Simon's true father—was not passed on to the next generations.

CHAPTER TWELVE

Sarah Kilby

1861–1924

Sarah Kilby is believed to have been born in 1861 in Culpeper County on the plantation of Malinda Kilby. To keep memories of family lines alive and honor beloved kin, Juliet most likely named Sarah after her grandmother. As the youngest of Juliet's children born in bondage, she may not have experienced the deprivations endured by her older siblings, but her observations as a child may have shaped lasting memories. Even though throughout her life Sarah would serve the demands of White overseers, she found dignity and respect beyond her position in life.

Sarah married James Reynolds, son of Horace and Jane Reynolds, on May 18, 1879.[1] Their ceremony was conducted in Woodville in Rappahannock County by Rev. A. Lewis.[2] The marriage license recorded her age as eighteen and his as twenty-one. James's occupation was noted as a farmhand. James signed the marriage license application by stating to the clerk who filled out the form that Sarah's parent was "Fanny [sic] Kilby." Maybe James did not know that Sarah was the daughter of Juliet, and perhaps she had been brought up after her mother's death under the care of Simon and his wife, Fannie. James did not provide Sarah's father's name for the application, and if Sarah ever knew the name of her biological father, she never provided it on any public document.

From their union came the birth of a daughter, Ella May, born in Luray, Virginia, on November 10, 1883.[3] The 1898 Winchester city directory and the 1900 U.S. census show that Sarah was living in that city with her daughter, Ella.[4] Sarah was the head of the household and a widow. She was a domestic most of her adult life and was noted as a cook in the homes of several women of the city. She rented her lodging at first, and toward the end of her life, she became a homeowner herself. The 1900 census recorded that Sarah had given birth to two children, only one (Ella) still living.[5]

Ella May (Reynolds) Honesty. (Photo courtesy of Roslyn Ella Honesty)

However, by the next census a decade later, the record showed three children born, all living.[6] There is no rectification for this count of children. However, of note is that Sarah reported that she had attended school and was able to read and write.[7]

Sarah must have kept in touch with her brother John, who informed her of his life in Pittsburgh (which will be told in a later chapter). Undoubtedly, she was happy when in 1917, John and his twenty-one-year-old daughter Julia Belle came to Winchester for a visit.[8] If John had visited in earlier years, the newspapers of the day did not take notice. If this was his first trip back to Virginia after such a long absence, surely it brought great joy to reminisce with his younger sister.

Daughter Ella Reynolds married Arthur Honesty in 1901.[9] Great-great grandchildren of Sarah, descendants of Ella and Arthur Honesty, live in Winchester today.

Sarah Kilby Reynolds died on Sunday, July 13, 1924. *The Daily Independent*, a Winchester newspaper of the time, published a front-page obituary titled "Old Time Colored Woman Dies Here" and noted that Sarah was "well-known and much liked." Sarah was eulogized at the Saint Stephen CME Church, where she had been a devoted member.[10]

CHAPTER THIRTEEN

Bettie Kilby

1867–1921

As a child of age three, her name was recorded as "Elizabeth."¹ Within a decade, she would grow into the girl "Betsy" and later the woman "Bettie," a familiar form of her given name that would be her recognized identity in adulthood.² Did her mother choose her given name at random, or perhaps was she named for a foremother, as was common practice? Names were one way of making permanent connections to one's ancestors, linking past to present, keeping memories alive. As historian and author Eric Foner explained, "To solidify a sense of family continuity, slaves frequently named children after cousins, uncles, grandparents, and other relatives."³ Bettie's sister, Sarah, had the same name as their grandmother, and Bettie may have been named after Betty, an enslaved woman of James Hawkins and perhaps her great-grandmother.⁴ Names were part of a legacy, often the only identity postbellum generations had to keep ancestral memories alive.

Bettie was a Kilby by family name and by all indications a sister to Sarah, James, John, and Simon. She grew up in the household of the aged Malinda and Bluford Thornhill, suffering the absence of affection and nurturing she would have received from her natural mother had Juliet been there.[5] Perhaps her sister or one of her brothers acted as a surrogate, but they could not protect her from the expectations of master or mistress. As brothers and then sister would eventually break away, Bettie, the young and vulnerable child, was left alone to serve Malinda and Bluford in their remaining days.

Juliet Ann, the mother to the other African American children in the Thornhill household, is believed to have died on August 9, 1867, perhaps soon after giving life to Bettie, thought to be born days or weeks earlier in July. No record proves Bettie to be a sibling (or half sibling) of Juliet's known children or even the biological daughter of Juliet. Circumstances—the common Kilby family name, a grouping that appears to be a family unit within the Thornhill household, and the coincidental birth date of Bettie and death date of Juliet—suggest that these are facts identifying kin.

Malinda Thornhill, ex-enslaver of Juliet and her four oldest children, died many years before the 1880 census.[6] Bettie (recorded as "Betsy" that year) was still a child of thirteen, and her brothers and sister were old enough to begin independent lives. They had not moved far, but the Thornhill household was nearly empty. Bluford, an older man of eighty-two, was alone, except for Bettie, whom the record shows as his cook. Laundress, seamstress, housekeeper? No doubt, he required her to do much more than prepare meals. Far from equals, they still depended upon each other for their respective needs: Bluford for all the tasks of housework and caregiving and Bettie for food, clothing, and shelter.

Bettie was only fifteen when Bluford Thornhill died.[7] He left her nothing. She was on her own. Where she lived for the next few years remains a mystery, though she likely remained in the immediate area. Perhaps Simon and Fannie looked after her.

In 1883, Bettie gave birth to a girl, Cora Blanche, and then in 1885 she gave birth to a boy whom she named Robert. Records do not show the name of the father of either child. Robert died a year later, 1886, the cause listed as "Cold."[8] Cora Blanche lived into adulthood. Her first marriage, in 1906, was to John Brown, by whom she had two children.[9] Her second marriage, in 1921, was to Lindsay Edward Wilson, with whom she would remain until her death in 1938.[10]

Bettie Kilby married Armstead Carr in Albemarle County, Virginia, in 1893. He was a widower about twenty years older than Bettie, and he had seven children by his first wife. The 1900 census shows Armstead, Bettie, Cora, and two of Armstead's children, Cornelius and Eunice, living in his hometown of Charlottesville.[11]

Bettie was the youngest of Juliet's children, and she was the first to pass away. The medical certificate of April 26, 1921, listed aortic insufficiency as the cause of death.[12]

Bettie Kilby Carr was buried in an unmarked grave in Oakwood Cemetery in Charlottesville, Virginia, where her husband would be buried ten years later.[13]

CHAPTER FOURTEEN

John Kilby

1857–1932

John Kilby was Juliet's second child, born about 1857. His name first appears in records in the 1865 suit brought by Mortimer Kilby against his mother, Malinda. At age thirteen, John appears on the 1870 U.S. census living with his siblings in the household group of Bluford and Malinda Thornhill.[1] Listed as a "farm laborer," John fell into the role demanded of him by his keepers and learned as a young child in bondage. If John was able to receive any schooling during his formative years, no record exists. Later censuses would record that he was not able to read or write, but he would surpass this limitation through persistence and determination to provide for his family.

Records of John's presence in Virginia for the two decades after 1870 have not been discovered. Sometime before 1890, John migrated to Allegheny City (now a section of Pittsburgh), Pennsylvania, an industrial city bustling with factories, ironworks, river traffic, packing houses, railroads, and immigrants from other states and other parts of the world.[2] The perceived limitless employment opportunity in a northern city as a contrast to the rural hardships and hostile atmosphere in Virginia must have become an irresistible attraction for John as he grew into manhood. Who or what influenced his decision to migrate, what drew him to Pittsburgh, and how he arrived are unanswered questions. However, John was likely not alone in making a choice to leave home in hopes of a better life. Other freedmen from rural Virginia left to seek better opportunities in Pittsburgh. John may have followed others there, or maybe he arrived earlier and wrote back to persuade others to join him in the city. In 1882, a correspondent for the *Alexandria Gazette* newspaper would report from Woodville in Rappahannock County, "The great Mecca, to which pretty much all the emigrants from out this section among the negroes go, is the great manufacturing centre of Pittsburg[h]."[3] Migration would not stop, as evidenced by the January 1890 newspaper story stating, "The negro men are leaving the county in such numbers as will make farmhands scarce, their destination being the ironworks at Pittsburg[h] and Harrisburg. Some 20 have left this neighborhood in the last few days, and more are going."[4] John would not be alone as he shared his experience with fellow Virginians making lives in this city of promise.

There were already more than 18,000 African Americans in Allegheny County at the time.[5] In Pennsylvania, his first occupation was recorded as a coachman.[6] Whether John was a driver employed by a business or a private employee for a well-to-do citizen, records do not tell. Later in life, John would be employed as a teamster delivering coal.[7] With the expectation of persistent employment and a steady income, John could find a wife and start a family.

On May 15, 1890, as a trace of rain fell on Pittsburgh, John married Virginia Frances Miles, daughter of David and Patsy Miles.[8] Virginia Frances had been born in 1867 in Amherst County, Virginia, though at the time of her marriage, she was living in Swissvale, another section of Pittsburgh.[9] Records do not indicate what brought her north. Virginia Frances was twenty-five at the time of their marriage.

With thoughts of starting a family, around 1892, John and Virginia moved temporarily to 4032 Penn Avenue in the Lawrenceville district (edging on the Bloomfield district) of Pittsburgh and then to 3906, two blocks away on the same street, where they would live for the following twenty-five years.[10] An insurance map showed that the row house was a three-story brick dwelling with a mansard roof.[11] John rented the second floor; other families lived above and below.[12] This building, the first long-term home for this Kilby family, exists today much the same as it did over a century ago.

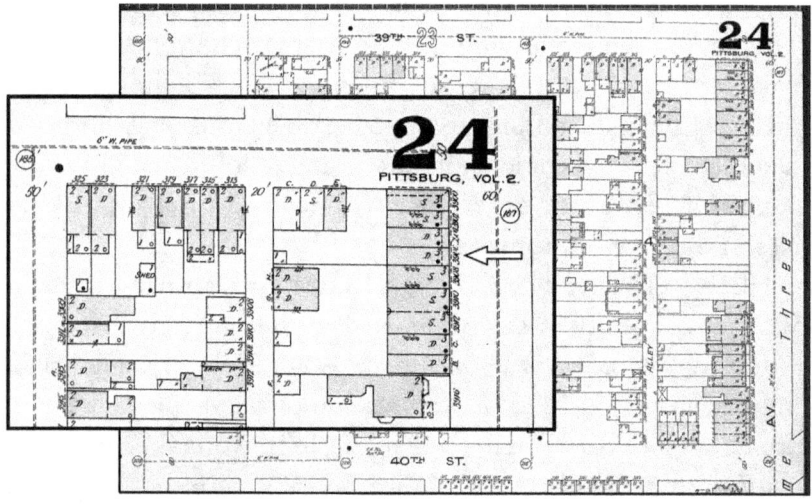

John Kilby's home at 3906 Penn Avenue, Pittsburgh, as noted on an 1892 Sanborn Fire Insurance Map.[13]
(Library of Congress, Geography and Map Division)

John and his young family watched from their front windows as the city and neighborhood modernized—paved streets, water and drainage lines, and electric and telephone lines. Sanitation was still a problem—like most residences, they had an exterior privy—but other conveniences were plentiful, and indoor plumbing would arrive in time. Across the street was the site of the Allegheny Arsenal, which became a public park in 1909. But more important to daily life, there was an electric trolley line at their front door, enabling them, with connections, to travel throughout the metropolitan area. This may have been the way John and his family were able to cross Bloomfield to their church, Carron Street Baptist Church.

A photograph taken in 1917 shows Penn Avenue just blocks from their home. Though empty in the foreground, deeper into the scene one sees a youngster on a tricycle, a woman pushing a baby carriage, other people strolling the sidewalk, a barber pole on the building where John and Virginia first moved and gave birth to their first child. Further in the distance, a trolley passes a horse-drawn cart on one side and a new-fangled "Tin Lizzy" on the other. Deep in the background, smoke from steel mills penetrate the gray haze that enveloped the city all the time.

Census records show that within several years of marriage, John and Virginia had their first child, a daughter born July 26, 1892, whom they named Flora Bernice.[14] Flora grew to marry Robert Monroe Walker, and they had one daughter, Frances Bernice Walker, born in 1921.[15] Flora lived in the home her father bought on Montier Street until she died on May 9, 1961.[16]

On March 22, 1895, Virginia prematurely gave birth to twins—one boy and one girl—but they both died the same day.[17]

John and Virginia's fourth child was born on March 31, 1896. Julia Belle was her name.[18] Julia went on to marry Zebedee Parrish, a World War I veteran.[19]

On November 19, 1899, Virginia once again gave birth to twins. The daughter they named Aronia. Tragedy struck the family again when Aronia died of pneumonia on January 9, 1902.[20]

The other twin was a son whom they named John.[21] When John became eighteen, he registered for the draft at the beginning of

Photograph taken in February 1917 looking west from the 4000 block of Penn Avenue in Pittsburgh.

(Photo courtesy of Archives & Special Collections,
University of Pittsburgh Library System)[22]

World War I. On his registration card he entered his name as John Ralph Kilby Jr. and listed his profession as a janitor.[23] There is no evidence that his father was born with or later chose a middle name, so John Ralph may have been called Junior as a loving gesture. The 1920 census refers to him as Ray and shows that he became a worker for an electric company.[24]

John Jr. apparently never married. He died in 1922.[25]

Virginia and John continued trying to increase their family size, and in April 1901, daughter Pattie Malinda Kilby was born. Once more, though, they suffered a loss. At the age of two, Pattie developed what a doctor described as a cold. For twenty-four days, she worsened, dying at home on February 2, 1903, from what the doctor later described as pertussis (whooping cough).[26] Pattie Malinda was buried in Allegheny Cemetery, where her father, mother, brother, and sisters would later rest.

In 1910, Virginia reported she had given birth to nine children in total, but no record of births or names for two additional children exists.[27] Virginia's childbearing years were over, and as the living children grew into adulthood, Virginia helped to support the family as a laundress for others.[28]

. . .

The Carron Street Baptist Church—founded in 1892 with its first pastor, Rev. Willis Duvall, the same minister who married John and Virginia two years prior—became the spiritual home for John and family.[29] John was reported to be a member and an officer in 1906.[30] The leadership of this church organized and directed the Emancipation Day celebration of 1910, "witnessed by more than 7,000" and "one of the most notable [celebrations] ever conducted by the colored people of Pittsburg[h]."[31]

The Kilby family's active participation over the following decade is documented within newspaper social columns, which, unlike in the South, typically did not refer to racial distinction of persons in stories. Pittsburgh newspapers reported activities of the church regularly, often mentioning John and especially Flora

Carron Street Baptist Church, Pittsburgh, c. 1902.[32]

and Julia as singers. Flora, in particular, was once reported as a soprano performing solo with an orchestra for a musical celebration, a likely indicator of remarkable talent.[33]

John and Virginia had firmly established their permanent home in Pittsburgh. However, John had not severed family ties altogether with those who remained in Virginia. The September 1917 social column of a Baltimore newspaper reported a visit by John Kilby and daughter Julia to his sister Sarah Reynolds, a resident of Winchester.[34] The two-sentence, concise notice only indicated that John had ended his visit with Sarah and "left for other parts of the state," presumably to visit Simon and Fannie and see how things had changed during his long absence. There was much to talk about in both households, stories to tell, and perhaps nephews and nieces to meet for the first time. The joy of being with family once again helped to put aside painful memories of their earliest years on the Thornhill plantation.

Virginia Kilby, too, had sought to reconnect with a sister with whom she had lost contact. In a poignant example of using a classified advertisement to locate a relative, so reminiscent of the period during Reconstruction when freed people sought information about long-separated loved ones, Virginia worded her inquiry, "Anyone knowing the whereabouts of Miss Sarah Anne Miles . . . please communicate with her sister. . . . Miss Sarah Miles was last heard of in Washington, D.C."[35] There is no indication that Virginia ever reunited with her sister.

John Kilby, the loving husband and father of seven children, died July 28, 1932, at the age of seventy-five.[36] Virginia Miles Kilby died June 28, 1936, at age seventy.[37] Father, mother, and son John were laid to rest in Allegheny Cemetery in Pittsburgh.[38]

Flora Kilby Walker lived until 1961, and Julia Kilby Parrish lived until 1963.[39] Descendants of Flora Kilby Walker live to this day.

Though financial prosperity would not reward John and Virginia in their northern home, they would meet and build lives together where they found happiness, respect, and dignity.

CHAPTER FIFTEEN

James Kilby

1860–1949

James Kilby was born about 1860. Perhaps neither James nor anyone else knew the exact date of his birth. In later years, he would vaguely remember some day and month and year he thought *might* be right, but no single date would persist. Official records would never show the same date twice. Recorded ages would be approximations. Birth anniversaries, as celebrated in White families, dates of personal significance imprinted in young minds and highlighted on such occasions, were not part of James's early experience or those of his kin.

James entered this world unceremoniously, unacknowledged as intended by his biological father, cherished perhaps only by his mother. Under the legal doctrine of *partus sequitur ventrem*, the basis for established law in the slave states until the end of the Civil War, the children of an enslaved woman were automatically deemed the property of her enslaver.[1] Thus, James was deemed born enslaved just as were Juliet's other children. James's name first appeared in writing along with Juliet and her other children in the 1865 suit brought by Mortimer Kilby.[2] The 1870 federal census, even with the erroneous recording of surnames, recorded James as age ten and already working as a laborer on the Thornhill farm.

No documents provide details of James's childhood life. Most likely, he learned at an early age the constricting limits of a slave existence, the expectations of unremitting physical labor and a deferential demeanor commanded of all in bondage, including torturing punishment for the smallest infraction. It would be easy to picture young James working alongside John and Simon to plant, maintain, and bring in crops, or maybe hauling grain to a nearby grist mill and returning with flour and ground corn for the Thornhill household. To Bluford and Malinda, James's singular priority would have been work. His emancipation at the age of five was conceptual only, for he was as dependent as before on the whims of his caregivers, his former owners. What was freedom when food and shelter and parental guidance were of top concern? Like it or not, after Juliet's death, Malinda and Bluford were the children's surrogate parents, and there they would stay until freedom's opportunity became apparent and independent decisions could be exercised. There is no evidence James was provided an opportunity to attend any school during his formative years. Fortitude was his teacher, and that would take him far.

On June 18, 1881, at age twenty-one, James married Mary Eliza Richardson, aged eighteen.[3] The ceremony in Woodville, Rappahannock County, was officiated by Rev. A. Lewis. Their marriage license recorded her name as Mary Eliza *Strother*, not Richardson. Strother was her stepfather's name. In the place on the form calling for parents' names, only the name of her mother, Eveline Strother, was entered. In their adult lives, Mary, her sister, and her two brothers, born before Eveline married a Strother, always used the surname Richardson.[4] There is no indication that Mary ever knew her biological father.

Mary's mother, brothers, and sister followed her to Rhode Island. But before Mary and James left Virginia, they started what would eventually become a large family. Daughter Elizabeth Kilby was their first child, born in 1882.[5] Later she would be known by more familiar names of Lacy or Lizzie. Daughter Lena Pauline was born in 1883, followed by a son, James Jr., in 1886.[6]

Any motivation to move away from rural Virginia is easily understood. The White racial bigotry and human disregard in rural Virginia posed significant barriers to African Americans wanting their rightful share of opportunity and prosperity. James had few options for employment to support a growing family. As historian and author Isabel Wilkerson put it, "They did what human beings looking for freedom, throughout history, have often done. They left."[7] Some before and many afterward would determine that the North offered a better life.

Perhaps James had heard from a northern recruiter looking for laborers of all trades. The Virginia planters, fearing the loss of cheap farm labor, threatened recruiters and their laborers who might be thinking of migrating with violence and arrests, frequently on the grounds of unpaid, trumped-up debts. Leaving had some danger. Nonetheless, Blacks heeded the call of fair wages paid on time and transportation to a new location. Records show that Mary Eliza's brother followed the same calling and path north.[8] Newport, Rhode Island, is where they would land and quickly take root.

Keith Stokes, a genealogist, historical researcher, and blogger, wrote this about Lindsay R. Walker: "[He] came to Newport from Culpepper [*sic*] County Virginia in 1860 and he would recruit other African American families to come to Newport after the Civil War."[9] Lindsay was the son of Lewis and Jane Walker, the same age as James, and perhaps a childhood playmate. Lindsay married Lena Richardson—sister to James's wife, Mary Eliza—in February, 1885, in Rappahannock County, and they soon departed for Newport.[10]

> Walker worked through an established employment office in Washington, D.C., that "would recruit down there [in Virginia]

on the basis of names he'd given them." Often, the recruits were laborers needed for the neighboring Middletown, Rhode Island, farms.[11]

Armstead Hurley was another African American with roots in Culpeper County who moved to Rhode Island.[12] He had learned the trade of painter and glazier before leaving for Newport in 1886. Hurley would continue his trade and become a prominent member of the Shiloh Baptist Church of Newport, which would become James and Mary's religious home, as well. Perhaps James and Mary Eliza had been persuaded by Lindsay Walker, or maybe they had known and followed Armstead Hurley in his decision to leave Virginia. Either appears a reasonable conclusion for their choosing this destination. By the following year, the Kilby family would be established in the North, and a new life would begin.

James and family became visible citizens of Newport, recorded in government and community documents and mentioned in the local newspapers as years passed. In 1887, James was recorded in the city directory as a resident having the catch-all occupation of "laborer." In all likelihood, Lindsay Walker helped James and

Shiloh Baptist Church of Newport, Rhode Island, c. 1900[13]

Mary find a place to board and find work as a start. Caring people there—even Whites—helped newcomers, something hard to imagine in Virginia of that day.

Within a year, James moved the family to new living quarters, perhaps because he was following employment prospects. For 1888 and the following year, James's residential address of record changed to a rooming house on the corner of Coggeshall Avenue and Casey Court.[14] The address happened to be a short distance—less than a quarter of a mile across an open lot—from the site of Cornelius Vanderbilt's mansion, Marble House, which began construction the same year, 1888.[15] Many hundreds of skilled and unskilled laborers were needed; perhaps James was among them. Records are absent as to whether his presence so close is mere coincidence, but maybe James had a part in constructing this historic mansion.

In 1893, James suffered an accident that could have had dire consequences. As reported in the local press, the horse he was riding slipped on a trolley car steel rail, flipped, and crushed James's leg on the way down.[16] James apparently recovered with no permanent injury.

After Elizabeth, Lena, and James Jr., James and Mary Eliza would have six more children while residing in Newport: John (1888), Richard (1890), Bessie (1892), Henry (1894), and Walter (1897). Madelene Alberta was their last child, born in 1900, but she died only three years later.[17]

As the family slowly grew in numbers, James advanced in employment. Idleness was certainly not in his character. Before the turn of the century, James would be employed by the City of Newport public works department, where he would work for the next half century. By 1910 he was a cement finisher, in 1920 and 1930 he was a paver, and the 1935 record shows he was a foreman.[18] The fact that James stuck with this employer for so long—and they with him—suggests he was satisfied and possibly even enjoyed his work. Respect was earned and given. Prejudices still existed between Whites and Blacks, but James and Mary found that ambition and fortitude worked to their favor. The contrast in opportunity and social acceptance between Virginia and New England could not have been greater. They were citizens in a different society.

Nine years after arriving in Rhode Island, James purchased a small lot in Newport proper. The year was 1896.[19] There was a mortgage to pay and food to put on the table, yet James was always able to provide what was needed. His house at number 5 Sheffield Avenue would be the permanent family home until his death, even providing shelter at various times for grown children and grandchildren. The stability of a permanent residence and steady employment would be the foundation for family life in what must have been a warm and comforting household.

The 1900 census record for James and family is extraordinary for what it reveals. James, as a "day laborer," an all-encompassing descriptor, was supporting his family while Mary was housekeeper and mother hen for their nine children, four of whom were attending school. James was given no opportunity for schooling in his early life, and his education remained incomplete throughout his life. Still, education was highly regarded in this Kilby household. The record that year shows that all but James could read and write, and the children over five at the time were "at school."[20]

By 1910, some of the older children had taken spouses, and some had begun work. Elizabeth, the oldest, married Thomas Johnson of Falls River, Massachusetts, in 1908. She would divorce before 1920 and be a laundress to private families.[21]

Lena Pauline Kilby married George Vieira in 1906. George served in the U.S. Navy from 1903 to 1923. He must have been away on duty in 1910, as Lena was living in her father's household at the time. George was back in Newport and heading the household for the 1920 census, where it shows he was a Navy cook.[22] Stability in the household set in after the first World War and would be a constant for over three decades.

James and Mary's second son, John, was newly married in 1909 to Gladys Gassaway, the two later living in her mother's household.[23] His employment as Pullman porter for the Pennsylvania Railroad would be an attractive start for a young man, but one that perhaps took him away from Gladys too long.[24] The marriage did not last. John was separated from Gladys in 1914 and remained separated until their assumed divorce in 1917.[25] In the month of May 1928, John remarried. It was the second marriage for his bride, Tula Henry, née Richards.[26]

Between 1913 and 1915, third son Richard Kilby found a marriage mate in a woman named Violet Green. They had a son together, Richard Jr., born in 1915. Their union lasted only a few years.[27]

Henry William, son number four, was about twenty-six when he married Elizabeth Jackson. They began a family immediately. Son James Henry was born in June 1921, and son Lawrence followed in January 1925.[28]

Walter was the youngest of James and Mary's five sons. He married Madeline Butler, familiarly known as May, in 1921. Their daughter, Hope Louise, was born in 1926.[29]

Three of James and Mary's sons served their country during the war years of 1917–19. The Selective Service Act of 1917 required all young men of U.S. citizenship to register for the newly established military draft. African Americans were not exempt. James Jr. registered that year as required.[30]

Henry also complied, a single man at the time, and was called to active U.S. Army service in April 1918. He served as private first class in the Headquarters Company, 367nd Infantry Regiment, of the 92nd Division, the famed "Buffalo Soldier Division." His unit took part in the Battle of the Argonne Forest, September 26 to November 11, 1918. He was honorably discharged in March 1919 after returning from France.[31]

On son John's draft registration card, he stated he was married and working as a Pullman porter for the Pennsylvania Railroad out of New York City.³² He served from October 1917 until honorably discharged in March 1919 in Company C of the same regiment and division as his brother, Henry.³³ Whether they ever saw each other while on the Western Front is not known. Richard enlisted in the U.S. Navy in February 1917 and was honorably discharged in August 1919, earning the rank of mate first class.³⁴ He served aboard the newly commissioned USS Arizona, the same ship sunk at the attack on Pearl Harbor twenty-three years later.³⁵ Walter, the fifth and youngest son, also registered for the draft, but his military service would not begin until World War II.³⁶

Lena's husband, George Vieira, joined the Navy in 1903 and only left after twenty years of service.³⁷ Though he was on duty away from their Newport home at various times, Newport became his primary duty station. After World War I, their home would be a haven for three children of Lena's brothers. George and Lena opened their home to her nephews, beginning with Richard Kilby Jr. around the time his father was in the Navy. Their first and only natural child, George Jr., was born in January 1921. Then, after Lena's brother Henry William Kilby died in 1926, they took in Henry's sons James Henry and Lawrence.³⁸

James Jr. was married in 1918 to Louise Levin, an immigrant from Italy.³⁹ At the time, he was working as a sanitation worker. Perhaps he found thrown-away items that still had some value, for Louise was described as a junk peddler on the next census. The family surely appreciated income from whatever source. The marriage did not last, for James filed for and was granted a divorce in 1928.⁴⁰ No children are known from this union. James later moved back to the home of his father and mother on Sheffield Avenue, caring for them until their deaths.⁴¹

As James and Mary Kilby established a permanent presence in Newport at the turn of the century, fellow African American citizens must have taken notice as the family grew. Adults spent their days working, and children were going to school. There was precious little time to relax. James and his family followed other families in attending regular worship services. And to participate even more in community activities and fraternal organizations within the African American community, James Kilby, the father, became a member of the Canonchet Lodge of the Grand United Order of Odd Fellows.[42] According to a 1917 article in the *Newport Mercury* newspaper, members elected him color bearer, and his brother-in-law James Richardson, who had also moved to Newport, accepted an elected position as well.[43] Later evidence would show that James was also a member of the Stone Mill Lodge of Masons.[44]

The children of James and Mary struggled as adults. They suffered less than ideal marriages, divorces and remarriages, and some instability in employment. Though not as bad as in Virginia and further south, racial discrimination in the northern states was prevalent. The war years (1917–1919) were especially hard on families trying to get a good start. When troubles came, the families of the new generation could count on the stability of the household on Sheffield Avenue, the loving home of parents James and Mary. The two worked hard to provide for their large family and claim a spot they could call all their own. It was more than a small house on a small city lot, it was a symbol of freedom, of full participation in a community, a refuge from a past branded with racial hatred and oppression. It was theirs, and pride was justified.

. . .

Mary Eliza Kilby died on Tuesday, January 11, 1944, at age eighty-one. A brief notice of her death was published in the local newspaper that stated she has been ill for a long time.[45]

James Kilby, the youngest of Juliet's three boys born into slavery, the sibling who would travel the farthest as a young man to escape the Jim Crow South, the devoted father of nine children and husband to Mary Eliza, died quietly on Thursday, September 29, 1949, at age eighty-nine.[46] He would sacrifice for his family so his children might have better lives, the lesson of love he surely learned from his mother. More extraordinary was the example he set as a father to his children, himself having grown up without the love and guidance from his own father. Through his personal strength, determination, and perseverance, and with the help of a vibrant community and a loving wife, James became a father figure to honor and emulate. He left no great fortune nor achieved notable fame, but his riches were measured by his legacy of respect and love.

The Newport community acknowledged one of their own in a tribute published about James Kilby's final rites.[47] The Odd Fellows, of which James was a long-time member, honored him in the first of three services. The Masons held a second ritual service a day later. Then the family, friends, and public filled the Shiloh Baptist Church at 25 School Street for one last service. Music was played, solos were sung, eulogies were recited, prayers were offered, and thanks were given for a life of sacrifice, service, universal respect, and commitment to family and community. James was laid to rest alongside Mary in unmarked graves in Braman Cemetery, a short distance from his home.[48]

James Kilby was just a teen when, in 1874, Frederick Douglass delivered his popular address, "Self-Made Men."[49] "Personal independence is a virtue and it is the soul out of which comes the sturdiest manhood. But there can be no independence without a large share of self-dependence, and this virtue cannot be bestowed. It must be developed from within," Douglass wrote. Though James would not have heard the orator's message, he only had to follow his own sense of independence, "from within," to live a life of self-realization, dignity, respect, and honor. And as I review the lives of James, his brothers and sisters, and Juliet before them, whether in large ways or small, throughout life or only at the moment, finding and then expressing their self-constituted independence was the essence of their freedom.

PART THREE

FACTS OF FAMILY

Right is of no Sex — Truth is of no Color — God is the Father of us all, and we are all Brethren.
— Frederick Douglass

CHAPTER SIXTEEN

Genetic Ties

The barest facts of most records—dates, names, ages, racial designations, an occasional news article mention—are all that are available for reconstructing personal identities from so long ago. These few facts, as essential as they are in genealogical research, are insufficient for fully describing the physical, biological, social, and emotional dimensions of relationships. The parent–child relationship was as critical to physical and emotional development in previous centuries as it is now. As a mother, Juliet, no doubt, did her best in rearing her children (when access was granted). But what, I ask, of an identity and role of the children's father (or fathers)? Juliet never specified the paternity of her children on any written document. During their lifetimes, Simon, John, James, Sarah, and Bettie never recorded a father's name on a public document, even if they had known the name. No family Bible of the era is known to exist. The third-hand information provided by family members as informants on death certificates is not corroborated by any other evidence and is highly suspect. Perhaps science can provide correct answers.

With no reliable identification of a father or fathers of Juliet's children, the possibility of paternity by a White enslaver must be considered. Lacking contrary evidence, this is a strong possibility. No evidence suggests the biological father of these children was—at least for the four oldest siblings—anyone *other* than a member of the enslaving family. The history of slavery is one of pervasive sexual assaults on enslaved African-descent women.[1] Such abuses in Virginia's Piedmont were no exception. It is extremely rare that the nature of the relationship between a male member of an enslaving family and an enslaved female, considered by one's owner, society, and the law to be chattel property, would have been loving and caring. Enslavers, their sons, overseers, and even male guests were free to sexually abuse female slaves without legal consequences, social stigma, or basic human regard. There is no evidence to suggest the sexual relationships that resulted in the births of Juliet's children—or for that matter, Juliet herself—were non-violent, respectful, and consensual. There is little doubt that Juliet was sexually coerced and even raped, again and again.

Who this man was (or men were) is a question that genealogy alone cannot answer. By using DNA test evidence, I *can* complete a part of the story, that of paternal genetic heritage.

Genetic genealogy is the combination of facts derived from DNA testing and traditional genealogy to suggest relationships. Malinda Kilby enslaved Simon, John, Sarah, and James at birth. These children may have simply adopted their first enslaver's family name, thinking it right but not knowing exactly why. Denied the ownership and identity of a family name before their freedom, Kilby would become the surname of their choice—or at least of record—as each became his or her own person. Bettie, born after the Civil War, also used the Kilby name. Was there a reason each chose this family name? Maybe Juliet wanted her children to carry a more closely tied identity, the surname of their biological father. Was a White Kilby male the father of Juliet's five children? Could there have been other fathers?

The Y-chromosome of DNA, the male-only chromosome, is passed from father to son, generation after generation, virtually unchanged. It follows male lineage and, under most circumstances, surnames. A Y-DNA genetic test can provide a possible answer to the question of paternity.

Table 2. Y-DNA 37-marker test results for four descendants of James Kilby (1740–1829), son of patriarch John Kilby (c. 1710–1772).[2]

Line No.	Kit I.D.	Proven Ancestor	DYS393	DYS390	DYS19	DYS391	DYS385	DYS426	DYS388	DYS439	DYS389i	DYS392	DYS389ii	DYS458	DYS459
1	–	James Kilby	13	25	14	11	11–14	12	12	11	13	13	30	16	9–10
2	503461	**Simon Kilby**	**13**	**25**	**14**	**11**	**11–14**	**12**	**12**	**11**	**14**	**13**	**31**	**16**	**9–10**
3	108633	Thomas Kilby	13	25	14	11	11–14	12	12	11	13	13	30	16	9–10
4	B51962	Leroy Kilby	13	25	14	11	11–14	12	12	11	13	13	30	16	9–10
5	140018	Joseph Kilby	13	25	14	11	11–14	12	12	11	13	13	30	17	9–10

Line No.	DYS455	DYS454	DYS447	DYS437	DYS448	DYS449	DYS464	DYS460	Y-CATA-H4	YCAII	DYS456	DYS607	DYS576	DYS570	CDY	DYS442	DYS438
1	11	11	25	15	18	28	12–17–17–17	11	11	19–22	16	15	17	16	37–38	13	12
2	**11**	**11**	**25**	**15**	**18**	**28**	**12–17–17–17**	**11**	**11**	**19–22**	**16**	**15**	**17**	**16**	**37–38**	**13**	**12**
3	11	11	25	15	18	28	12–17–17–17	11	11	19–22	16	15	17	16	37–38	13	12
4	11	11	25	15	18	28	12–17–17–17	11	11	19–22	16	15	17	16	36–38	13	12
5	11	11	25	15	18	28	12–17–17–17	11	11	19–22	16	15	17	16	38–38	13	12

The genealogical record has established the link between Juliet and Thomas Kilby. Thomas was the son of James Kilby. Joseph and Leroy were other sons, brothers of Thomas. Living descendants of each of these siblings are candidates for testing a paternity hypothesis for Juliet's children.

Three white Kilbys, proven to be descendants of Thomas, Leroy, and Joseph, and one proven living descendant of Simon Kilby, have taken Y-DNA tests through FamilyTreeDNA, a genetic testing company, and made their test results available.[3] Table 2 presents these test results. Other male descendants of the patriarch John Kilby have also tested, though their Kilby forefathers at the time lived in North Carolina and should not be considered as potential fathers of Juliet's children. Nonetheless, their test results are valuable in determining the characteristics of the Y-chromosome of the family line, the patriarch John Kilby, and the most recent common ancestor, James Kilby.

We do not have actual DNA from John Kilby or his son James. However, one can accurately predict their DNA characteristics from the mode values of Y-DNA markers from the eight living Kilby males who have tested and who are proven direct-line descendants of John Kilby through one of his sons.[4] The aggregate values of Y-DNA of multiple living male descendants are a proxy for the Y-DNA of their forefathers. This presents a good foundation for determining the Y-DNA marker pattern on this family line, a benchmark for comparison.

The full description of DNA's Y-chromosome and the process of Y-DNA testing is beyond the scope of this analysis. It is only necessary to find the pattern of marker values most closely matching one set to another to assess probable paternity. The fewer the number of differences—mutations, as genetic scientists call them—the closer the match and the greater the probability of paternity.

The test taker identified as kit 503461 in Table 2 is a direct descendant of Simon Kilby. His Y-DNA test results reveal that he descends from the R-M269 haplogroup, a group with European origins. His closest Y-DNA match, the match with the fewest number of differences (called "genetic distance"), the match with a white descendant of Thomas Kilby, identified as kit 108633, supports the theory that Simon's biological father was one of Thomas Kilby's sons.[5] Y-DNA testing can determine the branch one follows backward in time on a family tree; however, of several brothers, men who shared presumably identical Y-chromosomes,

Y-DNA cannot pinpoint which son fathered one or more of Juliet's children. The way genes are inherited and the possibilities of mutations across multiple generations, and the fact that individuals in question are long since dead and unavailable for testing, I cannot attribute paternity with absolute certainty to a single individual using Y-DNA testing alone. However, probability does not require absolute proof. With the positive Y-DNA match and other historical evidence to consider, I come to a reasoned conclusion that Simon's father was one of the sons of Thomas Kilby and that the most recent common ancestor (MRCA) between Simon's descendants and the white Kilby descendants who tested is James Kilby, son of the family patriarch John Kilby.

A question remains, who was the father of Juliet? One genealogical researcher conjectured that Thomas Kilby might have been Juliet's biological father. Though unrecorded, Juliet is reasoned to have been born sometime between late December 1833 and early 1834. Thomas was alive when Juliet was conceived, presumed to be around April of 1833. Sarah, Juliet's mother, was described at the time of James Hawkins's death and Thomas Kilby's purchase as a "girl," which suggests she may have only been in her teens. Though Thomas's sons were too young, Thomas himself, at the age of about forty-six, is a reasonable candidate as Juliet's biological father. But so are James Hawkins's sons, who may have had closer proximity and greater opportunity. Since Juliet did not inherit a Y-chromosome, which only exists in males, the Y-DNA test is useless for deriving the identity of Juliet's father.

. . .

Another type of DNA test, that of autosomal DNA (atDNA), might prove specific genetic relationships going back five or six generations, possibly farther. Of the forty-four autosomal chromosomes each human inherits from their parents, twenty-two come from the mother and twenty-two from the father. Each of Juliet Ann's children received half of their autosomal DNA from her and the other half from their father. However, each half is itself a random recombination from many earlier generations. To illustrate this, let us hypothesize that Juliet's half, that which Simon Kilby received, was made up of forty-seven percent from her mother's (Sarah's) DNA and fifty-three percent from her (unknown) father's DNA. Those percentages were themselves made up of smaller, unpredictable amounts of DNA from their respective ancestors, and so on until some distant ancestor's DNA is inherited in a very small amount or absent altogether. This is just an example, for we do not have Simon's DNA to analyze, and we cannot know the precise makeup of his autosomal DNA that came from many of his ancestors and what is missing from others.

If we assume Juliet's five children had the same biological father—not a proven assumption—each child's DNA would be similar to the others but not identical. One child may have inherited DNA from a distant ancestor that her siblings did not. Therefore, testing one or more descendants of each sibling helps clarify the relationship picture for all.

The autosomal DNA of a living fourth- or fifth-generation descendant of Simon Kilby may or may not include tiny bits of DNA from Simon's earlier ancestors. That is to say, a second- or third-great-granddaughter of Simon may or may not have traces of DNA from Simon's father, grandfather, or earlier ancestor. But on the other hand, she may. First cousins have a grandparent in common and inherit a substantial amount of DNA from that grandparent. Second cousins share a common great-grandparent and share measurable but a smaller amount of DNA. Third and fourth cousins usually share some DNA, but possibly do not. It is important to remember that two people may be genuinely related through a distant ancestor but have little or no common DNA. Genetics and genealogy must work together when trying to answer questions of long-ago family relationships.

A method is available for determining the identity of a common ancestor through autosomal DNA matching. It involves looking for multiple individuals who match each other on the same segments of DNA. This process is called triangulation. When a segment of DNA matches each of three or more persons, and they match each other as well, that matching segment may be attributed to an ancestral couple. Further analysis of triangulated segments might reveal the individual of that couple who passed that segment to descendants. We then might attribute a specific DNA segment to Sarah or any of Sarah's ancestors, or the father of Juliet's children or any of his ancestors. Using this method, we look for multiple descendants, male or female, of African or European descent, who have matching segments and then try to identify the origin of that DNA segment.

Several known descendants of Simon, John, James, and Sarah Kilby have each taken autosomal DNA tests.[6] Each has matched one or more individuals who have ancestry on the White Kilby family line. With descendants of John, James, and Sarah matching several descendants of their brother Simon, and matching descendants of a son of Thomas and Malinda, the proof of a Kilby biological father is established. Further analysis of matches and the respective genealogical trees advances the assumption of single common paternity. Considering other related facts, one Kilby male stands out as the likely father: James Franklin Kilby. On the surface, this is compelling evidence. However, the DNA these matches inherited may have come from or through another of Malinda's sons. The same DNA segments could have passed to any of Juliet's descendants through Joseph Mortimer Kilby. As interesting as the matches are and what they reveal about a genetic connection between Black Kilbys and White Kilbys, they provide no proof of any one son's paternity of Juliet's children.

Using the clues (not evidence) that DNA testing has provided so far, and the clues revealed in documentary evidence, we come closer to naming names. With additional descendant testing and availability of the results, and further analysis of existing and new data, it may be possible to definitively answer the question, who was the man (or men) who fathered Juliet's five children?

. . .

Where genealogy has, so far, failed to identify the parents of Sarah (Juliet's mother) and her ancestors' origin in Africa, genetic testing presented some inkling.

Mitochondrial DNA (mtDNA) exists in us all, male and female, but is passed on to offspring only through the mother. It only reveals information about the *direct* maternal family line.[7] Unless a rare mutation occurs at a single location in the full sequence of mitochondria, children's mtDNA is identical to their mother's, maternal grandmother's, maternal great-grandmother's, and so forth. Similar to Y-DNA, the frequency of mtDNA mutations is quite low, thus the pattern of mtDNA of a living person is likely identical to that of a maternal ancestor many generations ago.[8]

So, is there a person, male or female, who could be a direct-line *maternal* descendant of Sarah and Juliet, someone who could reveal more about Sarah through their mitochondrial DNA? The answer is Yes, a fourth-great-granddaughter of Sarah. From this living descendant, a mtDNA test identifies Sarah's maternal haplogroup, the specific branch of the maternal tree of humankind, as L3e2a.[9] This genetic branch dates from 5,000 to 15,000 years ago.[10] The origins of L3e2a are Central Africa and, by later expansion, West Africa.[11] With the migration of Africans within that continent over thousands of years, it is not currently possible using mtDNA to pinpoint an origin for Sarah's foremother who was involuntarily transported across the Atlantic. However, the autosomal DNA ethnicity estimates of nine known African Americans on the Kilby family tree suggest Central Africa (Nigeria) as their ancestors'—and Sarah's ancestors'—ethnic origin.[12]

. . .

Genetic testing presents to us the gift of scientific fact. The mitochondrial DNA of a direct-line maternal descendant of Sarah and Juliet Ann informs the family of a link to their ancestral origin in Africa. What Y-DNA testing proves conclusively is that Simon's father was a White man, a Kilby. Then, autosomal testing also connects Simon's brothers, John and James, and sister Sarah to a Kilby male father, almost certainly the same as Simon's. I hypothesize, without proof, that Juliet's daughter Bettie had a Kilby father, too. Thus, I may be a bit closer to answering the question of how the surname identities of Juliet's progeny came to be. Though I cannot tell for sure, I can surmise that Juliet's children knew their father was a Kilby, and they chose to use the Kilby surname as their hereditary birthright.

CHAPTER SEVENTEEN

Conclusion

As I began writing this book, and as an early draft appeared, it became clear that this was principally a story of two women of dramatically different circumstances. Malinda Kilby was born into relative wealth and, despite many subsequent hardships, always held the power and privilege of Southern White families. The other woman, Juliet Ann, came to life enslaved, bound by Malinda for thirty-one years, denied human rights and choices possible through freedom. Even with such contrasts, keep in mind that lives are complex, and absolute judgment is not yours or mine to make.

Joyce Libes, a Kilby family historian, wrote about Malinda: "[I]t can be said that this lady, Malinda Hawkins Kilby Thornhill, was a survivor! She managed all alone as a young widow to raise the nine children born to her and Thomas Kilby. . . . Credit must be given to her for managing as well as she did."[1] Libes's assessment of Malinda is certainly correct, but it is not evident that Libes knew anything about the lives of those individuals Malinda enslaved.

Malinda was a survivor, and yet at a high cost to others. She endured the suffering of losing a supportive husband in the prime of life, raising nine children by herself, overcoming great debt to retain Thomas's legacy, holding on through years of increasing privation as the Civil War came home, and enduring loneliness without a marriage companion. What Malinda had was White privilege, which she appreciated and used fully to her and her family's advantage. Her station in White society relieved many personal hardships, put the law on her side, provided social and political support, and ensured moral justification in enslaving Blacks. Without the income that free labor provided, she would likely have failed to retain the land she held, the prestige it conveyed, and the life it secured. Malinda survived, but only at the great expense of those she abused and of moral degeneration to herself and her family.

It is easy to be guilty of "presentism," casting judgment on people of the past using the standards of today.[2] Historian Andrew Delbanco writes of the "delicate and exacting" task of understanding and explaining "how people in the past could have failed to see what seems so clear to us in retrospect." He writes, "On the one hand, explanation can shade into excuse; on the other hand, passing judgment on the past can be a form of self-congratulation in the present."[3] How will we, how *should* we, process the facts of slavery practiced and perpetuated by Whites of the Kilby family? Was their sense of humanity and moral responsibility so different from our own? You and I must try to understand—not accept, not agree, just understand—their beliefs, moral codes, customs, laws, and institutions that allowed slavery to flourish. Frederick Douglass provides some sense of understanding in his autobiography as he writes about himself and his owner, "Our courses had been determined for us, not by us. We had both been flung, by powers that did not ask our consent, nor control. By this current he was a master, and I a slave."[4] He regarded his enslaver as he did himself, a "victim of the circumstances of birth, education, law, and custom."[5] What Douglass overlooks in this statement is the will one with power had to change, to act on different beliefs of right and wrong.

Even with the sin of enslaving human beings, and after considering the abuses and indignities that I describe in these pages, are there elements of humane treatment of Juliet Ann and her children to Malinda's credit? The straightforward answer from all the evidence is No. Separating Juliet from her mother at an early age and apparently hiring her away and thus separating her from her children as they were growing was cold-blooded, morally reprehensible, and cruel beyond understanding. The salient fact is, Malinda held Juliet and her children in absolute bondage, robbing each of their labor and freedom until forced emancipation brought some relief. No incidental acts of kindness toward Juliet, unrecorded and known only to them, compensate for the undeserved cruelty Malinda imposed on these human beings. A victim of circumstances, yes, but Malinda also had freedom of will to act humanely. Her legacy of a loving wife and mother should not be ignored, but her legacy must not ignore her life as an enslaver of human beings.

What survival tools did each have, and which did they use? Malinda had the power to buy and sell property, to incur debt and borrow against that property, to speak openly and publicly about her condition, to move about as she saw fit, to advance her and her children's position — in other words, she had free will. Juliet was denied all these, and she had to fight for agency in the exceedingly limited ways available to her. Religion may have been one survival tool for Juliet. Certainly, the love she gave and the love she received from her children must have helped her endure. If chicanery or guile in dealing with her oppressors helped Juliet, then these were justified given her situation.

Undeniably, despite the unimaginable cruelty of enslavement, Juliet Ann was a survivor. Being born into slavery, she was denied choices. And yet she endured. She endured the denial of direct love and caring of her natural mother for most of her life, the absence of a male parent and the knowledge of her own birthday, the denial of a personal identity. She endured her stolen labor, marginal nutrition, sub-adequate clothing, and housing unequal to that of Whites. Juliet *could* have received harsh, unforgiving physical punishment, though no record is left to tell. Not by choice, she was forced to serve others, and she endured the commands of Malinda, her sons and daughters, and their White family associates. She survived rape, not once but multiple times, and bore children who would remind her of her abuse, even as they gave her comfort and hope. Yes, Juliet was a survivor, a great survivor, a forgotten survivor who deserves recognition and honor for the dignity she earned and the life she led.

. . .

It seems that no genealogical research is fully complete or without contradictions and some mystery. As I searched public records for traces of the lives of Juliet Ann and her children, some details created great questions. As a conscientious family historian, I try to find multiple, independent confirmations to call a fact proven. But then there is the occasional record that confounds and challenges prior conclusions.

An example is an entry in the Madison County, Virginia, record of deaths in 1885.[6] There, I found an entry for "Kilby Jno [John]," age twelve, "colored" son of "Kilby Sim & Jane." Who was Jane? Was Sim Kilby, the recorded father and the person who reported the death, Juliet's son Simon?

Then there is the entry for "Kilby Geo," who died as a one-year-old child in October 1880.[7] In the nineteenth century, *Geo* was a shortened way of writing George. But the sex of the baby was recorded as female. Was this an error, or was her name perhaps Georgianna? The parents were "Simon Kilby & Ann." Who was Ann, and was this Juliet's son Simon?

There is a record for "Lucy Frances Kilby" of Rappahannock County who gave birth to a daughter on February 12, 1875, and named her Mary F. Kilby.[8] The father's name was not recorded. One question originates from the entry for the child's color—"white."

Was this Mary the first child of Simon and Fannie? There is no subsequent record of her existence. Was Mary the firstborn of Fannie, did she die young, or is this a mistaken entry?

In each case, these entries may be relatively accurate, only partially informative, or substantially inaccurate to the point of being misleading and genealogically useless. Inaccuracies in the public records do exist more often than one might assume. Information provided on documents by informants may have been second- or third-hand and not entirely accurate—maybe faulty recollections or intentional misinformation. This is not to say these "facts" should be disregarded, just that they need validation to determine reliability and relevancy.

The greatest mysteries are those about Sarah and daughter Juliet Ann. The tidbits of information about Sarah after coming into enslavement by Malinda Kilby are insufficient to detail her fate. Did Sarah ever see her daughter after removing from Malinda's household? Could she have survived to find freedom through emancipation?

And what about Betsy Kilby, earlier recorded with name Elizabeth and later known as Bettie, the child in the same Thornhill household as her apparent siblings? Was she, in fact, Juliet's daughter? The documentary evidence is persuasive but not conclusive.

Lastly, when and from what cause did Juliet Ann pass from her life? Where was she put to rest? It would be comforting to be able to place flowers upon her grave if only I knew where.

I pass the stories and facts gathered in these pages to that future historian who will further the research, answer the mysteries, and honor the memory of Sarah and her descendants for all generations to come.

. . .

So, as this narrative comes to a close, we—you and I, writer and reader—should speak to the voiceless dead to let them know they are remembered. Those who endured slavery struggled for a full measure of life's treasures despite all possibilities. We honor them with our memory of their being.

APPENDIX

Sarah's Descendants: The First Two Generations

1. Sarah[1] was born about 1816. She was baptized at New Salem Baptist Church, Culpeper County, Virginia, on July 6, 1834. Sarah died on some unknown date after 1838.

Daughter of Sarah:

+   2   i   **Juliet Ann**[2] was born in Culpeper County, Virginia, in early 1834, possibly late 1833. She is believed to have died on August 9, 1867.

First Generation

2. Juliet Ann[2] (*Sarah*[1]) was born in Culpeper County, Virginia, in early 1834, possibly late 1833. Juliet Ann was baptized at F.T. Baptist Church, Rappahannock County, Virginia, on September 17, 1865. She is believed to have died on August 9, 1867, at age 33.

Children of Juliet Ann:

+   3   i   **Simon³ Kilby** was born in Culpeper County, Virginia, in 1853. Simon also went by the name of Charles William Kilby. He died in Etlan, Madison County, Virginia, on October 4, 1924.

+   4   ii   **John Kilby** was born in Culpeper County about 1857. John died in Wilkinsburg, Allegheny County, Pennsylvania, on July 28, 1932.

+   5   iii   **James Kilby** was born in Culpeper County in 1860. He died in Newport, Rhode Island, on September 29, 1949.

+   6   iv   **Sarah Kilby** was born in Culpeper County in 1861. She died in Winchester on July 13, 1924. Sarah was buried in Winchester on July 16, 1924.

+   7   v   **Bettie Kilby** was born in Rappahannock County in 1867. She died in Charlottesville, Albemarle County, Virginia, on April 26, 1921.

Second Generation

3. Simon³ Kilby (*Juliet Ann²*, *Sarah¹*) was born on or about May 21, 1853, in Culpeper County, Virginia. Simon also went by the name of Charles William Kilby. Simon died in Etlan, Madison County, Virginia, on October 4, 1924, at age 71.

Simon married **Lucy Frances "Fannie" Wallace** on December 30, 1873, in Rappahannock County. They had nine children: Bertie, Hubert, James, John, Mattie, Thomas, Ophelia, Simon, and Robert. Fannie Wallace was born in Rappahannock County about 1855. She was the daughter of Walker Wallace and Martha Parks. Fannie died in Madison County on March 30, 1933, at age 77.

Children of Simon Kilby and Fannie Wallace:

    i   **Bertie[4] Kilby** was born in Virginia on May 15, 1876. She died in York, Livingston County, New York, on December 22, 1910, at age 34. Bertie married Oscar Albert Hill in 1900. They had five children: three sons and two daughters.

    ii   **Hubert Reid Kilby** was born in Virginia on February 14, 1881. He died in Etlan, Virginia, on December 16, 1949, at age 68. Hubert married Malinda Green Frye on August 7, 1904, in Madison County. They had eleven children: five sons and six daughters.

    iii   **James Oscar Kilby Sr.** was born in Virginia on September 21, 1882. James Oscar died in Banco, Madison County, Virginia, on July 19, 1948, at age 65. James Oscar married Catherline Thomas on February 1, 1922, in Madison County. They had six children: three sons and three daughters.

iv   **John Henry Kilby** was born in Madison County on June 4, 1884. He died in Rappahannock County on September 25, 1958, at age 74. John Henry married Mary Ella Smith on November 5, 1913, in Madison County. They had seven children: four sons and three daughters.

v   **Martha Ann "Mattie" Kilby** was born in Madison County on December 7, 1888. She died in Slate Mills, Rappahannock County, on March 22, 1946, at age 57. Martha Ann married Simuel Wright on March 25, 1905, in Madison County. They had six children: two sons and four daughters.

vi   **Thomas Kilby** was born in Virginia in January 1890. He died on a date unknown before April 1933.

vii   **Ophelia Kilby** was born in Madison County on June 24, 1892. She died in Madison County on January 28, 1972, at age 79. Ophelia married Major W. Washington about 1922. They had five children: one son and four daughters.

viii **Simon Kilby Jr.** was born in Virginia in April 1894. He died on a date unknown before April 1933.

ix   **Robert E. Kilby** was born in Madison County on April 25, 1896. He died in

Madison County on April 26, 1917, at age 21.

4. John³ Kilby (*Juliet Ann²*, *Sarah¹*) was born about 1857 in Virginia. He died in Wilkinsburg, Allegheny County, Pennsylvania, on July 28, 1932, at age 74 or 75. John married **Virginia Frances Miles** on May 15, 1890, in Allegheny County. They had seven children: Flora, Julia, John, Aronia, Pattie, and unnamed twins who died at birth. Virginia Frances Miles was born in Amherst County, Virginia, on December 18, 1867. She was the daughter of David Miles and Patsy _____. Virginia Frances died in Wilkinsburg on June 28, 1936, at age 68.

Children of John Kilby and Virginia Frances Miles:

    i   **Flora Belle⁴ Kilby** was born in Pittsburgh, Allegheny County, Pennsylvania, on July 22, 1892. She died in Wilkinsburg on May 9, 1961, at age 68. Flora Belle married Robert Monroe Walker about 1920. They had one daughter.

    ii   **(infant male) Kilby** was born in Pittsburgh on March 22, 1895. He died the same day.

    iii   **(infant female) Kilby** was born in Pittsburgh on March 22, 1895. She died the same day.

    iv   **Julia Belle Kilby** was born in Pittsburgh on March 31, 1896. She died in Braddock, Allegheny County, on June 10, 1963, at age 67. Julia Belle married Zebedee Parrish in August 1931 in Pittsburgh.

v   **John Ralph Kilby** was born in Pennsylvania on November 19, 1899. He died in Pennsylvania in 1922.

vi   **Aronia Kilby** was born in Pittsburgh on November 19, 1899. Aronia was a twin of John Ralph Kilby. She died in Pittsburgh on January 9, 1902, at age 2.

vii   **Pattie Malinda Kilby** was born in Pittsburgh in April 1901. She died in Pittsburgh on February 2, 1903.

5. James^3 Kilby (*Juliet Ann^2, Sarah^1*) was born in 1860 in Culpeper County, Virginia. James died in Newport, Rhode Island, on September 29, 1949, at age 88 or 89. James married **Mary Eliza Richardson** on June 18, 1881, in Rappahannock County, Virginia. They had nine children: Lizzie, Lena, James, John, Richard, Bessie, Henry, Walter, and Madelene. Mary Eliza Richardson was born in Rappahannock County in August 1862. She was the daughter of Eveline Strother, and she also went by the name of Eliza Strother. Mary Eliza died in Newport, Rhode Island, on January 11, 1944, at age 81.

Children of James Kilby and Mary Eliza Richardson:

i   **Elizabeth^4 "Lizzie" Kilby** was born in Virginia on October 11, 1882. She married Thomas Johnson in Fall River, Massachusetts, on May 7, 1908. They had one son.

ii **Lena Pauline Kilby** was born in Rappahannock County, Virginia, on October 6, 1883. She died in Newport, Rhode Island, on October 7, 1952, at age 69. Lena Pauline married George Wjenia Vieira in 1906. They had one son.

iii **James Kilby Jr.** was born in Rappahannock County on September 2, 1886. He died in Cranston, Rhode Island, in December 1974, at age 88. James married Louise Ferretti Levin on January 29, 1918, and divorced in October 1928.

iv **John L. "Johnie" Kilby** was born in Middletown, Rhode Island, on July 9, 1888. John died in New York, New York, on March 4, 1960, at age 71. John married Gladys Sterling Gassaway in Fall River, Massachusetts, on October 14, 1909, and divorced in 1927. He married Tula Richard in Queens, New York, on May 24, 1928.

v **Richard Kilby Sr** was born in Middletown, Rhode Island, on August 13, 1890. He died in Brooklyn, New York, on July 19, 1955, at age 64. Richard married Violet Green before 1915. They had one son. Richard married Helenia "Nellie" _____ sometime before 1930.

vi **Bessie Kilby** was born in Rhode Island in December of 1892. She died in Boston, Massachusetts, in 1966. Bessie married

William McPherson about 1910. They had no children. Bessie married David Augustus Mayers in Newport, Rhode Island, on February 8, 1912. They had five children.

vii **Henry William Kilby** was born in Rhode Island on November 5, 1894. Henry William died in Newport on March 24, 1926, at age 31. Henry William married Elizabeth Reeves Jackson about 1920. They had two children, both sons.

viii **Walter Radford Kilby** was born in Rhode Island on August 30, 1897. Walter died in Newport on December 17, 1979, at age 82. Walter first married Madeline Butler. They had two daughters. Walter and Madeline divorced. Walter married Maude Thompson on January 28, 1943.

ix **Madelene Alberta Kilby** was born in Rhode Island on February 22, 1900. She died in Newport on May 6, 1903.

6. Sarah³ Kilby (*Juliet Ann²*, *Sarah¹*) was born in 1861 in Culpeper County, Virginia. Sarah died in Winchester, Virginia, on July 13, 1924, at age 62 or 63. Sarah married **James Reynolds** on May 18, 1879, in Rappahannock County, Virginia. James Reynolds was born in Rappahannock County about 1858. He was the son of Horace Reynolds and Jane _____. James died on a date unknown before 1898.

APPENDIX 147

Children of Sarah Kilby and James Reynolds:

    i   **Ella May⁴ Reynolds** was born in Page County, Virginia, on November 10, 1883. She died in Winchester on August 28, 1936, at age 52. Ella May married Arthur Honesty. They had two sons.

    ii   **(unidentified) Reynolds**. In the 1900 census, Sarah Reynolds indicated a child born but not then living. This child has not been identified.

7. Bettie³ Kilby (*Juliet Ann²*, *Sarah¹*) was born in 1867 in Rappahannock County, Virginia. Bettie died in Charlottesville, Albemarle County, Virginia, on April 26, 1921, at age 53 or 54. She had two children by an unknown father. Bettie married **Armstead Carr** on September 7, 1893, in Albemarle County. They had no known children. Armstead Carr was born in Virginia about 1844. Armstead died in Charlottesville on February 7, 1931.

Children of Bettie Kilby and an unknown father:

    i   **Cora Blanche Kilby** was born in Rappahannock County on May 24, 1883. She died in Charlottesville on August 29, 1936, at age 51. Cora Blanch married John Brown in 1906. They had two children. Cora Blanch married Lindsay Edward Wilson on May 23, 1921.

    ii   **Robert⁴ Kilby** was born in Slate Mills, Rappahannock County, in 1885. He died in Slate Mills on September 19, 1886.

Notes

Some abbreviations used in notes:
- dwell   dwelling
- fam   family
- fol   folio
- pop   population
- sch   schedule
- twp   township

Genealogists and family historians require complete and often complex source citations. While the format used here may be unfamiliar to you, the citations conform to recommendations prescribed by genealogy professionals. One example: dates are written in DD/MONTH/YYYY format. Hopefully, these notations will enable accurate discovery of specific source material. Unless otherwise noted, all referenced websites were last accessed on March 10, 2021.

Chapter One: The Promise of Light

1. Gourdvine Neck is the place name given to the northwest region of Culpeper County bordered by Rappahannock and Madison counties, not to be confused with Gourdvine Fork, the peninsula at the confluence of the Thornton and Hazel rivers.
2. Rappahannock County, Virginia, Chancery Court Case no. 253, Kilby v. Thornhill, chancery bill, March 1865; Office of the Clerk of the Circuit Court, Washington, Virginia. The enslaved persons Juliet and her children Simon, John, James, and Sarah are referenced by name in this document.

For Malinda Kilby's age, see 1860 U.S. census, Culpeper County, Virginia, population schedule, Southern Division, p. 47, dwelling 39, family 37, Malinda Kilby; NARA microfilm publication M653, roll 1341. Malinda Kilby's given name, as found on most records, is spelled with an *a* or rarely with an *o*; however, on a few documents where her original signature can be found, she spelled it with an *e*.

3   "Virginia, Death Records, 1912–2014," database with images, *Ancestry* (https://www.ancestry.com), imaged certificate no. 29198, Charles W. [Simon] Kilby, died Madison County, 4 October 1924; citing "Virginia Department of Health; Richmond, Virginia; Virginia Deaths, 1912–2014."

4   John's birth year cannot be precisely determined but is derived from multiple sources. First, see Culpeper County, Virginia, Chancery Court Case no. 76, Joseph M Kilby v. Malinda Kilby Etc., chancery bill, 1859; digital images, Library of Virginia (LVA), *Virginia Memory* (https://www.lva.virginia.gov/chancery/case_detail.asp?CFN=047-1880-038), images 3–4 of 150. This document references "a negro woman & her two children . . . which [*sic*] have not been divided and are in the possession of [said] Malinda his mother." Also, 1870 U.S. census, Rappahannock County, Virginia, population schedule, Stonewall Township, pp. 31–32 (penned), line 38, dwelling 216 [blank, skipped number], family 216 [blank, skipped number], Bluford Thornhill household; NARA microfilm publication M593, roll 1674. This record references John Walker [John Kilby], age thirteen. Proof summary to correct this census record is provided in the narrative. Also, 1910 U.S. census, Allegheny County, Pennsylvania, population schedule, Pittsburgh Ward 6, enumeration district (ED) 356, sheet 11A, dwelling 178, family 241, Jno [John] Kilby household; NARA microfilm publication T624, roll 1301. Federal censuses of 1900, 1920, and 1930 record ages inconsistent with early records, which most likely indicates that John and his family members did not know his actual age and birth year.

5   Rappahannock County, Virginia, Marriage License and Return, James Kilby and Mary Eliza Strother, 18 June 1881; microfilm 178, Rappahannock County, "Marriage Certificates & Licenses,

1861–1889," chronologically ordered; LVA, Richmond. Note the age of husband recorded as twenty-one.

6 Rappahannock County, Virginia, Marriage License and Return, James Reynolds and Sarah Kilby, 18 May 1879; microfilm 178, Rappahannock County, "Marriage Certificates & Licenses, 1861–1889," chronologically ordered; LVA, Richmond. The age of Sarah Kilby is recorded as eighteen.

7 Culpeper County, Virginia, Marriage License and Return, Bluford Thornhill and Malinda Kilby, license issued 28 December 1864, marriage 3 January 1865; Office of the Clerk of the Circuit Court, Culpeper, Virginia.

8 "Virginia Marriages, 1785–1940," database, *FamilySearch* (https://www.familysearch.org/ark:/61903/1:1:XRHJ-JBZ), entry for Thomas Kilby and Matilda [Malinda] Hawkins, married in Culpeper County, 2 January 1817; Family History Library (FHL) microfilm 30927. For land holdings, see Culpeper County, Virginia, Deed Book OO: 264–65, Leroy Kilby and wife to Thomas Kilby, 20 August 1822; Office of the Clerk of the Circuit Court, Culpeper, Virginia.

9 Gourdvine Baptist Church (Culpeper County, Virginia), Minute Book, 1812–1832, p. 56; bound Photostat copy (negative), LVA, Richmond. For children of Thomas Kilby, see Culpeper County, Virginia, Chancery Court Case, Lucy J. Stringfellow Etc. v. Varinda J. G. Scott, 1890; deposition of James F. Kilby, 8 September 1889; digital images, LVA, *Virginia Memory* (https://www.lva.virginia.gov/chancery/case_detail.asp?CFN=047-1891-003), images 28–29 of 115.

10 Culpeper County, Virginia, Chancery Court Case no. 7, Adm[inistratrix] of Thomas Kilby v. Adm[inistrator] of James Hawkins, administrator qualification, Estate of Thomas Kilby, 19 May 1834; digital images, LVA, *Virginia Memory* (https://www.lva.virginia.gov/chancery/case_detail.asp?CFN=047-1840-019), images 72–73 of 85.

11 Culpeper Co., Va., Chancery Court Case no. 76, Joseph M Kilby v. Malinda Kilby Etc., chancery bill, 1859; digital images 3–5 of 150. Also, Rappahannock Co., Va., Chancery Court Case no. 253, Kilby v. Thornhill, chancery bill, March 1865.

12 Rappahannock Co., Va., Chancery Court Case no. 253, Kilby v. Thornhill, chancery bill, March 1865.
13 Culpeper County, Virginia, Deed Book 6: 233–34, Malinda Kilby to Cornelius Smith, deed of trust, 10 February 1843; Office of the Clerk of the Circuit Court, Culpeper, Virginia.

CHAPTER TWO: "MASTERS, MISTRESSES, AND SLAVES"

1 Malinda Hawkins's birth year is estimated based on her marriage date and census data. See "Virginia Marriages, 1785–1940," database, *FamilySearch*, entry for Thomas Kilby and Matilda [Malinda] Hawkins, married in Culpeper Co., 2 January 1817. Also, 1860 U.S. census, Culpeper Co., Va., pop. sch., Southern Division, p. 47, dwell. 39, fam. 37, Malinda Kilby.
2 Culpeper County, Virginia, Will Book N: 4–8, James Hawkins estate appraisement, 1833; Office of the Clerk of the Circuit Court, Culpeper, Virginia.
3 Ibid.
4 Ibid.
5 Nancy Lee Hawkins Kaleo, *Hawkins and Allied Families: A Genealogy and Family History* (University Park, Maryland: Wordsworth Ink, 1991), 22.
6 Culpeper County, Virginia, Will Book H: 196–97, Will of Matthew Hawkins, 27 May 1820; Office of the Clerk of the Circuit Court, Culpeper, Virginia. See also, Culpeper County, Virginia, Will Book H: 340, Matthew Hawkins inventory, 1833; Office of the Clerk of the Circuit Court, Culpeper, Virginia.
7 1810 U.S. census, Culpeper County, Virginia, population schedule, folio 97 (right, stamped), line 15, Jas [James] Hawkins; NARA microfilm publication M252, roll 68. 1820 U.S. census, Culpeper County, Virginia, population schedule, folio 80 (right), p. 41 (penned), line 2, James Hawkins; NARA microfilm publication M33, roll 133. Culpeper Co., Va., Will Book H: 196–97, Will of Matthew Hawkins, 27 May 1820.
8 Kaleo, *Hawkins and Allied Families*, 32.
9 F.T. Baptist Church (Rappahannock County, Virginia),

Minute Book, 1805–1855; bound Photostat copy (negative), LVA, Richmond. F.T. Baptist Church (Rappahannock County, Virginia), Minute Book, 1855–1878; bound photocopy of original, Virginia Baptist Historical Society, Richmond.

10 Virginia Auditor of Public Accounts, Personal Property Tax, Culpeper County, Virginia, Daniel Brown's district, 1804, p. 21; for James Kilby; Personal Property Tax microfilm 90, LVA, Richmond. James Kilby's sons Joseph and John are listed separately. Given that in the prior year, 1803, taxable males over age sixteen living with James were two in number and in 1804 there were three, this third son, for the first time over taxable age of sixteen, must be Thomas, the known fifth son of James and Lucy and thus making his year of birth about 1787.

11 Culpeper County, Virginia, Will Book B: 59, inventory of the estate of John Kilby, 28 May 1772; Office of the Clerk of the Circuit Court, Culpeper, Virginia.

12 Northern Neck Land Office, Northern Neck Grants G, p. 27, land grant, 29 January 1747 (old style), John Kilvy [Kilby] grantee; archive with digital image, *Library Of Virginia* (https://lva.primo.exlibrisgroup.com/permalink/01LVA_INST/18mtacj/alma990008561740205756).

13 Culpeper Co., Va., Will Book B: 59, inventory of the estate of John Kilby, 28 May 1772.

14 Culpeper County, Virginia, Will Book B: 57–58, will of John Kilby, 8 December 1770; Office of the Clerk of the Circuit Court, Culpeper, Virginia.

15 Culpeper Co., Va., Will Book B: 59, inventory of the estate of John Kilby, 28 May 1772.

16 Culpeper County, Virginia, Deed Books WW: 421–22; XX: 153–57; XX: 157–161; and 9: 209–10; heirs of James Kilby, real estate division and conveyances, 1830 and 1848; Office of the Clerk of the Circuit Court, Culpeper, Virginia. Through these deeds the complete family of James Kilby can be established.

17 Virginia Auditor of Public Accounts, Personal Property Tax Records, Culpeper County, Virginia, 1812–1863; Personal Property Tax microfilms 90, 91, 92, 92A, 472, 473, and 474, LVA, Richmond.

18 Virginia Auditor of Public Accounts, Personal Property Tax,

Culpeper County, Virginia, Daniel Brown's district, 1817, p. 30; for James Kilbe [Kilby] and Joseph Kilbe; Personal Property Tax microfilm 90, LVA, Richmond. In this record, James Kilby, the father is shown to enslave one person over age sixteen, the same as his son Joseph. James's sons Leroy Kilbey and Thomas Kilbe [Kilby], and James's nephew Armistead Kilbe, were not taxed for enslaved property this year. Also, see Virginia Auditor of Public Accounts, Personal Property Tax, Culpeper County, Virginia, Daniel Brown's district, years 1831–1834; for James Kilby sons: Joseph, Henry, Leroy, Thomas, St. Clair, and Thompson Albert; Personal Property Tax microfilm 91, LVA, Richmond. James Kilby was deceased, but each of his sons listed enslaved one or more persons and were taxed accordingly. Possible enslaved children were not included in the counts.

19 John Blankenbaker, *A List of the Classes in Culpeper County for January 1781 for Recruiting this State's Quota of Troops to Serve in the Continental Army* (Chadds Ford, Pennsylvania: privately published, 1999), 28. James Kilby is recorded among class no. 88.

20 Culpeper Co., Va., Will Book B: 59, inventory of the estate of John Kilby, 28 May 1772. Of note, "1 Servant Man 20£." Virginia Auditor of Public Accounts, Personal Property Tax Records, Culpeper County, Virginia, Daniel Brown's district, 1814, p. 23, line 4; for James Kilbee [Kilby], one slave age above twelve and below sixteen; Personal Property Tax microfilm 90, LVA, Richmond. The tax record for 1814 is but one record of James Kilby's slaveholdings.

21 Culpeper Co., Va., Deed Book OO: 264–65, Leroy Kilby and wife to Thomas Kilby, 20 August 1822.

22 "Virginia Marriages, 1785–1940," database, *FamilySearch*, entry for Thomas Kilby and Matilda [Malinda] Hawkins, married in Culpeper Co., 2 January 1817.

23 1820 U.S. census, Culpeper County, Virginia, population schedule, folio 84 (left), p. 48 (penned upper left), line 11, Thomas Kilby; NARA microfilm publication M33, roll 133. 1830 U.S. census, Culpeper County, Virginia, population schedule, folio 144 (left, penned), line 14, Th^{os} Kilber [Thomas

Kilby]; NARA microfilm publication M19, roll 197. One female child under age ten on 1820 census and one female child between age ten and fifteen on the 1830 census suggests that Martha Ann was born about 1818.

24 1860 U.S. census, Culpeper County, Virginia, population schedule, Southern Division, p. 20, dwelling 154, family 156, James F. Kilby, enumerated 1 August 1860; NARA microfilm publication M653, roll 1341. 1860 U.S. census, Culpeper County, Virginia, population schedule, Southern Division, p. 3, dwelling 28, family 22, James Kilby, enumerated 17 July 1860; NARA microfilm publication M653, roll 1341. Note that the James F. Kilby family was enumerated twice in Culpeper County in 1860; presumably they moved between enumerator visits.

25 Thomas L. Kilby, born c. 1832 and died August 1861, is a son of Thomas Kilby and should not be confused with his father. Thomas L. Kilby is not known to be an enslaver. For Hamilton Burgess Kilby's age see 1850 U.S. census, Culpeper County, Virginia, population schedule, folio 225 (front), p. 21 (penned upper right), dwelling 147, family 147, Melinda [Malinda] Kilby household; NARA microfilm publication M432, roll 941.

26 1820 U.S. census, Culpeper Co., Va., pop. sch., fol. 84 (left), p. 48 (penned upper left), line 11, Thomas Kilby.

27 Virginia Auditor of Public Accounts, Personal Property Tax Records, Culpeper County, Virginia, Daniel Brown's district, 1830, p. 15; for Thomas Kilby; Personal Property Tax microfilm 91, LVA, Richmond.

28 Before 1845, when forms started to be pre-printed, tax commissioners handwrote column headings. Even up until the end of slavery, label inconsistencies occurred. Variations and misinterpretations could have resulted in inaccurate data gathering. For example, one column for "Slaves above 16 years of age" and a separate column for "Slaves above 12 years of age" could have been misinterpreted and resulted in recording errors. It appears in some instances that commissioners recorded only the slaves between the ages of twelve and sixteen in the latter count.

29 Culpeper County, Virginia, Will Book N: 19, James Hawkins estate sales accounting, Thomas Kilby purchases, returned 16 September 1833; Office of the Clerk of the Circuit Court, Culpeper, Virginia.
30 Culpeper Co., Va., Will Book N: 4–8, James Hawkins estate appraisement, 1833.
31 Culpeper Co. Va., Chancery Court Case no. 7, Adm. of Thomas Kilby v. Adm. of James Hawkins, commissioner's report filed 1 May 1840; digital images 39–43 of 85.
32 Culpeper County, Virginia, Deed Books ZZ: 467–69; ZZ: 470–71; 1: 69–70; 1: 70–72; and 1: 73–75; heirs of James Hawkins to Armistead Brown, Bluford Thornhill, Aaron House, and Albert Hawkins, May 1833; Office of the Clerk of the Circuit Court, Culpeper, Virginia.
33 Culpeper Co. Va., Chancery Court Case no. 7, Adm. of Thomas Kilby v. Adm. of James Hawkins, chancery bill, July 1839; digital image 6 of 85.
34 Culpeper Co. Va., Chancery Court Case no. 7, Adm. of Thomas Kilby v. Adm. of James Hawkins, James Hawkins estate appraisement, 1833; digital image 58 of 85.
35 Culpeper Co. Va., Chancery Court Case no. 7, Adm. of Thomas Kilby v. Adm. of James Hawkins, James Hawkins estate account of sales, 1833; digital image 63 of 85.
36 Ibid.
37 Culpeper County, Virginia, Will Book N: 8–19, James Hawkins estate sale accounting, 1833; Office of the Clerk of the Circuit Court, Culpeper, Virginia.
38 Culpeper Co. Va., Chancery Court Case no. 7, Adm. of Thomas Kilby v. Adm. of James Hawkins, chancery bill, July 1839; digital images 4–7 of 85.
39 1830 U.S. census, Culpeper County, Virginia, population schedule, folio 127 (left, penned), line 18, Jas [James] Hawkins; NARA microfilm publication M19, roll 197.
40 Gourdvine Baptist Church (Culpeper Co., Va.), Minute Book, 1812–1832, p. 56.
41 Culpeper Co. Va., Chancery Court Case no. 7, Adm. of Thomas Kilby v. Adm. of James Hawkins, administrator qualification, Estate of Thomas Kilby, 19 May 1834; digital

images 72–73 of 85. Also, Culpeper County, Virginia, Will Book N: 141, Thomas Kilby estate inventor and appraisement, 1834; Office of the Clerk of the Circuit Court, Culpeper, Virginia.

42 The Commonwealth of Virginia, *The Code of Virginia: With the Declaration of Independence and Constitution of the United States and the Declaration of Rights and Constitution of Virginia, 1849*, title 35, ch. 127, § 7, p. 533–34; online archive, *Internet Archive* (https://archive.org/details/codevirginiawit00virggoog/page/n580).

43 Judy Russell, Central New Jersey, to Timothy Kilby, e-mail, 19 April 2018, "Legal requirement for widow administratrix to maintain custody of minor children"; privately held by Kilby, Fairfax, Virginia. Ms. Russell, CG, CCL, is a nationally-known expert and blogger of *The Legal Genealogist*. Consulting her regarding legal responsibilities Malinda may have had toward the Thomas Kilby estate and his children's rights therein, and any requirement to establish trusts or guardianships, Ms. Russell felt that Malinda had dower rights and "as long as nobody was bothered by [Malinda's authority over her children], and the kids were young enough not to want (and be legally entitled to) their share now, it's not at all surprising that the court didn't force a guardianship."

44 Culpeper Co., Va., Will Book N: 141, Thomas Kilby estate inventor and appraisement, 1834.

Chapter Three: The Land

1 Culpeper Co., Va., Deed Book OO: 264–65, Leroy Kilby and wife to Thomas Kilby, 20 August 1822. Leroy, an older brother of Thomas, had purchased the tract four years earlier, though there is no record he ever lived on or worked this land.

2 Culpeper Co., Va., Will Book N: 141, Thomas Kilby estate inventor and appraisement, 1834.

3 Virginia Auditor of Public Accounts, Land Tax Records, Culpeper County, Virginia, Daniel Brown's district, 1823, p. 28, line 24; for Thomas Kilbee [Kilby]; Land Tax microfilm 80, LVA, Richmond.

4 Virginia Auditor of Public Accounts, Land Tax Records,

Culpeper County, Virginia, tax years 1824–1841; for Thomas Kilbee [Kilby]; Land Tax microfilms 80 and 81, LVA, Richmond.

5   Culpeper County, Virginia, Deed Book 1: 152–53, Presley N. Smith and wife to Thomas Kilby, 25 September 1833; Office of the Clerk of the Circuit Court, Culpeper, Virginia.

6   Culpeper County, Virginia, Deed Book 1: 268–69, Thomas Kilby & Malinda his wife to Julius M. Hunt, 25 December 1833; Office of the Clerk of the Circuit Court, Culpeper, Virginia.

7   Culpeper Co., Va., Chancery Court Case no. 76, Joseph M Kilby v. Malinda Kilby Etc., deposition of Joseph M. Kilby, 30 August 1870; digital image 56 of 150. Also, Culpeper County, Virginia, Deed Book 20: 155, Thomas Kilby heirs to John Scott, 12 April 1852; Office of the Clerk of the Circuit Court, Culpeper, Virginia.

Chapter Four: Years of Tension, Years of Toil

1   Culpeper County, Virginia, Law Order Book 2, 1835–1839, p. 83, Presley N. Smith against Melinda Kilby administratrix of Thomas Kilby, 14 June 1836; microfilm reel 64, LVA, Richmond.

2   Culpeper Co., Va., Deed Book OO: 264–65, Leroy Kilby and wife to Thomas Kilby, 20 August 1822. Culpeper Co., Va., Deed Book 1: 152–53, Presley N. Smith and wife to Thomas Kilby, 25 September 1833.

3   Culpeper County, Virginia, Law Order Book 2, 1835–1839, p. 129, Same [James Kemper] against Melinda Kilby administratrix of Thomas Kilby, 25 November 1836; microfilm reel 64, LVA, Richmond.

4   Ibid.

5   Culpeper Co. Va., Chancery Court Case no. 7, Adm. of Thomas Kilby v. Adm. of James Hawkins, chancery bill, July 1839; digital images 4–7 of 85.

6   Culpeper Co. Va., Chancery Court Case no. 7, Adm. of Thomas Kilby v. Adm. of James Hawkins, commissioner's report filed 1 May 1840; digital image 34 of 85.

7   1840 U.S. census, Culpeper County, Virginia, population schedule, division allotted to James W. Broadus, folio 257 (left), p. 37 (penned), line 9, Melinda [Malinda] Kilby household; NARA microfilm publication M704, roll 554.
8   Virginia Auditor of Public Accounts, Personal Property Tax Records, Culpeper County, Virginia, Daniel Brown's district, 1840, p. 10, line 23; for Melinda Kilbee [Malinda Kilby], one enslaved person above age sixteen; Personal Property Tax microfilm 92, LVA, Richmond.
9   Virginia Auditor of Public Accounts, Personal Property Tax Records, Culpeper County, Virginia, Robert Brown's district, 1841, p. 9, line 5; for Melinda Kilbee [Malinda Kilby], one enslaved person above age sixteen; Personal Property Tax microfilm 92, LVA, Richmond. Virginia Auditor of Public Accounts, Personal Property Tax Records, Culpeper County, Virginia, Robert Brown's district, 1842, unnumbered page; for Matilda Kilbee [Malinda Kilby]; Personal Property Tax microfilm 92, LVA, Richmond. The record for 1842 indicates that Malinda held no enslaved person over age sixteen. Taxes were not levied and public records were not kept for enslaved children.
10 Culpeper Co., Va., Deed Book 6: 233–34, Kilby to Smith, deed of trust, 10 February 1843.
11 Culpeper County, Virginia, Deed Book 7: 14–15, Melinda [Malinda] Kilby to Thomas J. Griffin, deed of trust, 11 March 1844; Office of the Clerk of the Circuit Court, Culpeper, Virginia. Culpeper County, Virginia, Deed Book 7: 354–55, Malinda Kilby to Thomas J. Griffin, deed of trust, 1 September 1845; Office of the Clerk of the Circuit Court, Culpeper, Virginia.
12 Culpeper Co., Va., Chancery Court Case no. 76, Joseph M Kilby v. Malinda Kilby Etc., chancery bill, 1859; digital image 3 of 150.
13 Ibid.
14 Ibid.
15 Ibid.
16 Culpeper Co., Va., Chancery Court Case no. 76, Joseph M Kilby v. Malinda Kilby Etc., chancery bill, 1859; digital image

3 of 150. Also, see Rappahannock Co., Va., Chancery Court Case no. 253, Kilby v. Thornhill, chancery bill, March 1865.

17 Culpeper Co., Va., Chancery Court Case no. 76, Joseph M Kilby v. Malinda Kilby Etc., chancery bill, 1859; digital images 3–5 of 150. Culpeper Co., Va., Chancery Court Case, Lucy J. Stringfellow v. Scott, deposition of James F. Kilby; digital images 28–29 of 115. These two cases provide interesting details of the many transactions, the buying and selling of land and interests in future inheritances among the Thomas Kilby family members.

18 1860 U.S. Census, Culpeper Co., Va., pop. sch., Southern Division, p. 47, dwell. 39, fam. 37, Malinda Kilby.

19 1860 U.S. Census, Culpeper Co., Va., pop. sch., Southern Division, p. 47, dwell. 39, fam. 37, Joseph M. Kilby. 1860 U.S. census, Culpeper County, Virginia, population schedule, Northern Division, p. 62, dwelling 505, family 461, line 3, Joseph M. [Kilby], enumerated 9 August 1860; NARA microfilm publication M653, roll 1341. Note the different handwriting style on these two pages. Though each page specifies Thomas Hill as the enumerator, William A. Hill, perhaps a brother, was also an assistant marshal and enumerator for other county divisions. It appears that there were two different enumerators, neither one knowing they were recording the same person twice.

20 1860 U.S. census, Culpeper County, Virginia, pop. sch., Northern Division, p. 62, dwell. 505, fam. 461, line 4, Francis Chesterfield [Kilby].

21 Eugene M. Scheel, Culpeper: A *Virginia County's History through 1920* (Culpeper, Virginia: The Culpeper Historical Society, 1982), 173 and 176.

22 "Affairs on the Rappahannock–Depredations of the Enemy–The Approaching Conflict," *Richmond (Virginia) Dispatch*, 1 August 1862, p. 1, col. 1; image copy, *Newspapers.com* (https://www.newspapers.com).

23 Charles L. Perdue, Thomas E. Barden, and Robert K. Phillips, ed., *Weevils in the Wheat* (Charlottesville: University of Virginia Press, 1976), 294.

24 "Compiled Service Records of Confederate Soldiers Who

Served in Organizations from the State of Virginia," records for Joseph M. Kilby, Pvt., Co. G, 7th Virginia Infantry; database with images, *Fold3* (https://www.fold3.com/ image/10753646); citing NARA microfilm publication M324, roll 458.

25   David F. Riggs, *7th Virginia Infantry* (Lynchburg, Virginia: H.E. Howard, 1982), 83.

26   "Compiled Service Records of Confederate Soldiers Who Served in Organizations from the State of Virginia," record for Joseph M. Kilby, Pvt., Co. G, 7th Virginia Infantry; database with image, *Fold3* (https://www.fold3.com/image/10753851); citing NARA microfilm publication M324, roll 458.

27   "Compiled Service Records of Confederate Soldiers Who Served in Organizations from the State of Virginia," record for [Hamilton] Burgess Kilby, Pvt., Co. B, 4th Battalion, Infantry, Local Defense (Naval Battalion; Navy Department Battalion); database with image, *Fold3* (https://www.fold3.com/image/9645334); citing NARA microfilm publication M324, roll 417.

28   "Confederate Papers Relating to Citizens or Business Firms, 1861–1865," file for James F. Kilby; database with images, *Fold3* (https://www.fold3.com/image/267317356); citing NARA microfilm publication M346, roll 547.

29   "Confederate Papers Relating to Citizens or Business Firms, 1861–1865," file for Bluford Thornhill; database with images, *Fold3* (https://www.fold3.com/image/54806456); citing NARA microfilm publication M346, roll 1026.

30   Daniel A. Grimsley, *Battles in Culpeper County, Virginia, 1861–1865* (Culpeper, Virginia: Raleigh Travers Green, 1900), 15, 19, and 24.

Chapter Five: Prelude to Freedom

1   United States, War Record Office, *The War of the Rebellion* (Washington: Govt. Print Office, 1893); online archive, *Internet Archive* (https://archive.org/details/warofrebellion431unit_0/page/676/mode/2up), p. 677.

2   "Register of Deaths," 1864, district of Albert Brady,

unnumbered page, line 11, Lucy Thornhill, 28 December 1864, pneumonia; microfilm reel no. 25, LVA, Richmond. "Virginia Deaths and Burials, 1853–1912," database, *FamilySearch* (https://familysearch.org/ark:/61903/1:1:XR92-SZZ), entry for Lucy Thornhill, death at F. T. Church, Rappahannock, Virginia, 28 December 1864; FHL microfilm 2048582. Note that there are no burials at the site of F.T. Baptist Church. Lucy Thornhill's burial location is undetermined but may be at one of several Thornhill family graveyards in the vicinity of the church.

3 F.T. Baptist Church (Rappahannock Co., Va.), Minute Book, 1855–1878, p. 4.
4 Culpeper Co., Va., Marriage License and Return, Bluford Thornhill and Malinda Kilby, license issued 28 December 1864, marriage 3 January 1865.
5 Ibid.
6 Rappahannock Co., Va., Chancery Court Case no. 253, Kilby v. Thornhill, chancery bill, March 1865.
7 Ibid.
8 Ibid.

CHAPTER SIX: FRACTURED LIVES, INDOMITABLE SPIRITS

1 Culpeper Co. Va., Chancery Court Case no. 7, Adm. of Thomas Kilby v. Adm. of James Hawkins, administrator qualification, Estate of Thomas Kilby, 19 May 1834; digital images 72–73 of 85. Culpeper Co., Va., Will Book N: 141, Thomas Kilby estate inventor and appraisement, 1834. Culpeper Co., Va., Deed Book 6: 233–34, Kilby to Smith, deed of trust, 10 February 1843. Reference is made within to "one negro girl named Juliet Ann."
2 William Waller Hening, ed., *The Statutes at Large; Being a Collection of All the Laws of Virginia from the First Session of the Legislature, in the Year 1619* (New York: R. & W. & G. Bartow, 1823), 2: 170; online archive, *Internet Archive* (https://archive.org/stream/statutesatlargeb02virg#page/170/mode/2up).
3 After conducting an extensive search for existent court records, no evidence of court records, trusts, or decrees regarding

Malinda Kilby's legal guardianship of her minor children has been found. Opinion from a legal expert regarding the absence of public record was provided in Russell to Kilby, e-mail, 19 April 2018.

4   Culpeper Co., Va., Will Book N: 4–8, James Hawkins estate appraisement, 1833.

5   Virginia Auditor of Public Accounts, Personal Property Tax Records, Culpeper County, Virginia, Daniel Brown's district; 1835, p. 7, line 34; and 1836, p. 8, line 2; each for Melinda Kilbee [Malinda Kilby]; Personal Property Tax microfilm 91, LVA, Richmond. Virginia Auditor of Public Accounts, Personal Property Tax Records, Culpeper County, Virginia, Daniel Brown's district, 1837, p. 8, line 5; for Melinda Kilbee [Malinda Kilby]; Personal Property Tax microfilm 92, LVA, Richmond.

6   Culpeper Co., Va., Will Book N: 19, James Hawkins estate sales accounting, Thomas Kilby purchases, 1833. In this document Sarah is referred to as a "girl." Culpeper Co., Va., Will Book N: 141, Thomas Kilby estate inventor and appraisement, 1834. In this document of the following year Sarah is referred to as a "woman."

7   Culpeper Co., Va., Will Book N: 4–8, James Hawkins estate appraisement, 1833. The description of Sarah as a "girl" implies someone of young age. Also, Culpeper Co., Va., Will Book N: 19, James Hawkins estate sales accounting, Thomas Kilby purchases, 1833.

8   According to panel on exhibit at the National Museum of African American History and Culture, Washington, District of Columbia, Africans captured and transported to the Chesapeake region of the colonies and later states, which includes Virginia, came primarily from Biafra, Gold Coast, Central Africa, or Senegambia. Though importation of Africans was not halted entirely with the passage of the Act Prohibiting Importation of Slaves of 1807, births among the enslaved within U.S. borders had increased to the point that importation was not necessary to meet labor needs.

9   Culpeper County, Virginia, Will Book N: 19, James Hawkins estate sales accounting, Thomas J. Hawkins purchases, returned

16 September 1833; Office of the Clerk of the Circuit Court, Culpeper, Virginia.

10 The date of Sarah's impregnation and the conception of Juliet can be estimated as nine months before Juliet's birth, which is itself estimated to be between September 1833, when the sale from the James Hawkins estate occurred, and February 1834, when Thomas Kilby died. See Culpeper Co. Va., Chancery Court Case no. 7, Adm. of Thomas Kilby v. Adm. of James Hawkins, James Hawkins estate account of sales, 1833; digital image 63 of 85. No child of Sarah is identified nor is a child named Juliet among the enslaved property in this record. See also Culpeper Co., Va., Will Book N: 141, Thomas Kilby estate inventor and appraisement, 1834. Reference is made to Juliet Ann as the child of Sarah. The month of the death of James Hawkins can only be estimated as February or March 1833. See Culpeper Co., Va., Will Book N: 4–8, James Hawkins estate appraisement, 1833.

11 Culpeper Co. Va., Chancery Court Case no. 7, Adm. of Thomas Kilby v. Adm. of James Hawkins, chancery bill, July 1839; digital images 4–7 of 85.

12 Gourdvine Baptist Church (Culpeper Co., Va.), Minute Book, 1812–1832, pp. 56 & 62.

13 The existent Gourdvine Baptist Church minute books—two volumes: 1812–1832 and 1835–1853—include extensive lists of enslaved persons and their enslavers as members or attendees. A page-by-page reading of the volumes found no entry for any enslaved person associated with any Kilby member. For independent review of these significant volumes, see Gourdvine Baptist Church (Culpeper County, Virginia), Minute Books, 1812–1832 and 1835–1853 [two volumes]; bound Photostat copies (negative), LVA, Richmond.

14 Woodford B. Hackley, *Historical Sketch of the Jeffersonton Baptist Church: An Address Delivered on Homecoming Day, August 21, 1932* (publisher not identified, 1932), 23–24.

15 New Salem [Baptist] Church (Culpeper County, Virginia), Records, 1834–1873, p. 3; bound Photostat copy (negative), LVA, Richmond.

16 Ibid, p. 23.

17 Ibid, p. 24.
18 1850 U.S. census, Culpeper Co., Va., pop. sch., fol. 225 (front), p. 21 (penned upper right), dwell. 147, fam. 147, Melinda [Malinda] Kilby household. For Mary Stringfellow, see 1850 U.S. census, Culpeper County, Virginia, population schedule, folio 225 (front), p. 21 (penned), dwelling 149, family 149, Mary Stringfellow household; NARA microfilm publication M432, roll 941. For Mary Stringfellow's church membership, see New Salem [Baptist] Church (Culpeper Co., Va.), Records, 1834–1873, p. 105.
19 Culpeper County, Virginia, Will Book N: 262–63, Will of William S. Field, 12 February 1835, Office of the Clerk of the Circuit Court, Culpeper, Virginia.
20 Virginia Auditor of Public Accounts, Personal Property Tax Records, Culpeper County, Virginia, Daniel Brown's district, 1836, p. 8, line 2; for Melinda Kilbee [Malinda Kilby], one enslaved person aged sixteen or above; Personal Property Tax microfilm 91, LVA, Richmond. Virginia Auditor of Public Accounts, Personal Property Tax Records, Culpeper County, Virginia, Daniel Brown's district; 1837, p. 8, line 5; and 1838, page number illegible, line 35; each for Melinda Kilbee [Malinda Kilby]; Personal Property Tax microfilm 92, LVA, Richmond.
21 Virginia Auditor of Public Accounts, Personal Property Tax Records, Culpeper County, Virginia, Daniel Brown's district, 1838, p. 10, line 31; for Mary Stringfellow, one enslaved person aged sixteen or above; Personal Property Tax microfilm 92, LVA, Richmond.
22 Virginia Auditor of Public Accounts, Personal Property Tax Records, Culpeper County, Virginia, years 1839–1850; Personal Property Tax microfilm reels 92 and 92A, LVA, Richmond. During this twelve-year period Mary Stringfellow was taxed each year for owning one enslaved person aged sixteen or above.
23 1850 U.S. census, Culpeper County, Virginia, slave schedule, p. 9 (unmarked), line 20, right column, Mary Stringfellow; NARA microfilm publication M432, roll 985.
24 1840 U.S. census, Culpeper Co., Va. pop. sch., division allotted

to James W. Broadus, fol. 257 (left), p. 37 (penned), line 9, Melinda [Malinda] Kilby household.

25 Culpeper Co., Va., Chancery Court Case no. 76, Joseph M Kilby v. Malinda Kilby Etc., deposition of Joseph M. Kilby, 30 August 1870; digital image 56 of 150. Reference is made here to the death of Martha Ann Kilby in 1839.

26 1840 U.S. census, Culpeper Co., Va. pop. sch., division allotted to James W. Broadus, fol. 257 (left), p. 37 (penned), line 9, Melinda [Malinda] Kilby household.

27 Culpeper Co., Va., Deed Book 6: 233–34, Kilby to Smith, deed of trust, 10 February 1843. Culpeper Co., Va., Deed Book 7: 14–15, Melinda [Malinda] Kilby to Thomas J. Griffin, deed of trust, 11 March 1844. Culpeper Co., Va., Deed Book 7: 354–55, Malinda Kilby to Thomas J. Griffin, deed of trust, 1 September 1845.

28 Culpeper Co., Va., Deed Book 6: 233–34, Kilby to Smith, deed of trust, 10 February 1843.

29 "Virginia, Compiled Marriages, 1740–1850," database, *Ancestry* (https://www.ancestry.com), Louisa Kilby and John Q. Adams, 23 December 1843, Chesterfield [Culpeper] County, and Missouri E. Kilby and James Adams, 1 February 1843, Chesterfield [Culpeper] County; citing Jordan R. Dodd, et al., *Early American Marriages: Virginia to 1850* (Bountiful, Utah: Precision Indexing Publishers).

30 1850 U.S. census, Culpeper Co., Va., pop. sch., fol. 225 (front), p. 21 (penned upper right), dwell. 147, fam. 147, Melinda [Malinda] Kilby household.

31 1850 U.S. census, Culpeper County, Virginia, slave schedule; NARA microfilm publication M432, roll 985. An extended search for Malinda Kilby as enslaver uncovered no record.

32 Virginia Auditor of Public Accounts, Personal Property Tax Records, Culpeper County, Virginia, Robert Brown's district, 1850, p. 10, line 28, Malinda Kilby; Personal Property Tax microfilm 92A, LVA, Richmond.

33 Virginia Auditor of Public Accounts, Personal Property Tax Records, Culpeper County, Virginia, Robert Brown's district; 1851, p. 12, line 15; 1852, p. 12, line 25; 1853, p. 23, line 27; 1854, p. 25, line 3; each for Malinda Kilby, one enslaved

person age sixteen or above; Personal Property Tax microfilm 472, LVA, Richmond. Virginia Auditor of Public Accounts, Personal Property Tax Records, Culpeper County, Virginia, Robert Brown's district; 1856, p. 23, line 19; 1857, p. 23, line 29; both for Malinda Kilby, one enslaved person age sixteen or above; Personal Property Tax microfilm 473, LVA, Richmond.

34 To determine the probable birth year for Simon Kilby, multiple sources must be referenced. See Rappahannock County, Virginia, "Rappahannock Co. Marriages, 1871–1879," unnumbered box, folder for 1873, Simon Kilby and Lucy Frances Wallace, application for marriage license, 29 December 1873; Office of the Clerk of the Circuit Court, Washington, Virginia. Next, see 1860 U.S. census, Culpeper County, Virginia, slave schedule, Southern Division, p. 30, Molinda [Malinda] Kilby, "slave owner;" NARA microfilm publication M653, roll 1389. Entry in column set 2, line 16 is believed to be that of Simon Kilby and reports age as seven. Culpeper County, Virginia, Deed Book 14: 127, [James] Franklin Kilby to Hamilton B. Kilby, deed of conveyance of Charles William [Simon], 10 March 1858; Office of the Clerk of the Circuit Court, Culpeper, Virginia. For the person named James Walker, age eighteen, see 1870 U.S. census, Rappahannock Co., Va., pop. sch., Stonewall Twp., pp. 31–32 (penned), line 38, dwell. 216 [blank, skipped number], fam. 216 [blank, skipped number], Bluford Thornhill household. As Juliet is believed to have been born in early 1834 and Simon to have been born in 1853, Juliet must to have been around nineteen years of age at Simon's birth.

35 Culpeper Co., Va., Deed Book 14: 127, [James] Franklin Kilby to Hamilton B. Kilby, deed of conveyance of Charles William [Simon], 10 March 1858.

36 Culpeper County, Virginia, Deed Book 14: 127, [James] Franklin Kilby to Hamilton B. Kilby, deed of conveyance of Julet [sic], 10 March 1858; Office of the Clerk of the Circuit Court, Culpeper, Virginia. In this quoted passage, written exactly as it appears in the deed book, there appear numbers of what we would today describe as grammatical errors; for example, lists not separated by commas.

37 The Commonwealth of Virginia, *The Code of Virginia: With the Declaration of Independence and Constitution of the United States and the Declaration of Rights and Constitution of Virginia*, 1849, title 35, ch. 123, § 10, p. 524; online archive, *Internet Archive* (https://archive.org/details/codevirginiawit00virggoog/page/n572).
38 1860 U.S. census, Culpeper Co., Va., pop. sch., Southern Division, p. 3, dwell. 28, fam. 22, James Kilby. James Franklin Kilby's occupation was recorded as overseer.
39 Madison County, Virginia, Deed Book 68: 128–31, Simon Kilby heirs-at-law to Flora Belle Aylor, 14 November 1945; Office of the Clerk of the Circuit Court, Madison, Virginia.
40 1860 U.S. census, Culpeper Co., Va., pop. sch., Southern Division, p. 3, dwell. 28, fam. 22, James Kilby. For Thomas Kilby, see 1850 U.S. census, Orange County, Virginia, population schedule, folio 259 (front), line 12, Thomas Kilby; NARA microfilm publication M432, roll 967.
41 Craig M. Kilby, notes for James Franklin "Frank" Kilby, database as GEDCOM-format file, record collection of the author, Fairfax, Virginia. Though an otherwise meticulous genealogist, Craig Kilby provided no source citation for this notation.
42 Joyce Colleen Libes, *John Kilby of Culpeper County, Virginia: A Report of Some of His Descendants* (self-pub, 1992), 19.
43 New Salem [Baptist] Church (Culpeper Co., Va), Records, 1834–1873, p. 50.
44 1860 U.S. census, Culpeper County, Virginia, slave schedule, district of Thos Hill, Ass't Marshall [Northern District], p. 32, Jas [James] Kilby; NARA microfilm publication M653, roll 1389. The record indicates that James Franklin Kilby hired an eight-year-old female from F. Brown of Culpeper.
45 1850 U.S. census, Orange Co., Va., pop. sch., fol. 259 (front), line 12, Thomas Kilby. Culpeper Co., Va., Chancery Court Case no. 76, Joseph M Kilby v. Malinda Kilby Etc., summon to Thomas L. Kilby, 30 May 1857; digital image 95 of 150.
46 1860 U.S. census, Culpeper County, Virginia, population schedule, Town of Fairfax, p. 67, dwelling 52, family 52, Arther Edmond household; for H.B. Kilby with occupation of carpenter; NARA microfilm publication M653, roll 1341.

47 Culpeper Co., Va., Chancery Court Case no. 76, Joseph M Kilby v. Malinda Kilby Etc., chancery bill, 1859; digital image 3 of 150.
48 The 1850 U.S. census slave schedule was thoroughly searched, though no entry for Malinda Kilby was recorded that year. Malinda may have hired out Juliet during 1850, which could account for no record under her name for that year.
49 1860 U.S. census, Culpeper Co., Va., slave schedule, Southern Division, p. 30, Molinda [Malinda] Kilby.
50 The story of the design of the 1850 and 1860 census slave schedules is told in David E. Patterson, "The 1850 and 1860 Census, Schedule 2, Slave Inhabitants," *Afrigeneas Library*, 16 May 2015 (https://www.afrigeneas.com/library/slave_schedule2.html).
51 "Virginia Marriages, 1785–1940," database, *FamilySearch* (https://www.familysearch.org/ark:/61903/1:1:X5YN-XPK), entry for William Apperson and Frances M. Glasscock, married in Culpeper County, 1 January 1857; FHL microfilm 30978.
52 1860 U.S. census, Culpeper County, Virginia, slave schedule, Southern Division, p. 24, William C. Apperson, "slave owner;" NARA microfilm publication M653, roll 1389.
53 Virginia Auditor of Public Accounts, Personal Property Tax Records, Culpeper County, Virginia, St. Pierre Gibson's district, 1862, p. 13, line 13; for Malinda Kilby; Personal Property Tax microfilm 474, LVA, Richmond.
54 Ibid.
55 Virginia Auditor of Public Accounts, Personal Property Tax Records, Culpeper County, Virginia, John L Eggborn's district, 1863, p. 13, lines 7; for Malinda Kilby; Personal Property Tax microfilm 474, LVA, Richmond.

CHAPTER SEVEN: WHAT NAME SHALL WE USE?

1 Herbert Gutman, *The Black Family in Slavery and Freedom, 1750–1925* (New York: Pantheon Books, 1976), 230.
2 U.S. Congress, *Executive Documents Printed by Order of the House of Representatives During the First Session of the Thirty-*

Ninth Congress, 1865–'66 (Washington, D.C.: Government Printing Office, 1866), for Freedmen's Bureau General Order no. 8, 11 August 1865, Section III, paragraph 7; digital image copy, *Google Books* (https://www.google.com/books/edition/United_States_Congressional_serial_set/pWpHAQAAIAAJ?hl=en&gbpv=1&pg=PA109). Also, specific to Virginia, "Virginia, Freedmen's Bureau Field Office Records, 1865–1872," microfilm images, *FamilySearch* (https://familysearch.org/ark:/61903/3:1:S3HT-D897-FLX?cc=1596147&wc=9LMV-RMQ%3A1078518802%2C1078519003), Madison Courthouse (assistant subassistant commissioner) > Roll 110, Circulars and general and special orders received, Jan 1865–Aug 1868 > image 185 of 358; citing NARA microfilm publication M1913.

3   Leon F. Litwack, *Been in the Storm So Long: The Aftermath of Slavery* (New York: Alfred A. Knopf, 1979), 271.

4   F.T. Baptist Church (Rappahannock Co., Va.), Minute Book, 1855–1878, pp. 10–13 and 78–80. By matching first names, baptism dates, exclusion and restoration dates, dismissions, and death dates, the author was able to determine former enslavers for thirty-eight formerly enslaved church members. Of ninety-four African American members in 1866, forty percent could be matched with former enslavers. Of these thirty-eight individuals, *none* took the enslavers surname as their own. Of the remaining African American members, some were free people of color, some had recently joined, some could not be connected to an enslaver who was also a church member, and some may have chosen an enslaver's surname as their own. However, a clear preference for new surnames was evident. Further research would be needed to determine if this phenomenon was widespread or local only to this church community.

5   Litwack, *Been in the Storm So Long*, 272.

6   Herbert Gutman, *The Black Family in Slavery and Freedom, 1750–1925* (New York: Pantheon Books, 1976), 232.

7   Ralph Ellison, *Shadow and Act* (New York: Quality Paperback Book Club, 1994), 149.

8   1870 U.S. census, Rappahannock Co., Va., pop. sch., Stonewall

Twp., pp. 31–32 (penned), line 38, dwell. 216 [blank, skipped number], fam. 216 [blank, skipped number], Bluford Thornhill household. The form fields for dwelling and family number were inadvertently left blank for this separate household, whereas sequential numbering should have been recorded as dwelling 216 and family 216.
9 Virginia Auditor of Public Accounts, Personal Property Tax Records, Rappahannock County, Virginia, 1866, not paginated, alphabetically listed; for Lewis Walker, at Jno [John] S. Buckner; Personal Property Tax microfilm 719, LVA, Richmond.
10 Virginia Auditor of Public Accounts, Personal Property Tax Records, Rappahannock County, Virginia, 1867, not paginated, alphabetically listed; for Lewis Walker, at John Walden; Personal Property Tax microfilm 719, LVA, Richmond.
11 Virginia Auditor of Public Accounts, Personal Property Tax Records, Rappahannock County, Virginia, 1868, not paginated, alphabetically listed; for Lewis Walker, at A.T. Walden; Personal Property Tax microfilm 719, LVA, Richmond.
12 1870 U.S. census, Rappahannock County, Virginia, population schedule, Stonewall Township, pp. 30–31 (penned), line 40, dwelling/family 209, Lewis Walker household; NARA microfilm publication M593, roll 1674.
13 1870 U.S. census, Rappahannock Co., Va., pop. sch., Stonewall Township, pp. 30–31 (penned), line 40, dwell./fam. 209, Lewis Walker household. See also, Madison County, Virginia, Will Book 4: 560–61, Lewis Walker will, 1 July 1899, recorded 8 November 1920; Office of the Clerk of the Circuit Court, Madison, Virginia. Madison County, Virginia, Will Book 5: 316–19, Lewis Walker estate accounting, recorded July1923; Office of the Clerk of the Circuit Court, Madison, Virginia.
14 Madison County, Virginia, Deed Book 34: 370–71, Lewis Walker and Mary J. Walker to Simon Kilby, 13 September 1898; Office of the Clerk of the Circuit Court, Madison, Virginia. Madison County, Virginia, Deed Book 37: 102, Lewis Walker and Mary J. Walker to Charles W. Kilby, 1

July 1901; Office of the Clerk of the Circuit Court, Madison, Virginia.
15 1870 U.S. census, Rappahannock Co., Va., pop. sch., Stonewall Twp., pp. 31–32 (penned), line 38, dwell. 216 [blank, skipped number], fam. 216 [blank, skipped number], Bluford Thornhill household.
16 John Philip Colletta, *Only a Few Bones: A True Account of the Rolling Fork Tragedy and its Aftermath* (Washington, DC: Direct Descent, 2015 [New Edition]), 392.
17 1880 U.S. census, Rappahannock County, Virginia, population schedule, Stonewall District, enumeration district (ED) 131, p. 34 (penned), line 13, Betsy Kilby in Bluford Thornhill household; NARA microfilm publication T9, roll 1386.
18 F.T. Baptist Church (Rappahannock Co., Va.), Minute Book, 1805–1855. F.T. Baptist Church (Rappahannock Co., Va.), Minute Book, 1855–1878.
19 F.T. Baptist Church (Rappahannock Co., Va.), Minute Book, 1805–1855, pp. 6–8, 29–36. F.T. Baptist Church (Rappahannock Co., Va.), Minute Book, 1855–1878, pp. 10–13, 78–80.
20 F.T. Baptist Church (Rappahannock Co., Va.), Minute Book, 1805–1855, p. 18. F.T. Baptist Church (Rappahannock Co., Va.), Minute Book, 1855–1878, p. 4.
21 F.T. Baptist Church (Rappahannock Co., Va.), Minute Book, 1855–1878, pp. 72, 76.
22 Ibid, p. 13.
23 A. Paul Thompson, F.T. Baptist Church 1778–1978 (Orange, Virginia: Green Publishers, 1979), 18.
24 Ibid.
25 F.T. Baptist Church (Rappahannock Co., Va.), Minute Book, 1855–1878, pp. 39–40.
26 Ibid, pp. 78–79.
27 Ibid, p. 78.
28 Ibid, p. 13.
29 Ibid, p. 80.
30 Upon Simon Kilby's death his daughter, Mattie [Martha Ann] Wright, the informant identified on Simon's death certificate, gave the name Julia Luby as Simon's mother, a curious surname

unsupported by any corroborating evidence. Furthermore, she gave his father's name as "Nimrod Kilby (col)" with no evidence a man of this name ever existed.
31 Gregory A. Wills, *Democratic Religion: Freedom, Authority, and Church Discipline in the Baptist South, 1785–1900* (New York: Oxford University Press, 1997), 66 and 81.
32 F.T. Baptist Church (Rappahannock Co., Va.), Minute Book, 1805–1855. Among the many charges brought against enslaved women found in this book are the following: Daphney, 18 January 1823, p. 93; Kizzia, about 1826, p. 115; Charlotte, 14 July 1827, for "having a bastard child," p. 120; Charlotte and Nancy, for "sin of uncleanness," about 1831, p. 156.
33 F.T. Baptist Church (Rappahannock Co., Va.), Minute Book, 1855–1878, p. 78.
34 P.M. Finks to Clerk of the Court, certification document, 29 December 1873; with Rappahannock Co., Va., "Rappahannock Co. Marriages, 1871–1879," unnumbered box, folder for 1873, Simon Kilby and Lucy Frances Wallace, 29 December 1873.
35 1880 U.S. census, Rappahannock Co., Va., pop. sch., Stonewall District, ED 131, p. 34 (penned), line 13, Betsy Kilby in Bluford Thornhill household.
36 Rappahannock County, Virginia, "Marriage Certificates & Licenses, 1861–1889," no. 43, Simon Kilby and Lucy Frances Wallace, 30 December 1873; image, microfilm reel no. 178, LVA, Richmond.
37 P.M. Finks to Clerk of the Court, certification document, 29 December 1873.
38 "Pennsylvania, Death Certificates, 1906–1967," database with images, *Ancestry* (https://www.ancestry.com), imaged certificate no. 64870, John H Kilby, died Allegheny County, 28 July 1932; citing "Pennsylvania Historic and Museum Commission; Harrisburg, Pennsylvania." See another example, "Old-Time Colored Woman Dies Here," *The (Winchester, Virginia) Daily Independent*, 14 July 1924, p. 1, col. 6; LVA microfilm no. 286, roll for <1924:1:2–9:18,20–10:13,15–12:31>, LVA, Richmond.

39 Rappahannock Co., Va., Chancery Court Case no. 253, Kilby v. Thornhill, chancery bill, March 1865.
40 Madison Co., Va., Deed Book 68: 128–31, Simon Kilby heirs-at-law to Flora Belle Aylor, 14 November 1945.
41 "Our Colored Folk," *Madison County (Virginia) Eagle*, 14 April 1933, p. 8, col. 6; LVA microfilm no. 276, roll for <1933:1:1–9:22, 10:6–1934:5:18, 6:1–12:14,28>, LVA, Richmond.
42 Culpeper Co., Va., Deed Book 14: 127, [James] Franklin Kilby to Hamilton B. Kilby, deed of conveyance of Charles William [Simon], 10 March 1858.

CHAPTER EIGHT: TRANSITION TO FREEDOM

1 Records of the Field Offices for the State of Virginia, Bureau of Refugees, Freedmen, and Abandoned Lands, National Archives and Records Administration, 1865–1872; NARA microfilm publication M1913, rolls 69, 70, 102, 103, and 110.
2 Wilma King, *Stolen Children: Slave Youth in Nineteenth-Century America* (Bloomington: Indiana University Press, 2011), 335–338.
3 Ibid. The author conducted an image-by-image search through this entire set looking for records pertaining to the subjects of this research.
4 *Contracts and Indentures in Greene and Madison Counties, 1865–1867*, Records of the Field Offices for the State of Virginia, Bureau of Refugees, Freedmen, and Abandoned Lands, National Archives and Records Administration, 1865–1872; image, *FamilySearch* (https://www.familysearch.org/ark:/61903/3:1:S3HT-D897-X6P), image 527 of 587; citing NARA microfilm publication M1913, roll 110. Many similar apprenticeship agreements can be found among the Freedmen's Bureau records for Madison, Rappahannock, and Culpeper counties.
5 Mary Niall Mitchell, *Raising Freedom's Child: Black Children and Visions of the Future after Slavery* (New York: New York University Press, 2008), 144.
6 The Commonwealth of Virginia, *The Code of Virginia, Second*

Edition, Including Legislation to the Year 1860, title 35, ch. 126, §4, p. 585; online archive, *Internet Archive* (https://archive.org/details/codeofvirginiain00virg/page/585).

7   1870 U.S. census, Rappahannock Co., Va., pop. sch., Stonewall Twp., pp. 31–32 (penned), line 38, dwell. 216 [blank, skipped number], fam. 216 [blank, skipped number], Bluford Thornhill household.

8   *Register of Letters Received and Endorsements Received and Sent, May–Nov. 1867 and Feb. 1868*, Records of the Field Offices for the State of Virginia, Bureau of Refugees, Freedmen, and Abandoned Lands, National Archives and Records Administration, 1865–1872, p. 215 [stamped]; image, *FamilySearch* (https://www.familysearch.org/ark:/61903/3:1:S3HT-D897-FRQ), image 12 of 17; citing NARA microfilm publication M1913, roll 110.

9   Rappahannock Co., Va., "Rappahannock Co. Marriages, 1871–1879," unnumbered box, folder for 1873, Simon Kilby and Lucy Frances Wallace, 29 December 1873.

10 Nazareth Baptist Church (Boston, Virginia), "A History of Nazareth Baptist Church," *Nazareth Baptist Church Celebrates One Hundred Twenty-Five Years of Serving the Lord*, 10 July 2004, self-published and unpaginated. Also, Nazareth Baptist Church, record books, selected records, 1943-87; Nazareth Baptist Church, Boston, Virginia.

11 "The Kuklux Klan," *The Native Virginian (Orange Court House, Virginia)*, 3 April 1868, p. 2, col. 3; image copy, Library of Congress, *Chronicling America: Historic American Newspapers* (https://chroniclingamerica.loc.gov/lccn/sn94051044/1868-04-03/ed-1/seq-2/)

12 "K. K. K.," *The Native Virginian (Orange Court House, Virginia)*, 3 April 1868, p. 2, col. 6; image copy, Library of Congress, *Chronicling America: Historic American Newspapers* (https://chroniclingamerica.loc.gov/lccn/sn94051044/1868-04-03/ed-1/seq-2/)

13 "See It! If you have to lose a day!!," *Madison (Virginia) Exponent*, 21 September 1923, p. 2, col. 5; LVA microfilm no. 274, roll for <1923:1:12,26, 2:2–3:16, 4:13–6:29, 7:20–27, 8:17–9:21, 10:5,26, 11:2–12:28>, LVA, Richmond.

14 "Letter from Rappahannock," *Alexandria Gazette and Virginia Advertiser*, 15 February 1893, p. 2, col. 5; image copy, Library of Congress, *Chronicling America: Historic American Newspapers* (https://chroniclingamerica.loc.gov/lccn/sn85025007/1893-02-15/ed-1/seq-2/).

15 "Swift Retribution: A Lascivious Negro Hanged to a Convenient Tree" *Delaware Gazette and State Journal*, 7 August 1884, p. 1, col. 2; image copy, Library of Congress, *Chronicling America: Historic American Newspapers* (https://chroniclingamerica.loc.gov/lccn/sn88053046/1884-08-07/ed-1/seq-1/).

CHAPTER NINE: WHO WILL BE REMEMBERED?

1 F.T. Baptist Church (Rappahannock Co., Va.), Minute Book, 1855–1878, p. 76.

2 The author conducted an extensive search of existent newspapers, public records, private accounts, cemeteries, and burial grounds but found no death record for Malinda Thornhill beyond the single record of the F.T. Baptist Church. Also see Culpeper Co., Va., Chancery Court Case, Stringfellow v. Scott, deposition of James F. Kilby; digital image 30 of 115. The statement in this deposition by James F. Kilby that his mother had died "about 12 years ago" (1877) is not corroborated with any evidence.

3 F.T. Baptist Church (Rappahannock County, Virginia), Minute Book, 1878–1894, leather bound original book, p. 205; Virginia Baptist Historical Society, Richmond.

4 Culpeper Co., Va., Chancery Court Case, Stringfellow v. Scott, deposition of James F. Kilby; digital image 29 of 115.

5 For Albert Chesterfield Kilby' death see New Salem [Baptist] Church (Culpeper Co., Va.), Records, 1834–1873, p. 106. For Hamilton Burgess Kilby's disappearance and presumed death see Culpeper Co., Va., Chancery Court Case, Lucy J. Stringfellow v. Scott, deposition of James F. Kilby, 8 September 1889; digital image 29 of 115.

6 Culpeper Co., Va., Chancery Court Case, Stringfellow v. Scott, deposition of James F. Kilby; digital image 29 of 115.

7   Bureau of Land Management, "Land Patents," database with image, *General Land Office Records* (https://glorecords.blm.gov/search/), search for Joseph M. Kilby, Ransom County, North Dakota. *FindAGrave* (http://findagrave.com), memorial page for Joseph M. Kilby (1830–1888), Find A Grave Memorial no. 62753051, citing Oakwood Cemetery, Lisbon, Ransom County, North Dakota.
8   Culpeper Co., Va., Chancery Court Case, Stringfellow v. Scott, deposition of James F. Kilby; digital image 29 of 115.
9   Culpeper County, Virginia, Will Book Z: 292–93, will of James F. Kilby, dated 24 December 1895, proved 17 October 1898, Office of the Clerk of the Circuit Court, Culpeper, Virginia.
10 Culpeper County, Virginia, Deed Book 24: 463–64, deed of trust, James F. Kilby to C.S. Jones, 1 January 1880; Office of the Clerk of the Circuit Court, Culpeper, Virginia. See also, Culpeper Co., Va., Chancery Court Case, Stringfellow v. Scott, deposition of James F. Kilby; digital image 29 of 115.

CHAPTER TEN: ONE FAMILY, SEPARATE PATHS

1   1870 U.S. census, Rappahannock Co., Va., pop. sch., Stonewall Twp., pp. 31–32 (penned), line 38, dwell. 216 [blank, skipped number], fam. 216 [blank, skipped number], Bluford Thornhill household.
2   Litwack, *Been in the Storm So Long*, 258.
3   F.T. Baptist Church (Rappahannock Co., Va.), Minute Book, 1878–1894, p. 205.

CHAPTER ELEVEN: SIMON KILBY

1   "Madison County Has Scored a Glorious Success," *Madison County (Virginia) Eagle*, 10 October 1924, p. 1, cols. 4–7 and p. 4, cols. 1–3; LVA microfilm no. 276, roll for <1924:1:4–2:22, 3:7–4:4,18–8:22, 9:5–1925:6:12,26–12:25>, LVA, Richmond.
2   Ibid, p. 1, col. 5 and p.4, col. 3.
3   "Madison County Has Scored a Glorious Success," p. 1, cols. 4–7, p. 4, cols. 1–3; "Madison Gala Day," p. 4, col. 3;

and "Observations of an On Looker," p. 4, col. 5; all for 10 October 1924, *Madison County (Virginia) Eagle*; LVA microfilm no. 276, roll for <1924:1:4–2:22, 3:7–4:4,18–8:22, 9:5–1925:6:12,26–12:25>, LVA, Richmond.
4 "Virginia, Death Records, 1912–2014," database with images, *Ancestry.com*, certificate 29198, Charles W. Kilby, 4 October 1924.
5 Ibid.
6 Frederick Douglass, *Narrative of the Life of Frederick Douglass*, in *Autobiographies* (New York: Literary Classics of the United States, 1994), 15.
7 "Virginia, Death Records, 1912–2014," database with images, *Ancestry.com*, certificate 29198, Charles W. Kilby, 4 October 1924. The 1853 date of birth is confirmed through the synthesis of information found in the following two sources. 1860 U.S. census, Culpeper Co., Va., slave schedule, Southern Division, p. 30, Molinda [Malinda] Kilby. Rappahannock Co., Va., Chancery Court Case no. 253, Kilby v. Thornhill, chancery bill, March 1865.
8 Edward Ball, *Slaves in the Family* (New York: Farrar, Straus and Giroux, 1998), 278.
9 1850 U.S. census, Rappahannock County, Virginia, population schedule, folio 128 (back), dwelling 611, family 611, Bluford Thornhill household, for Sarah A Thornhill and Paskiel [Paschal] Finks; NARA microfilm publication M432, roll 972. *Find A Grave*, database and images (http://findagrave.com), memorial page for Sarah Ann Thornhill Finks (1826–1889), Find A Grave Memorial no. 87769245, citing Finks Family Cemetery, Culpeper, Culpeper County, Virginia. Note that the Cemetery location is incorrect; it is in Rappahannock County.
10 *Map of Culpeper, Madison and Rappahannock* (Virginia: Chief Engineer's Office D.N.V, 1864); digital image, *Library of Congress* (https://www.loc.gov/item/2012590169/).
11 1870 U.S. census, Madison County, Virginia, population schedule, Robertson District, p. 49 (penned), dwelling 322, family 329, Walker Wallace household; NARA microfilm publication M593, roll 1662.

12 F.T. Baptist Church (Rappahannock Co., Va.), Minute Book, 1855–1878, pp. 55, 58, 59. Also, see pp. 78 and 79 of the same volume showing that Walker Wallace had become a baptized member of the church in 1844 and Martha Wallace in 1866—they remained church members throughout their lives. The record shows that Walker remained the church sexton until his death in 1898.

13 1870 U.S. census, Madison Co., Va., pop. sch., Robertson District, p. 49 (penned), dwell. 322, fam. 329, Walker Wallace household.

14 Rappahannock County, Virginia, "Marriage Certificates & Licenses, 1861–1889," no. 43, Simon Kilby and Lucy Frances Wallace, 30 December 1873; image, microfilm reel no. 178, LVA, Richmond. Conclusion is drawn from the minister's return statement of the marriage occurring at the "residence of the bride" and the clerk's record for place of marriage at "Paschal M Finks in Rappk County."

15 "Letter from Rappahannock," *Alexandria* (Virginia) *Gazette*, 24 March 1886, p. 2, col. 6; image copy, Library of Congress, *Chronicling America: Historic American Newspapers* (https://chroniclingamerica.loc.gov/lccn/sn85025007/1886-03-24/ed-1/seq-2/).

16 As example, see Madison County, Virginia, Chancery Court Case, Exr. of Elliott Finks v. Mary H Huffman Etc., chancery bill, 1875; digital images, LVA, *Virginia Memory* (https://www.lva.virginia.gov/chancery/case_detail.asp?CFN=113-1895-001), images 2–9 of 166. Undetermined is whether Paschal was properly trained and officially authorized to prepare documents with statements of legal standing, such as those for Simon Kilby and Fannie Wallace.

17 Martha Wallace, marriage consent, 29 December 1873; with Rappahannock Co., Va., "Rappahannock Co. Marriages, 1871–1879," unnumbered box, folder for 1873, Simon Kilby and Lucy Frances Wallace, 29 December 1873.

18 P.M. Finks to Clerk of the Court, certification document, 29 December 1873; with Rappahannock Co., Va., "Rappahannock Co. Marriages, 1871–1879," unnumbered

box, folder for 1873, Simon Kilby and Lucy Frances Wallace, 29 December 1873.
19 "Circular 11," *Circulars and General and Special Orders Received, Jan 1865–Aug 1868*, Records of the Field Offices for the State of Virginia, Bureau of Refugees, Freedmen, and Abandoned Lands, National Archives and Records Administration, 1865–1872, order of 19 March 1866, p. 3; image, *FamilySearch* (https://www.familysearch.org/ark:/61903/3:1:S3HT-D897-NQ5), image 184 of 358; citing NARA microfilm publication M1913, roll 110.
20 As Paschal M. Finks was married to Sarah Ann Thornhill, a daughter of Bluford Thornhill, through marriage Finks had familial connections to Malinda (Kilby) Thornhill's sons, one of whom is considered the biological father of Simon Kilby.
21 Rappahannock Co., Va., "Rappahannock Co. Marriages, 1871–1879," unnumbered box, folder for 1873, Simon Kilby and Lucy Frances Wallace, 29 December 1873.
22 Ibid.
23 James Wilson Kilby and Patricia Kilby-Robb, *The Kilby Legacy: I Stretch My Hands to Thee* (USA, Kilby Publications, 1999), 2–9. Also, Betty Kilby Fisher, *Wit, Will & Walls* (Euless, Texas: Cultural Innovations, 2002), 2–5.
24 Virginia, Bureau of Vital Statistics, "Old Births Index, 1867–1879: Griggs-Roscher," p. 410; for "fem, Simon, Fanny, 15 May 1876, Rapp."; microfilm, reel 003, City of Fairfax Public Library, Fairfax, Virginia. 1900 U.S. census, Rappahannock County, Virginia, population schedule, Hawthorne division, enumeration district (ED) 50, sheet 177B, dwelling/family 12, line 70, Bertie Hill; NARA microfilm T623, roll 1724.
25 1900 U.S. census, Madison County, Virginia, population schedule, Robertson District, enumeration district (ED) 39, sheet 5B, dwelling/family 90, line 61, Hubert Kilby in George E. Dulaney household; NARA microfilm T623, roll 1717.
26 1900 U.S. census, Madison County, Virginia, population schedule, Robertson District, enumeration district (ED) 38, sheet 3B, dwelling/family 57, line 84, Oscar Kilby in Lemuel Hoffman household; NARA microfilm T623, roll 1717.
27 1900 U.S. census, Madison County, Virginia, population

schedule, Robertson District, enumeration district (ED) 38, sheet 70A (stamped), sheet 6 (penned), dwelling/family 108, Simeon [Simon] Kilby household; NARA microfilm T623, roll 1717.

28 1900 U.S. census, Madison Co., Va., pop. sch., Robertson District, ED 38, sheet 70A (stamped), sheet 6 (penned), dwell./fam. 108, Simeon [Simon] Kilby household. 1910 U.S. census, Madison County, Virginia, population schedule, Robertson District, enumeration district (ED) 48, sheet 2B, dwelling/family 39, Charles W. Kilby household; NARA microfilm T624, roll 1635.

29 1900 U.S. census, Madison Co., Va., pop. sch., Robertson District, ED 38, sheet 70A (stamped), sheet 6 (penned), dwell./fam. 108, Simeon [Simon] Kilby household. 1910 U.S. census, Madison Co., Va., pop. sch., Robertson District, ED 48, sheet 2B, dwell./fam. 39, Charles W. Kilby household. "Virginia, Death Records, 1912–2014," database with images, *Ancestry* (https://www.ancestry.com), imaged certificate no. 12368, Robert E Kilby, died Madison County, 26 April 1917; citing "Virginia Department of Health; Richmond, Virginia; Virginia Deaths, 1912–2014."

30 1900 U.S. census, Madison Co., Va., pop. sch., Robertson District, ED 38, sheet 70A (stamped), sheet 6 (penned), dwell./fam. 108, Simeon [Simon] Kilby household. 1910 U.S. census, Madison Co., Va., pop. sch., Robertson District, ED 48, sheet 2B, dwell./fam. 39, Charles W. Kilby household. It is possible that one son (Simon Jr. or Thomas) died before 1900 and the other before 1910, though there is no evidence to support this hypothesis.

31 This photo was identified in 1980 by Mrs. Karin Bivins to be of Simon (a.k.a. Charles William) Kilby. While positive identification through a second source is sought, no one the author has approached since has either confirmed or disputed this photo's identification.

32 1900 U.S. census, Madison Co., Va., pop. sch., Robertson District, ED 38, sheet 70A (stamped), sheet 6 (penned), dwell./fam. 108, Simeon [Simon] Kilby household.

33 1900 U.S. census, Madison Co., Va., pop. sch., Robertson District, ED 38, sheet 70A (stamped), sheet 6 (penned), dwell./fam. 108, Simeon [Simon] Kilby household.

34 Madison County, Virginia, Deed Book 34: 370, A.L. [Abraham Lemuel] Hoffman To Simon Kilby, 18 March 1898; Office of the Clerk of the Circuit Court, Madison, Virginia. Madison County, Virginia, Deed Book 34: 370–71, Lewis Walker and Mary J. Walker his wife to Simon Kilby, 13 September 1898; Office of the Clerk of the Circuit Court, Madison, Virginia.

35 Madison County, Virginia, Deed Book 30: 542, Lewis Walker and Jane his wife to Walker Wallace, 11 June 1885; Office of the Clerk of the Circuit Court, Madison, Virginia. Madison County, Virginia, Deed Book 37: 102, Lewis Walker and Mary J. Walker his wife to Charles W. Kilby, 1 July 1901; Office of the Clerk of the Circuit Court, Madison, Virginia.

36 Madison Co., Va., Deed Book 34: 370–71, Lewis Walker and Mary J. Walker his wife to Simon Kilby, 13 September 1898.

37 Madison Co., Va., Deed Book 37: 102, Lewis Walker and Mary J. Walker his wife to Charles W. Kilby, 1 July 1901.

38 Nazareth Baptist Church, "A History of Nazareth Baptist Church," *Nazareth Baptist Church Celebrates One Hundred Twenty-Five Years of Serving the Lord.*

39 Madison County, Virginia, Register of Marriages, unpaginated, chronologically ordered page, Oscar Hill and Berta Kilby, December 1904; LVA microfilm reel no. 27, LVA, Richmond.

40 1910 U.S. census, Livingston County, New York, population schedule, York Township, enumeration district (ED) 67, sheet 1A, dwelling/family 1, Oscar Hill household; NARA microfilm publication T624, film 987.

41 "Virginia Marriages, 1785–1940," database, *FamilySearch* (https://www.familysearch.org/ark:/61903/1:1:XRD9-L8Z), entry for Sim Wright and Martha Kilby, married in Madison County, 25 March 1905; FHL microfilm 32595.

42 1920 U.S. census, Madison County, Virginia, population schedule, Robertson District, enumeration district (ED) 62, sheet 3A, dwelling/family 38, Simeon Wright household;

NARA microfilm publication T625, film 1897. 1930 U.S. census, Rappahannock County, Virginia, population schedule, Hawthorne District, enumeration district (ED) 79–3, sheet 3A, dwelling 51, family 52, Simuel Wright household; NARA microfilm publication T626, film 2457.

43 Madison County, Virginia, Marriage Register 2, 1905–1938, p. 57 (stamped), Major Washington to Ophelia Kilby, 8 March 1922; LVA microfilm reel no. 57, LVA, Richmond.

44 1940 U.S. census, Madison County, Virginia, population schedule, Robertson District, enumeration district (ED) 57–10, sheet 15A, dwelling 240, Ophelia Washington household; NARA microfilm publication T627, film 4275.

45 Madison County, Virginia, Marriage Register 1, 1793–1905, p. 240 (penned), Hubert Kilby to Linda Fry, 6 August 1904; LVA microfilm reel no. 57, LVA, Richmond.

46 Ibid.

47 "Virginia, Death Records, 1912–2014," database with images, *Ancestry* (https://www.ancestry.com), imaged certificate no. 28251, Hubert Reid Kilby, died Madison County, 16 December 1949; citing "Virginia Department of Health; Richmond, Virginia; Virginia Deaths, 1912–2014." "Hubert Reid Kilby," *Madison County (Virginia) Eagle*, 22 December 1949, p. 8, col. 1–2; LVA microfilm no. 276, roll for <1948:1:8–9:3.17–1952:5:22>, LVA, Richmond.

48 1930 U.S. census, Madison County, Virginia, population schedule, Robertson District, enumeration district (ED) 57–5, sheet 10A, dwelling 185, family 186, J. Oscar Kilby household; NARA microfilm publication T626, film 2450. 1940 U.S. census, Madison County, Virginia, population schedule, Robertson District, enumeration district (ED) 57–9, sheet 6A, dwelling 108, line 36, Oscar Kilby household; NARA microfilm publication T627, film 4275.

49 "Hubert Reid Kilby," *Madison County Eagle*, 22 December 1949, p. 8, col. 1–2. Also, *Find A Grave*, database and images (http://findagrave.com), memorial page for Hubert Reid Kilby (1881–1949), Find A Grave Memorial no. 186060372, citing Nazareth Baptist Church Cemetery, Boston, Culpeper County, Virginia.

50 Madison County, Virginia, Marriage Register 2, 1905–1938, p. 57 (stamped), James Oscar to Catherine Thomas, 1 February 1922; LVA microfilm reel no. 57, LVA, Richmond.

51 1900 U.S. census, Madison Co., Va., pop. sch., Robertson District, ED 38, sheet 3B, dwell./fam. 57, line 84, Oscar Kilby in Lemuel Hoffman household. 1910 U.S. census, Madison County, Virginia, population schedule, Robertson District, enumeration district (ED) 48, sheet 3A, dwelling/family 39, line 1, James O. Kilby; NARA microfilm publication T623, film 1635. Madison County, Virginia, Deed Book 40: 535–36, W.M. Mitchell and C.F. Mitchell his wife to Oscar Kilby, 4 March 1911; Office of the Clerk of the Circuit Court, Madison, Virginia. Madison County, Virginia, Deed Book 47: 315–16, John T. Brown, administrator, to Oscar Kilby, 23 May 1924; Office of the Clerk of the Circuit Court, Madison, Virginia.

52 Madison County, Virginia, Deed Book 40: 178–79, Sarah A. Barbour and Geo. Barbour her husband to James Oscar Kilby, 16 October 1909, recorded 16 October 1909; Office of the Clerk of the Circuit Court, Madison, Virginia.

53 Lodge Number 2121, The Grand United Order of Off Fellows, membership application book, entry for James O Kilby, 1911, p. 94; private collection of Mrs. Nancy Williams Garnett, Madison, Virginia.

54 Madison County, Virginia, List of Voters Registered in Madison County, unpaginated, alphabetically listed, James O. Kilby, 24 September 1918; Office of the Clerk of the Circuit Court, Madison, Virginia.

55 Madison Co., Va., James Oscar to Catherine Thomas, 1 February 1922.

56 1940 U.S. census, Madison Co., Va., pop. sch., Robertson District, ED 57-9, sheet 6A, dwell. 108, line 36, Oscar Kilby household.

57 1900 U.S. census, Madison Co., Va., pop. sch., Robertson District, ED 38, sheet 70A (stamped), sheet 6 (penned), dwell./fam. 108, Simeon [Simon] Kilby household.

58 1910 U.S. census, Rappahannock County, Virginia, population schedule, Hawthorne District, enumeration district (ED) 60,

sheet 7B, dwelling 120, family 122, line 91, John Kilby in Andra [Andrew] Finks household; NARA microfilm publication T624, roll 1643.

59 1880 U.S. census, Rappahannock County, population schedule, Stonewall District, enumeration district (ED) 131, p. 34 (penned), dwelling 276, family 289, Paschal M. Finks household; NARA microfilm publication T9, film 1386. The Finks household included three non-White "servant" persons in 1880. 1900 U.S. census, Rappahannock County, Virginia, population schedule, Hawthorn District, enumeration district (ED) 50, sheet 5B, dwelling 86, family 87 (corrected), Andrew J. Finks household; NARA microfilm publication T623, film 1724. Three non-White "servants" are part of the Andrew Finks household in 1900. 1910 U.S. census, Rappahannock Co., Va., pop. sch., Hawthorne District, ED 60, sheet 7B, dwell. 120, fam. 122, line 91, John Kilby in Andra [Andrew] Finks household. John Henry Kilby was a "servant" to Andrew Finks in 1910.

60 Madison County, Virginia, Marriage Register 2, 1905–1938, p. 29 (stamped), John H. Kilby to M.E. Smith, 5 November 1913; LVA microfilm reel no. 57, LVA, Richmond.

61 1930 U.S. census, Rappahannock County, Virginia, population schedule, Hawthorne District, enumeration district (ED) 79–5, sheet 3A, dwelling 50, family 51, Emma Finks household for John H. Kilby family; NARA microfilm publication T626, film 2457. 1940 U.S. census, Rappahannock County, Virginia, population schedule, Hawthorne District, enumeration district (ED) 79–5, sheet 3A, dwelling 31, Eda Finks household for John Kilby family; NARA microfilm publication T627, film 4287.

62 "Virginia, Death Records, 1912–2014," database with images, *Ancestry* (https://www.ancestry.com), imaged certificate no. 6853, Ella Kilby, died Rappahannock County, 8 March 1945; citing "Virginia Department of Health; Richmond, Virginia; Virginia Deaths, 1912–2014." "Virginia, Death Records, 1912–2014," database with images, *Ancestry* (https://www.ancestry.com), imaged certificate no. 23831, John Henry Kilby, died Rappahannock County, 25 September 1958; citing "Virginia

Department of Health; Richmond, Virginia; Virginia Deaths, 1912–2014."

63 *Find A Grave*, database and images (http://findagrave.com), memorial page for John Henry Kilby (1884–1958), Find A Grave memorial no. 156115877, and memorial page for Mary Ella Smith Kilby (1887–1945), Find A Grave memorial no. 156115933, both citing Nazareth Baptist Church Cemetery, Boston, Culpeper County, Virginia.

64 "Virginia, Death Records, 1912–2014," database with images, *Ancestry.com*, certificate 29198, Charles W. Kilby, 4 October 1924.

65 Ibid.

66 "Virginia, Death Records, 1912–2014," database with images, *Ancestry* (https://www.ancestry.com), imaged certificate no. 6981, Lucy Frances Kilby, died Madison County, 30 March 1933; citing "Virginia Department of Health; Richmond, Virginia; Virginia Deaths, 1912–2014."

67 "Our Colored Folks," *Madison County (Virginia) Eagle*, 14 April 1933, p. 8, col. 6; LVA microfilm no. 276, roll for <1933:1:1–9:22, 10:6–1934:5:18, 6:1–12:14,28>, LVA, Richmond.

68 "Virginia, Death Records, 1912–2014," database with images, *Ancestry.com*, certificate 6981, Lucy Frances Kilby, 30 March 1933.

69 "Virginia, Death Records, 1912–2014," database with images, *Ancestry.com*, certificate 29198, Charles W. Kilby, 4 October 1924.

70 Ibid. Martha "Mattie" Wright, Simon's daughter, was the informant who thought Simon's father was named Nimrod. A thorough search found no male named Nimrod Kilby, exact or similar. Similarly, no direct or indirect evidence was found to conclude that Juliet, recorded as Julia Luby on the form, ever used that surname. The conclusion is that Mattie was misinformed.

Chapter Twelve: Sarah Kilby

1 Rappahannock Co., Va., Marriage License and Return, James Reynolds and Sarah Kilby, 18 May 1879.
2 Ibid.
3 "Virginia, Death Records, 1912–2014," database with images, *Ancestry* (https://www.ancestry.com), imaged certificate no. 20098, Ella Honesty, died Frederick County, 28 August 1936; citing "Virginia Department of Health; Richmond, Virginia; Virginia Deaths, 1912–2014."
4 *J. Frank Eddy & Bro's. Directory of Winchester Virginia, 1898–1899* (Winchester, Virginia: Enterprise Publishing Company, 1899), 76; Handley Library, Winchester, Virginia. 1900 U.S. census, Frederick County, Virginia, population schedule, Winchester City Ward 3, enumeration district (ED) 94, sheet 117A (stamped), sheet 12 (penned), dwelling 252, family 267, Sarah Reynolds household; NARA microfilm T623, roll 1740.
5 1900 U.S. census, Frederick Co., Va., pop. sch., Winchester City Ward 3, ED 94, sheet 117A (stamped), sheet 12 (penned), dwell. 252, fam. 267, Sarah Reynolds household; NARA microfilm T623, roll 1740.
6 1910 U.S. census, Winchester, Virginia, population schedule, Winchester Ward 1, enumeration district (ED) 106, sheet 163B (stamped), sheet 9B (penned), dwelling 172, family 186, Sarah Reynolds household; NARA microfilm publication T624, roll 1640.
7 Ibid.
8 "Winchester Notes," *The (Baltimore) Afro-American*, 15 September 1917, p. 2, col. 1; online archive, *MyHeritage* (https://www.myheritage.com/ : accessed 5 January 2019).
9 1910 U.S. census, Winchester, Virginia, population schedule, Winchester Ward 1, enumeration district (ED) 106, sheet 6B, dwelling 139, family 152, line 88, Ella M. Honesty in Arthur Honesty household; NARA microfilm publication T624, roll 1640. This record indicated she had been married for nine years.

10 "Old-Time Colored Woman Dies Here," *The (Winchester, Virginia) Daily Independent*, 14 July 1924, p. 1, col. 6; LVA microfilm no. 286, roll for <1924:1:2–9:18,20–10:13,15–12:31>, LVA, Richmond.

Chapter Thirteen: Bettie Kilby

1. 1870 U.S. census, Rappahannock County, Virginia, population schedule, Stonewall Township, p. 32 (penned), line 2, dwelling 216 [blank, skipped number], family 216 [blank, skipped number], for Elizabeth Walker in Bluford Thornhill household; NARA microfilm publication M593, roll 1674.
2. 1880 U.S. census, Rappahannock Co., Va., pop. sch., Stonewall District, ED 131, p. 34 (penned), line 13, Betsy Kilby in Bluford Thornhill household. 1900 U.S. census, Albemarle, Virginia, population schedule, Court House Precinct, enumeration district (ED) 1, sheet 3 (stamped), dwelling 49, family 52, line 23, Bettie E Carr; NARA microfilm publication T623, roll 1697.
3. Eric Foner, Forever Free: *The Story of Emancipation and Reconstruction* (New York: Alfred A. Knopf, 2005), 16.
4. Culpeper Co. Va., Chancery Court Case no. 7, Adm. of Thomas Kilby v. Adm. of James Hawkins, James Hawkins estate appraisement, 1833; digital image 58 of 85.
5. King, *Stolen Children*, 334.
6. F.T. Baptist Church (Rappahannock Co., Va.), Minute Book, 1855–1878, p. 76.
7. F.T. Baptist Church (Rappahannock Co., Va.), Minute Book, 1878–1894, p. 205.
8. Virginia Bureau of Vital Statistics, Deaths, Rappahannock County, 1853–1896; "Register of Deaths," 1886, p. 2; Robert Kilby, 19 September 1886; LVA microfilm reel no. 25, LVA, Richmond.
9. 1910 U.S. census, Albemarle, Virginia, population schedule, Court House Precinct, enumeration district (ED) 1, sheet 17A, dwelling 300, family 318, line 29, Cora Brown in Armstead Carr household; NARA microfilm publication M624, roll 1619.

10 "Virginia, Death Records, 1912–2014," database with images, *Ancestry* (https://www.ancestry.com), imaged certificate no. 19359, Cora Blanche Wilson, died Charlottesville, Virginia, 29 October 1936; citing "Virginia Department of Health; Richmond, Virginia; Virginia Deaths, 1912–2014."
11 1900 U.S. census, Albemarle, Virginia, population schedule, Court House Precinct, enumeration district (ED) 1, sheet 3 (stamped), dwelling 49, family 52, Armstead Carr household; NARA microfilm publication T623, roll 1697.
12 "Virginia, Death Records, 1912–2014," database with images, *Ancestry* (https://www.ancestry.com), imaged certificate no. 7231, Bettie Carr, died Charlottesville, Virginia, 26 April 1921; citing "Virginia Department of Health; Richmond, Virginia; Virginia Deaths, 1912–2014."
13 Ibid. For Armstead, see "Virginia, Death Records, 1912–2014," database with images, *Ancestry* (https://www.ancestry.com), imaged certificate no. 2959, Armstead Carr, died Charlottesville, Virginia, 7 February 1931; citing "Virginia Department of Health; Richmond, Virginia; Virginia Deaths, 1912–2014."

CHAPTER FOURTEEN: JOHN KILBY

1 1870 U.S. census, Rappahannock County, Virginia, population schedule, Stonewall Township, p. 32 (penned), line 2, dwelling 216 [blank, skipped number], family 216 [blank, skipped number], for John Walker in Bluford Thornhill household; NARA microfilm publication M593, roll 1674.
2 "Pennsylvania, County Marriages, 1885–1950," database with image, *FamilySearch* (https://familysearch.org/ark:/61903/1:1:VF9F-CPR), entry for John Kilby and Virginia F. Miles, married in Allegheny (City), Pennsylvania, 15 May 1890; FHL microfilm 878583.
3 "Letter from Rappahannock," *Alexandria* (Virginia) *Gazette*, 29 June 1882, p. 1, col. 3; image copy, Library of Congress, *Chronicling America: Historic American Newspapers* (https://chroniclingamerica.loc.gov/lccn/sn85025007/1882-06-29/ed-1/seq-1/).

4   "Letter from Rappahannock," *Alexandria* (Virginia) *Gazette*, 2 January 1890, p. 3, col. 1; image copy, Library of Congress, *Chronicling America: Historic American Newspapers* (https://chroniclingamerica.loc.gov/lccn/sn85025007/1890-01-02/ed-1/seq-3/).

5   "The Cry of Freedom," *Pittsburgh* (Pennsylvania) *Dispatch*, 30 July 1898, p. 8, col. 1; image copy, Library of Congress, *Chronicling America: Historic American Newspapers* (https://chroniclingamerica.loc.gov/lccn/sn84024546/1889-07-30/ed-1/seq-8/).

6   "Pennsylvania, County Marriages, 1885–1950," database, *FamilySearch*, entry for John Kilby and Virginia F. Miles, married 15 May 1890.

7   1920 U.S. census, Allegheny County, Pennsylvania, population schedule, Wilkinsburg Ward 1, District 859, sheet 18A, dwelling 313, family 400, John Kilby household; NARA microfilm publication T625, roll 1530.

8   "Pennsylvania, County Marriages, 1885–1950," database, *FamilySearch*, entry for John Kilby and Virginia F. Miles, married 15 May 1890. "The Weather," *Pittsburgh* (Pennsylvania) *Dispatch*, 16 May 1890, p. 6, col. 7; image copy, Library of Congress, *Chronicling America: Historic American Newspapers* (https://chroniclingamerica.loc.gov/lccn/sn84024546/1890-05-16/ed-1/seq-6/).

9   "Pennsylvania, County Marriages, 1885–1950," database, *FamilySearch*, entry for John Kilby and Virginia F. Miles, married 15 May 1890.

10 The birth of Flora Kilby and address of 4039 Penn Avenue is recorded in Allegheny County, Pennsylvania, "Pennsylvania Births and Christenings, 1709–1950," register 44, p. 521, 26 July 1892; image, *FamilySearch* (https://familysearch.org/ark:/61903/3:1:3QS7-99V6-5DMR), FHL microfilm 7612144, image 372 of 718. See also, 1900 U.S. census, Allegheny County, Pennsylvania, population schedule, Pittsburgh Ward 16, enumeration district (ED) 189, sheet 155A (stamped), sheet 6 (penned), dwelling 75, family 121, John Kilby household; NARA microfilm publication T623, roll 1360.

11 Sanborn-Perris Map Company, *Sanborn Fire Insurance Map from*

Pittsburgh, Allegheny County, Pennsylvania, 1893, vol. 2, sheet 24; digital image, *Library of Congress* (https://www.loc.gov/resource/g3824pm.g3824pm_g07911189302/?sp=27&r=0.717,0.034,0.283,0.189,0).

12 1900 U.S. census, Allegheny Co., Pa., pop. sch., Pittsburgh Ward 16, ED 189, sheet 155A (stamped), sheet 6 (penned), dwell. 75, fam. 121, John Kilby household.

13 Sanborn-Perris, *Sanborn Fire Insurance Map from Pittsburgh*, 1893.

14 1900 U.S. census, Allegheny County, Pennsylvania, population schedule, Pittsburgh Ward 16, enumeration district (ED) 189, sheet 155A (stamped), sheet 6 (penned), dwelling 75, family 121, line 44, Flora B. Kilby; NARA microfilm publication T623, roll 1360.

15 Allegheny County, Pennsylvania, "Pennsylvania, County Marriages, 1885–1950," database with image, *FamilySearch* (https://familysearch.org/ark:/61903/1:1:VF7H-CJQ), entry for Frances Bernice Walker and Burton Lee Younger, 5 December 1942; FHL microfilm 1992316. This record includes the date of birth and parents of Frances Walker.

16 "Pennsylvania, Death Certificates, 1906–1967," database with images, *Ancestry* (https://www.ancestry.com), imaged certificate no. 41856, Flora Walker, died Allegheny County, 9 May 1961; citing "Pennsylvania Historic and Museum Commission; Harrisburg, Pennsylvania."

17 Allegheny County, Pennsylvania, "Pennsylvania, Pittsburgh City Deaths, 1870–1905," database with image, *FamilySearch* (https://www.familysearch.org/ark:/61903/1:1:XZ7R-LVD), entry for Infant Kilby (male), death on 22 March 1895; FHL microfilm 505855. Allegheny County, Pennsylvania, "Pennsylvania, Pittsburgh City Deaths, 1870–1905," database with image, *FamilySearch* (https://www.familysearch.org/ark:/61903/1:1:XZ7R-LVF), entry for Infant Kilby (female), death on 22 March 1895; FHL microfilm 505855.

18 "Pennsylvania, Death Certificates, 1906–1967," database with images, *Ancestry* (https://www.ancestry.com), imaged certificate no. 057088-63, Julia K. Parrish, died Allegheny County, 10 June 1963; citing "Pennsylvania Historic and Museum Commission; Harrisburg, Pennsylvania."

19 Ibid. Also, "Pennsylvania, WWI Veterans Service and Compensation Files, 1917–1919, 1934–1948," database with images, *Ancestry* (https://www.ancestry.com), application 233225, Zeb Parrish; citing "World War I Veterans Service and Compensation Files, 1934–1948," RG 19, Series 19.91, Pennsylvania Historical and Museum Commission, Harrisburg, Pennsylvania.

20 Allegheny County, Pennsylvania, "Pennsylvania, Pittsburgh City Deaths, 1870–1905," p. 431, Aronia Kilby (female), death on 9 January 1902; database with images, *FamilySearch* (https://www.familysearch.org/ark:/61903/3:1:939V-8GQ4-LL), FHL microfilm 4672775, image 252 of 692.

21 1900 U.S. census, Allegheny County, Pennsylvania, population schedule, Pittsburgh Ward 16, enumeration district (ED) 189, sheet 155A (stamped), sheet 6 (penned), dwelling 75, family 121, line 47, John R. Kilby; NARA microfilm publication T623, roll 1360.

22 "Penn Avenue," 21 February 1917, photograph; Pittsburgh City Photographer Collection, 1901–2002, Archives & Special Collections, University of Pittsburgh Library System; image, *Historic Pittsburgh* (https://historicpittsburgh.org/islandora/object/pitt%3A715.174878.CP).

23 "United States World War I Draft Registration Cards, 1917–1918," database with images, *FamilySearch* (https://www.familysearch.org/ark:/61903/1:1:K6KJ-7TV), entry for John Ralph Kilby Jr, 1917–1918; citing Pittsburgh City no 6, Pennsylvania, United States, NARA microfilm publication M1509; FHL microfilm 1908113.

24 1920 U.S. census, Allegheny Co., Pa., pop. sch., Wilkinsburg Ward 1, District 859, sheet 18A, dwell. 313, fam. 400, John Kilby household.

25 Allegheny Cemetery, Compiler, "Allegheny Cemetery, Pittsburgh, Allegheny County, Pennsylvania," record for John Kilby Jr., death in 1922; database, *Interment.net* (http://www.interment.net/data/us/pa/allegheny/allegcem/records-kes-kir.htm).

26 Allegheny County, Pennsylvania, "Pennsylvania, Pittsburgh City Deaths, 1870–1905," p. 568, Pattie Malinda Kilby,

death on 2 February 1903; database with images, *FamilySearch* (https://www.familysearch.org/ark:/61903/3:1:939V-8P91-J1), FHL microfilm 4672778, image 412 of 694.
27 1910 U.S. census, Allegheny County, Pennsylvania, population schedule, Pittsburgh Ward 6, enumeration district (ED) 356, sheet 11A, dwelling 178, family 241, line 46, [Virginia] Frances Kilby; NARA microfilm publication T625, roll 1301.
28 1920 U.S. census, Allegheny Co., Pa., pop. sch., Wilkinsburg Ward 1, District 859, sheet 18A, dwell. 313, fam. 400, John Kilby household. Virginia Frances Kilby's occupation is recorded as laundress.
29 "A New Baptist Church," *The Pittsburgh (Pennsylvania) Dispatch*, 13 May 1892, p. 9, col. 4; image copy, Library of Congress, *Chronicling America: Historic American Newspapers* (https://chroniclingamerica.loc.gov/lccn/sn84024546/1892-05-13/ed-1/seq-9/).
30 "Funeral of Negro Gets Into Court," *The Pittsburgh (Pennsylvania) Daily Post*, 7 July 1906, p. 11, col. 5; digital images, *Newspapers.com* (https://www.newspapers.com). This article references John Kilby as an officer of "the Carron Street Colored [*sic*] Baptist Church" and one of four defendants in an assault case, subsequently acquitted.
31 "Big Celebration at Pittsburg," *The Broad Ax (Salt Lake City, Utah)*, 19 November 1910, p. 3, col. 3; image copy, Library of Congress, *Chronicling America: Historic American Newspapers* (https://chroniclingamerica.loc.gov/lccn/sn84024055/1910-11-19/ed-1/seq-3/).
32 "Interesting Brick Architecture in Pittsburgh, Pa.," *The BrickBuilder*, Vol II, no. 12, December 1902, p. 254; image copy, *Archive.org* (https://archive.org/details/brickbuild11p8unse/).
33 "Afro-American Notes," *The Pittsburgh (Pennsylvania) Press*, 28 May 1916, "Society Section," p. 3, col. 3; digital images, *Newspapers.com* (https://www.newspapers.com/image/143692668/); referencing "Miss Flora Kilby, soprano," singing at a musicale and reception.
34 "Winchester Notes," *The (Baltimore) Afro-American*, 15 September 1917, p. 2, col. 1.

35 "Classified," *The Pittsburgh (Pennsylvania) Courier*, 20 September 1924, p. 9, col. 2; digital images, *Newspapers.com* (https://www.newspapers.com/image/40062624/).

36 "Pennsylvania, Death Certificates, 1906–1967," database with images, *Ancestry.com,* certificate no. 64870, John H Kilby, 28 July 1932.

37 "Pennsylvania, Death Certificates, 1906–1967," database with images, *Ancestry* (https://www.ancestry.com), imaged certificate no. 57189, Virginia Kilby, died Allegheny County, 28 June 1936; citing "Pennsylvania Historic and Museum Commission; Harrisburg, Pennsylvania."

38 Allegheny Cemetery, Compiler, "Allegheny Cemetery, Pittsburgh, Allegheny County, Pennsylvania," record for John H. Kilby, death in 1932; database, *Interment.net* (http://www.interment.net/data/us/pa/allegheny/allegcem/records-kes-kir.htm).

39 "Pennsylvania, Death Certificates, 1906–1967," database with images, *Ancestry.com*, certificate no. 41856, Flora Walker, 9 May 1961. "Pennsylvania, Death Certificates, 1906–1967," database with images, *Ancestry.com*, certificate no. 057088-63, Julia K. Parrish, 10 June 1963.

CHAPTER FIFTEEN: JAMES KILBY

1 *Wikipedia* (https://en.wikipedia.org/), "Partus sequitur ventrem," 19 June 2020.

2 Rappahannock Co., Va., Chancery Court Case no. 253, Kilby v. Thornhill, chancery bill, March 1865.

3 Rappahannock Co., Va., Marriage License and Return, James Kilby and Mary Eliza Strother, 18 June 1881. For Mary Richardson's surname, see 1870 U.S. census, Madison County, Virginia, population schedule, Robertson District, p. 97A (stamped), p. 47 (penned), dwelling 309, family 315, William Strother household for Eliza Richardson and Lena Richardson; NARA microfilm publication M593, roll 1662.

4 1870 U.S. census, Madison Co., Va, pop. sch., Robertson District, p. 97A (stamped), p. 47 (penned), dwell. 309, fam. 315,

William Strother household for Eliza Richardson and Lena Richardson.
5   1900 U.S. census, Newport County, Rhode Island, population schedule, Newport City Ward 2, enumeration district (ED) 216, sheet 14A, dwelling 282, family 311, James Kilby household; NARA microfilm publication T623, roll 1505. Elizabeth was recorded as Lacy on this census.
6   1900 U.S. census, Newport Co., R.I., pop. sch., Newport City Ward 2, ED 216, sheet 14A, dwell. 282, fam. 311, James Kilby household.
7   Isabel Wilkerson, *The Warmth of Other Suns* (New York: Random House, 2010), i5.
8   1920 U.S. census, Newport County, Rhode Island, population schedule, Newport City Ward 2, enumeration district (ED) 44, sheet 12A, dwelling 219, family 240, James R Richardson household; NARA microfilm publication T625, roll 1670.
9   Keith Stokes, *Gilded Age Newport in Color* (http://www.gildedageincolor.com/), section "Biographies," for Lindsay R. Walker.
10 "Virginia Marriages, 1785–1940," database, *FamilySearch* (https://www.familysearch.org/ark:/61903/1:1:X518-DYX), entry for Lindsay Richard Walker and Lena Richardson, married in Rappahannock County, 12 February 1885; FHL microfilm 2048472. 1870 U.S. census, Madison Co., Va, pop. sch., Robertson District, p. 97A (stamped), p. 47 (penned), dwell. 309, fam. 315, William Strother household for Eliza Richardson and Lena Richardson. 1880 U.S. census, Rappahannock County, Virginia, population schedule, Stonewall District, enumeration district (ED) 131, p. 356 (stamped), p. 35 (penned), dwelling 299, family 313, William Strother household; NARA microfilm publication T9, roll 1386. Myra Beth Young Armstead, *Lord, please don't take me in August: African Americans in Newport and Saratoga Springs, 1870–1930* (Chicago: University of Illinois Press, 1999), p. 53.
11 Armstead, *Lord, please don't take me in August*, p. 53.
12 Henry N. Jeter, *Shiloh Baptist Church and Her History* (Providence, Rhode Island: Remington Printing Company, 1901), 89.

13 Ibid, 10
14 Sampson, Murdock & Company, compiler, *Newport, Rhode Island, City Directory, 1888*, database, *Ancestry* (https://www.ancestry.com), entry for James Kilby, p. 122.
15 L. J. Richards & Co., *Atlas of the City of Newport, Rhode Island*, 1893, "Plate B;" digital image, item US14667, *Historic Map Works* (http://www.historicmapworks.com).
16 "Gossip of the Vicinity," *Fall River (Massachusetts) Daily Herald* (Fall River, Massachuettes), 18 October 1893, p. 6, col. 5; digital images, *Newspapers.com* (https://www.newspapers.com/image/616921528).
17 1900 U.S. census, Newport Co., R.I., pop. sch., Newport City Ward 2, ED 216, sheet 14A, dwell. 282, fam. 311, James Kilby household. For Madelene Kilby's death, see "Rhode Island Deaths and Burials, 1802–1950," database with image, *FamilySearch* (https://www.familysearch.org/ark:/61903/1:1:F86S-1YL), entry for Madelene Alberta Kilby, death in Newport, 6 May 1903; FHL microfilm 1906587.
18 1910 U.S. census, Newport County, Rhode Island, population schedule, Newport City Ward 2, enumeration district (ED) 39, sheet 5B, dwelling 94, family 95, James Kilby; NARA microfilm publication T624, roll 1437. 1920 U.S. census, Newport County, Rhode Island, population schedule, Newport City Ward 2, enumeration district (ED) 44, sheet 12A, dwelling 218, family 239, James Kirbey [Kilby]; NARA microfilm publication T625, roll 1670. 1930 U.S. census, Newport County, Rhode Island, population schedule, Newport City Ward 2, enumeration district (ED) 3–14, sheet 18B, dwelling 390, family 452, James Kilby household; NARA microfilm publication T626, roll 2169. "Rhode Island State Census, 1935," database with image, *Ancestry* (https://www.ancestry.com), entry for James Kilby, computer card 395365; citing "Rhode Island State Census, 1935, Microfilm, New England Historic Genealogical Society, Boston, Massachusetts."
19 "Real Estate Sales and Rentals," *The Newport (Rhode Island) Mercury*, 20 June 1896, p. 4, col. 3, describing lot purchase of

James Kilby; digital images, *Newspapers.com* (https://www.newspapers.com/image/24359675).

20 1900 U.S. census, Newport Co., R.I., pop. sch., Newport City Ward 2, ED 216, sheet 14A, dwell. 282, fam. 311, James Kilby household.

21 1920 U.S. census, Newport County, Rhode Island, population schedule, Newport City Ward 3, enumeration district (ED) 50, sheet 11A, dwelling 191, family 291, line 23, Lizzie Johnson; NARA microfilm publication T625, roll 1670.

22 1920 U.S. census, Newport County, Rhode Island, population schedule, Newport City Ward 1, enumeration district (ED) 42, sheet 16A, dwelling 299, family 361, line 16, Lena P. Vieira; NARA microfilm publication T625, roll 1670.

23 "Massachusetts, Marriage Records, 1840–1915," database with images, *Ancestry* (https://www.ancestry.com/imageviewer/collections/2511/images/41262_b139548-00234), for John Kilby and Gladys S. Gassaway, married in Fall River, 14 October 1909; citing "New England Historic Genealogical Society; Boston, Massachusetts; Massachusetts Vital Records, 1911–1915." 1910 U.S. census, Suffolk County, Massachusetts, population schedule, Boston City, Ward 18 Precinct 4, sheet 5B, dwelling 49, family 113, Nora A Gassaway household, John L Kilby; NARA microfilm publication T624, roll 621.

24 "WWI Draft Registration Cards," database with images, *Fold3* (https://www.fold3.com/image/568713854), imaged card for John Kelby [Kilby], Newport, Rhode Island; citing "World War I Selective Service System Draft Registration Cards, 1917–1918," RG 163, NARA microfilm publication M1509.

25 "Libel for Divorce," *Fall River (Massachusetts) Evening News*, 2 July 1917, p. 4, col. 4; digital image, *Newspapers.com* (https://www.newspapers.com/image/603353709).

26 "New York, New York, Extracted Marriage Index, 1866–1937," database, *Ancestry* (https://www.ancestry.com), certificate no. 1151, John Kilby and Lulu [Tula] Henry, married in Queens, New York, 24 May 1928; citing "Index to New York City Marriages, 1866–1937," New York City Department of Records/Municipal Archives, New York, New York.

27 1925 New York State Census, Kings County, Brooklyn, Election District 10, Assembly District 10, p. 17, line 32, Richard Kilby and wife Violet Kilby; database with image, *Ancestry* (https://www.ancestry.com); citing "State Population Census Schedules, 1925," New York State Archives, Albany, New York. 1930 U.S. census, New York County, New York, population schedule, Manhattan Borough, enumeration district (ED) 31-1043, p. 2A, family 32, lines 45 and 46, Violet Jackson and Richard Kilby [Jr]; NARA microfilm publication T626, roll 1578.

28 Though no specific marriage documentation was found, the marriage of Henry William Kilby and Elizabeth Reeves Jackson in 1920 is inferred through the following records: Sampson, Murdock & Company, compiler, *The Newport, Rhode Island, City Directory*, 1920, database with images, *Ancestry* (https://www.ancestry.com), entry for Henry W Kilby, p. 267; also subsequent year by the same title, 1921, entry for Henry W Kilby, p. 263. "Rhode Island State Census, 1925," database with image, *Ancestry* (https://www.ancestry.com), entry for Henry M Kilby, Newport, enumeration district 47, p. 11, dwelling 76, lines 9–12; citing "Rhode Island State Census, 1925, Microfilm, New England Historic Genealogical Society, Boston, Massachusetts."

29 No specific marriage documentation for Walter Kilby and Madeline Butler was found. Their marriage in 1920 or 1921 is inferred through the following records: Sampson, Murdock & Company, compiler, *The Newport, Rhode Island, City Directory*, 1920, database with images, *Ancestry* (https://www.ancestry.com), entry for Walter E [R] Kilby, p. 267; also subsequent year by the same title, 1921, entry for Walter R Kilby, p. 263. The birth of daughter Hope Louise Kilby is documented in Social Security Administration, "U.S., Social Security Applications and Claims Index, 1936–2007," database, *Ancestry* (https://www.ancestry.com), entry for Hope Louise Kilby, SS no. 038-16-1352.

30 "WWI Draft Registration Cards," database with images, *Fold3* (https://www.fold3.com/image/569619590), imaged card for James Kilby, Newport, Rhode Island; citing "World War I

Selective Service System Draft Registration Cards, 1917–1918," RG 163, NARA microfilm publication M1509.

31 "WWI Draft Registration Cards," database with images, *Fold3* (https://www.fold3.com/image/569619591), imaged card for Henry William Kilby, Newport, Rhode Island; citing "World War I Selective Service System Draft Registration Cards, 1917–1918," RG 163, NARA microfilm publication M1509. "Headstone Applications, 1925–1963," database with images, *Fold3* (https://www.fold3.com/image/320883940), imaged application for Henry William Kilby, Newport, Rhode Island; citing "Applications for Headstones for U.S. Military Veterans, 1925–1941," RG 92, NARA microfilm publication M1916.

32 "WWI Draft Registration Cards," database with images, *Fold3* (https://www.fold3.com/image/568713854), imaged card for John Kelby [Kilby], Manhattan, New York, New York; citing "World War I Selective Service System Draft Registration Cards, 1917–1918," RG 163, NARA microfilm publication M1509, roll 1786971.

33 "WWI New York Army Cards," database with images, *Fold3* (https://www.fold3.com/image/322564777), imaged card for John Kilby, New York City, New York; citing "New York State Abstracts of World War I Military Service, 1917–1919," New York State Archives, Albany.

34 "U.S. National Cemetery Interment Control Forms, 1928–1962," database with images, *Ancestry* (https://www.ancestry.com/interactive/2590/40479_2421402106_0470-00748), imaged card for Richard Kilby, Long Island National Cemetery, Farmingdale, New York; citing "Interment Control Forms, 1928–1962," RG 92, NARA.

35 "World War I Statements of Military Service, 1917-1918," record for Richard Kilby; image, Rhode Island State Digital Archives (https://sosri.access.preservica.com/uncategorized/IO_a3a13999-aa7e-4685-96d1-b67604f6f1e1/).

36 "WWI Draft Registration Cards," database with images, *Fold3* (https://www.fold3.com/image/569619592), imaged card for Walter Kilby, Newport, Rhode Island; citing "World War I Selective Service System Draft Registration Cards, 1917–1918," RG 163, NARA microfilm publication M1509, roll 1852396.

"WWII Draft Registration Cards," database with images, *Fold3* (https://www.fold3.com/image/657829153), imaged card for Walter Radford Kilby, Newport, Rhode Island; citing "Selective Service Registration Cards, World War II," RG 147, NARA.

37 "U.S., Headstone Applications for Military Veterans, 1925–1963," database with images, *Ancestry* (https://www.ancestry.com), imaged card for George Wjenio Vieira, Braman Cemetery, Newport, Rhode Island; citing "Applications for Headstones for U.S. Military Veterans, 1925–1941," RG 92, NARA microfilm publication M1916.

38 "Headstone Applications, 1925–1963," database with images, *Fold3*, Henry William Kilby. 1930 U.S. census, Newport County, Rhode Island, population schedule, Newport City Ward 1, enumeration district (ED) 3-9, sheet 5A, dwelling 94, family 95, GeorgeVieiro [Vieira]; NARA microfilm publication T626, roll 2169.

39 1920 U.S. census, Newport County, Rhode Island, population schedule, Newport City Ward 2, enumeration district (48), sheet 13A, dwelling 225, family 298, James Kilby household; NARA microfilm publication T625, roll 1670.

40 "Divorces Granted," *Newport (Rhode Island) Mercury and Weekly News*, 5 October 1928, p. 3, col. 8, for James Kilby Jr. vs. Louise Ferretti Levin Kilby; digital images, *Newspapers.com* (https://www.newspapers.com/image/24494814).

41 1930 U.S. census, Newport County, Rhode Island, population schedule, Newport City Ward 2, enumeration district (ED) 3-14, sheet 18B, dwelling 390, family 452, line 91, James Kilby Jr; NARA microfilm publication T626, roll 2169.

42 "Election of Officers," *Newport (Rhode Island) Mercury*, 19 January 1917, p. 6, col. 4, for James Kilby and James Richardson, Canonchet Lodge, Grand United Order of Odd Fellows; digital images, *Newspapers.com* (https://www.newspapers.com/image/16203122/).

43 Ibid.

44 "James Kilby, 87, Dies; Ex-highway Worker," *Newport (Rhode Island) Mercury and Weekly News*, 7 October 1949, p. 3, col. 2,

obituary for James Kilby; digital images, *Newspapers.com* (https://www.newspapers.com/image/16374572).

45 "Mrs. James Kilby Dies," *Newport (Rhode Island) Mercury*, 14 January 1944, p. 3, col. 7, for Mary Eliza Kilby; digital images, *Newspapers.com* (https://www.newspapers.com/image/16210411)

46 "Rhode Island Deaths and Burials, 1802–1950," database with image, *FamilySearch* (https://familysearch.org/ark:/61903/1:1:F8CS-YR5), entry for James Kilby, death in Newport, 29 September 1949; FHL microfilm 2229193.

47 "James Kilby, 87, Dies; Ex-highway Worker," *Newport (Rhode Island) Mercury and Weekly News*, 7 October 1949, obituary for James Kilby.

48 "Rhode Island Deaths and Burials, 1802–1950," database with image, *FamilySearch*, entry for James Kilby, death in Newport, 29 September 1949.

49 Frederick Douglass, "Self-Made Men, Address Before the Students of the Indian Industrial School at Carlisle, Pa.," 1874, p. 15; archive with digital images, *Library of Congress* (https://www.loc.gov/item/mfd.29002/).

Chapter Sixteen: Genetic Ties

1 Thavolia Glymph, *Out of the House of Bondage: The Transformation of the Plantation Household* (New York: Cambridge University Press, 2008), 59. King, *Stolen Children*, 254, 270-71. William Dusinberre, *Strategies for Survival: Reflections of Bondage in Antebellum Virginia* (Charlottesville: University of Virginia Press, 2009), 156. These are but three of the many accounts of rampant sexual abuse of enslaved females.

2 Y-DNA 37 marker values for James Kilby (1740–1829), line 1, the most recent common ancestor of the group, are derived from eight known direct-line male descendants of John Kilby. Values that deviate from this James Kilby reference are highlighted. This table is derived, in part, from "Y-DNA Colorized Chart," *Kilby Surname FamilyTree DNA Project*; database, FamilyTreeDNA (https://www.familytreedna.com/public/kilby/)?iframe=yresults).

3   "Y-DNA Colorized Chart," *Kilby Surname FamilyTree DNA Project*; database, FamilyTreeDNA. Eight European-American males genealogically proven as descending from John Kilby of Culpeper (Lineage 1) tested at the 37-marker or higher level of the Y-chromosome and are participants of the Kilby Surname FamilyTreeDNA Project. The Y-DNA markers of three genealogically proven descendants of James Kilby—kits B51962 (the author), 108633, and 140018—were compared to the Y-DNA markers of a genealogically proven African American descendant of Simon Kilby who provide his results privately to the author. This descendant has not chosen to join the project or make his results public; therefore, personally identifying information is withheld.

4   "Y-DNA Colorized Chart," *Kilby Surname FamilyTree DNA Project.*

5   The possibility of a Kilby male other than a son of Thomas Kilby as the biological father of Simon must not be disregarded, even with the stronger evidence otherwise. The genetic distance, the number of mutation differences, in the Y-DNA markers is greater with descendants on other family lines, and this reduces—but does not eliminate—Kilby cousins as the biological father. One oral record suggested that Simon's father was Andrew Jackson Kilby, son of Leroy Kilby and a nephew of Thomas Kilby, but no evidence has ever been uncovered to support this assertion.

6   With permission from several AncestryDNA.com testers, the author viewed autosomal DNA match lists, centimorgan and segment counts, and known and predicted family trees to make comparisons. The names of these testers are withheld for reasons of privacy. Testers included known descendants of Juliet Ann and descendants of Thomas and Malinda Kilby through sons James Franklin Kilby and Joseph Mortimer Kilby, as well as White descendants on collateral Kilby lines.

7   "What is the direct maternal lineage?" *FamilyTreeDNA* (https://learn.familytreedna.com/mtdna-testing/direct-maternal-lineage/).

8   Roberta Estes, "Mitochondrial DNA Mutation Rates and Common Ancestors," *DNAeXplained-Genetic Genealogy*, 5

December 2014 (https://dna-explained.com/2014/12/05/mitochondrial-dna-mutation-rates-and-common-ancestors/).
9   *FamilyTreeDNA* (Houston, Texas), "mtDNA – Mutations, Haplogroup L3e2a," sample 931852; prepared for anonymous, Philadelphia, Pennsylvania.
10 Rebekah Canada, "Encyclopedia of MtDNA Origins | Haplogroup," *Haplogroup.org* (https://haplogroup.org/encyclopedia-of-mtdna-origins/), entry for haplogroup L3e2a.
11 Antonio Salas et al., "The Making of the African MtDNA Landscape," *The American Journal of Human Genetics* 71, no. 5 (1 November 2002): 1082–1111; full text copy, *ScienceDirect* (https://www.sciencedirect.com/science/article/pii/S0002929707604030).
12 The ethnicity estimates for nine African Americans related to each other on the Kilby Family tree are on average twenty-nine percent Nigeria, eighteen percent Cameron/Congo/Southern Bantu, and three percent Senegal.

CHAPTER SEVENTEEN: CONCLUSION

1   The Church of Jesus Christ of Latter-day Saints [LDS], "User Submitted Genealogies," database, *FamilySearch* (https://www.familysearch.org/tree/person/details/LWMC-7M3), for Malinda Hawkins; collaborate note by "jlibes2722688" [Joyce Libes] titled "Malinda Hawkins may have been much," 26 August 2013.
2   Henry Wiencek, Master of the Mountain (Farar, Straus and Giroux: New York, 2012), 5.
3   Andrew Delbanco, *The War Before the War* (New York: Penguin Press, 2018), 55.
4   Frederick Douglass, *Life and Times of Frederick Douglass*, in *Autobiographies* (New York: Literary Classics of the United States, 1994), 876.
5   Ibid, 875.
6   Virginia Bureau of Vital Statistics, Deaths, Madison County, Robertson District, 1853–1896; "Register of Deaths," 1885, no page number, line 31; Kilby Jno, July 1885; LVA microfilm reel no. 18, LVA, Richmond.

7   Virginia Bureau of Vital Statistics, Deaths, Madison County, Robertson District, 1853–1896; "Register of Deaths," 1880, no page number, line 29; Kilby Geo, October 1880; LVA microfilm reel no. 18, LVA, Richmond.

8   Virginia Bureau of Vital Statistics, Deaths, Rappahannock County, 1853–1896; "Register of Births," 1875, p. 90 (stamped), line 16, Kilby Mary F, 12 February 1875; LVA microfilm reel no. 28, LVA, Richmond.

Bibliography

Armstead, Mary Beth Young. *Lord, Please Don't Take Me in August: African Americans in Newport and Saratoga Springs, 1870–1930.* Chicago: University of Illinois Press, 1999.

Ayers, Edward L. *The Promise of the New South: Life After Reconstruction.* New York: Oxford University Press, 1992.

Ball, Edward. *Slaves in the Family.* New York: Farrar, Straus and Giroux, 1998.

Blankenbaker, John. *A List of the Classes in Culpeper County for January 1781 for Recruiting this State's Quota of Troops to Serve in the Continental Army.* Chadds Ford, Pennsylvania: privately published, 1991.

Colletta, John Philip. *Only a Few Bones: A True Account of the Rolling Fork Tragedy and its Aftermath.* New Edition. Washington, DC: Direct Descent, 2015.

Delbanco, Andrew. *The War Before the War: Fugitive Slaves and the Struggle for America's Soul from the Revolution to the Civil War.* New York: Penguin Press, 2018.

Deutsch, Stephanie. *You Need a Schoolhouse.* Evanston, Illinois: Northwestern University Press, 2011.

Douglass, Frederick. *Life and Times of Frederick Douglass*. In *Autobiographies*. New York: Literary Classics of the United States, 1994.

———. *Narrative of the Life of Frederick Douglass*. In *Autobiographies*. New York: Literary Classics of the United States, 1994.

Du Bois, W.E.B. *The Souls of Black Folk*. Mineola, New York: Dover Publications, 1994.

Dusinberre, William. *Strategies for Survival: Reflections of Bondage in Antebellum Virginia*. Charlottesville, Virginia: University of Virginia Press, 2009.

Ellison, Ralph. *Shadow and Act*. New York: Quality Paperback Book Club, 1994.

F.T. Baptist Church. *Minute Book, 1805–1855*. Rappahannock County, Virginia.

———. *Minute Book, 1855–1878*. Rappahannock County, Virginia.

———. *Minute Book, 1878–1894*. Rappahannock County, Virginia.

Fisher, Betty Kilby. *Wit, Will & Walls*. Euless, Texas: Cultural Innovations, 2002.

Foner, Eric. *Forever Free: The Story of Emancipation and Reconstruction*. New York: Alfred A. Knopf, 2005.

Glymph, Thavolia. *Out of the House of Bondage: The Transformation of the Plantation Household*. New York: Cambridge University Press, 2008.

Gourdvine Baptist Church. *Minute Book, 1812–1832.* Culpeper County, Virginia.

———. *Minute Book, 1835–1853.* Culpeper County, Virginia.

Grimsley, Daniel A. *Battles in Culpeper County, Virginia, 1861–1865.* Culpeper, Virginia: Raleigh Travers Green, 1900.

Hening, William Waller, ed. *The Statutes at Large; Being a Collection of All the Laws of Virginia from the First Session of the Legislature, in the Year 1619.* New York: R. & W. & G. Bartow, 1823.

Jacobs, Harriet A. *Incidents in the Life of a Slave Girl: Written by Herself.* Edited by Jean Fagan Yellin. Cambridge, Massachusettes: Harvard University Press, 1987.

Jeter, Henry N. *Shiloh Baptist Church and Her History.* Providence, Rhode Island: Remington Printing Company, 1901.

Jones-Rogers, Stephanie. *They Were Her Property.* New Haven: Yale University Press, 2019.

Kaleo, Nancy Lee Hawkins. *Hawkins and Allied Families: A Genealogy and Family History.* University Park, Maryland: Wordsworth Ink, 1991.

Kilby, James Wilson and Kilby-Robb, Patricia. *The Kilby Legacy: I Stretch My Hands to Thee.* USA: Kilby Publications, 1999.

King, Wilma. *Stolen Childhood: Slave Youth in Nineteenth-Century America.* Second Edition. Bloomington, Indiana: Indiana University Press, 2011.

Kleinberg, S.J. *The Shadow of the Mills: Working-Class Families in Pittsburgh, 1870–1907.* Pittsburgh: University of Pittsburgh Press, 1989.

Libes, Joyce Colleen. *John Kilby of Culpeper County, Virginia: A Report on Some of His Descendants.* Self-published, 1992.

Litwack, Leon F. *Been in the Storm So Long: The Aftermath of Slavery.* New York: Alfred A. Knopf, 1979.

Mitchell, Mary Niall. *Raising Freedom's Child: Black Children and Visions of the Future after Slavery.* New York: New York University Press, 2008.

Morgan, Lynda J. *Emancipation in Virginia's Tobacco Belt, 1850–1870.* Athens, Georgia: University of Georgia Press, 1992.

———. *Known for My Work: African American Ethics from Slavery to Freedom.* Gainesville, Florida: University Press of Florida, 2016.

New Salem Baptist Church. *Records, 1834-1873.* Culpeper County, Virginia.

Patterson, David E. "The 1850 and 1860 Census, Schedule 2, Slave Inhabitants." Afrigeneas Library, May 16, 2015. https://www.afrigeneas.com/library/slave_schedule2.html.

Riggs, David F. *7th Virginia Infantry.* Second Edition. Lynchburg, Virginia: H.E. Howard, 1982.

Scheel, Eugene M. *Culpeper: A Virginia County's History Through 1920.* Culpeper, Virginia: The Culpeper Historical Society, 1982.

Scott, Emmett J. *Scott's Official History of the American Negro in the World War*. 1919. Archive.org. https://archive.org/details/scottsofficialhiooscot/.

Stokes, Keith. *Gilded Age Newport in Color*. http://www.guildedageincolor.com/.

Thompson, A. Paul. *F.T. Baptist Church 1778–1978*. Orange, Virginia: Green Publishers, 1979.

Wiencek, Henry. *Master of the Mountain: Thomas Jefferson and His Slaves*. New York: Farrar, Straus and Giroux, 2012.

Wilkerson, Isabel. *Caste: The Origins of Our Discontents*. New York: Random House, 2020.

———. *The Warmth of Other Suns*. New York: Random House, 2010.

Wills, Gregory A. *Democratic Religion: Freedom, Authority, and Church Discipline in the Baptist South, 1785-1900*. New York: Oxford University Press, 1997.

Zaborney, John J. *Slaves For Hire: Renting Enslaved Laborers in Antebellum Virginia*. Baton Rouge, Louisana: Louisana State University Press, 2012.

Index

absence, 29, 31, 49, 62, 84, 100-101, 111, 136
abuse, 126, 135-136
accident, accidental, 17, 26, 117
accomplishment, achievement, xix, 79, 84, 87, 122
accusation, 46, 65
activities, 3, 28, 61, 87, 110, 121
administrator/administratrix, 6, 16-17, 27-28, 30-31, 41, 48, 90
advantages, 9, 87, 89, 135
affection, 17, 102
Africa, 132
agreement, 30, 73
Alexandria Gazette, 76, 105
Allegheny Cemetery, 110, 112
ambition, 5, 12, 77, 89, 118
ancestors, xviii, xix, 24, 101, 128-132
Andrew (enslaved by James Hawkins), 15-16
Apperson, William C., 53-54
appointed, 17-18, 65, 90
apprenticeship, 72
archives, xviii, xx, 109
Argonne Forest, Battle of, 119
article, 74-76, 87, 121, 125
assault, 39, 45, 74, 76, 126

assessment, 23, 29, 134
associates, xviii, 12, 42, 84, 137
atDNA. *See* autosomal DNA
attitudes, xviii, 11, 64, 76, 92
auction, 14-15
authority, 49, 57, 61, 72, 84, 87
autonomy, 92, 94
autosomal DNA (atDNA), 129-132
Bagby, George, 74
Ball, Edward, 88
baptism, 46, 64, 66-67, 73
Baptist, 10, 38, 45-46, 52, 57, 63-67, 73-74, 90, 92, 94, 96-97, 107, 110-111, 116, 122
bargain, 28, 42, 46, 50
bartering, 89
battles, 3, 77
behavior, 77, 79
beliefs, xviii, xx, 10, 14, 32, 34, 37, 47-48, 62, 77, 91-92, 96, 98, 102, 135-136
benefit, 10, 42, 53, 89, 92
Ben (enslaved by James Hawkins), 15-16
Betty (enslaved by James Hawkins), xxi, 15-16, 44, 101
bigotry, 74, 115

biological, xviii, 16, 97, 99, 102, 113–114, 125–126, 128–131
birthday, 88, 137
Birth of a Nation, 76
birthright, xviii, 133
Bloomfield, 106–107
bondage, xviii, 11–13, 30, 32–33, 35, 39, 45, 48, 56, 71, 97–98, 104, 114, 136
bonds, 16–17, 84
Braman Cemetery, 122
brick, 22, 24–26, 106
Brown, Joshua, 74
Buckner, John Strother, 60
Buffalo Soldier Division, 119
buildings, 20, 23–24, 53, 94, 106–107
buried, 85, 97, 103, 110
Butler, Madeline. *See* Kilby, Madeline
cabin, 3, 20–21, 23–24, 30
Canonchet Lodge of GUOOF, 121
capitation tax, 11
carpenter, carpentry, 53, 96
Carr, Armstead, 103
Carr, Bettie (Kilby), 103. *See also* Kilby, Bettie
Carron Street Baptist Church, 107, 110–111
censuses, 11, 13–14, 58, 62, 69; 1820 census, 13; 1830 census, 16, 44; 1840 census, 29, 48; 1850 census, 47–49, 53; 1860 census, 32–33, 48, 51, 53–54; 1870 census, 59, 60–63, 88, 104, 113; 1880 census, 63, 67, 85, 102; 1900 census, 93, 99, 103, 107, 118; 1910 census, 93, 96, 100; 1920 census, 110, 118, 120
certificate: birth, 88; death, 68, 87, 103
chancery court, 6, 30, 32, 38–39, 53, 69
charges, charged, 27, 34, 46, 52, 55, 65–67
chattel, 6, 15, 28, 30, 42, 47, 51, 126
choice, xix, xx, 1, 20, 41–42, 57–58, 62, 66, 69, 76, 83–84, 101, 105, 116, 126, 134, 136–137
Christmas, 36, 91
chromosomes, 129
church, 10, 21, 37–38, 45–48, 52, 57, 63–67, 73–74, 78, 90, 92, 94, 96–97, 100, 107, 110–111, 116, 122
church discipline, 65. *See also* excluded from a church congregation
Civil War, 3, 5, 33–36, 38–39, 55, 59–60, 63, 71, 73–74, 76–78, 88–89, 113, 115, 126, 135
clerk, 37, 64, 91–92, 98
clothe, clothing, 8, 28, 71–72, 84, 102, 137
coachman, 105
coerce, 72, 92, 126
collateral, 6, 49
Colletta, John Philip, 62
commissioner, 55
community, xvii, xviii, 12, 33, 38, 43–44, 71, 74, 86, 90, 116, 121–122
Community League, 86–87
concealment, 46

conditions, 30, 72-73, 92
Confederacy, 33, 55
Confederate, 34, 36, 39, 86
Confederate Army, 34, 36, 39, 86
Confederate States, 34
Connor, John, 46
consent, 68, 91, 135
contract, 61, 72, 89
control, xvii, 4, 6, 18, 27, 47-48, 50, 76, 88, 135
cook, 54, 63, 67, 85, 99, 102, 119
couple, 64, 73, 90, 92-96, 131
courage, 76, 96
court, 4, 15, 17-18, 27-28, 31-32, 37-38, 41, 72, 78, 91, 117
courthouse, 50
crops, 8, 10, 18, 20-21, 27-30, 32, 49, 78, 89, 114. *See also* grain
cruelty, 17, 48, 50, 78, 136
Daily Independent, The, 100
danger, 115
deaths, deceased, 28, 31-33, 37, 44, 48, 64, 66-68, 87, 120, 137
debt, 6, 17, 27-29, 43, 45, 49, 79, 115, 135-136
decisions, 14, 27, 32, 41-42, 65, 69, 84, 90, 105, 114, 116
deeds: deeds in general, 58; deeds of trust (mortgage), 29-30, 41, 49; land deeds, 20, 69; deeds of sale, 50-51, 69
Delbanco, Andrew, 135
demand, 3, 61, 82, 92, 104
denial, xvii, 40, 126, 134, 136-137
dependency, 17, 27, 89, 102, 114
deprived, 7, 88
determination, 6, 76, 94, 96, 104, 122

devoted, 100, 121
dignity, xix, 57, 96, 98, 112, 122, 137
dismission from a church congregation, 73
dispute, 6, 31, 41
divorce, 118-121
Douglass, Frederick, 83, 88, 122-123, 135
duties, 5, 28, 63
Duvall, Rev. Willis Duvall, 110
education, 73, 92, 118, 135
Ellison, Ralph, 58
emancipation, xvii, 40, 56, 73, 78, 84, 89, 114, 136, 138
Emancipation Day, 110
Emancipation Proclamation, 39
employment, employee, employer, 53-54, 68, 71, 92, 104-105, 115, 117-119, 121
endurance, xvii, 9, 13, 77, 88, 94, 98, 135-138
enfranchisement, 92
enlist, 33-34, 120
enslaved, xvii, xviii, xix, 6, 8-14, 16-19, 23-24, 26, 29, 32-33, 39, 41-50, 53, 55, 59-60, 63, 69, 71, 84, 87, 101, 113, 126, 134
enslavement, 14, 72, 138
enslaver, xvii, xix, 4, 6, 9-11, 13-14, 17, 34, 36, 42-43, 45, 47-48, 50, 54, 56-57, 60, 62-63, 69, 78, 84-85, 89, 92, 113, 126, 135-136
enumerate, enumerator, 29, 53, 61
escape, 5, 34, 39, 121

estate, 6, 8-10, 14, 16, 19, 23, 27-32, 38, 41, 43, 46, 48, 50-51, 69, 78, 90
European-descended, xx
Evans, Bessie Belle Hawkins, 51
excluded from a church congregation, 52, 64-66, 74
exploited, 73, 84
FamilyTreeDNA, 127
farmer, 12, 95-96
farmhand, 90, 96, 98, 105
farming, 8, 11, 27, 29, 42, 71, 90, 94
Finks, Andrew, 96
Finks, Paschal, 68, 89-92, 96
Fitzhugh, John, 76
Five Forks, Battle of, 34
Foner, Eric, 101
forebears, xix, 101, 132
forefathers, 128
France, 119
freedmen (male and female), 57-58, 61, 72-73, 89, 92, 105
Freedmen's Bureau (Bureau of Refugees, Freedmen, and Abandoned Lands), 57, 72-73, 89
freedom, 3, 5-6, 35-36, 39-40, 56-57, 63-64, 70-72, 76-77, 81, 83, 85, 114-115, 121-122, 126, 134, 136, 138
freed people, 6, 40, 57, 59, 71-72, 74, 77, 89, 92, 112
Frye, Malinda Green. *See* Kilby, Malinda Green
Frye, Oliver, 95
F.T. Baptist Church, 38, 57, 63-66, 73, 90, 92

F.T. Valley, 63
F.T. Village, 63
Gassaway, Gladys. *See* Kilby, Gladys
genealogical research, xviii, xix, xx, xxi, 48, 125, 137-138
genealogy, xviii, xx, xxi, 48, 126, 130, 132
genetic, xviii, xxi, 125-129, 131-132
genetic genealogy, xviii, xxi, 126
Gettysburg, 34
Gillison, Wesley, 74
Glasscock, James, 46
Glasscock, Susannah, 46
Gourdvine Baptist Church, 45
Gourdvine Neck, 3-4, 9, 36, 38, 56, 74
grain: corn, 21, 30, 34, 114; rye, 18, 21; wheat, 18, 21, 30
Grand United Order of Odd Fellows (GUOOF), 96, 121-122
grievance, 6, 33, 72
Grimsley, Rev. Aldridge, 38, 73, 92
guardian, 18, 91
Gufson, Herbert, 58
haplogroup, 128, 132
hardship, xvii, 7, 89, 97, 104, 134-135
Hawkins, Albert, 44
Hawkins, Augustine, 15-16, 28, 44, 60
Hawkins, James, 8-9, 14-16, 28, 43-44, 129
Hawkins, Malinda, 8-10, 13. *See also* Kilby, Malinda (Hawkins)

INDEX

Hawkins, Matthew, 9, 44
Hawkins, Sarah, 8
Hawkins, Thomas J., 16, 44
Hazel River, 4
healing, 40
help, helping, xxi, 9, 28, 32, 91-92, 110, 112, 116-117, 136
Henrietta _____, 66
Henry (enslaved by James Hawkins and Thomas Kilby), 15-16, 18, 23, 26, 28-30, 42-43, 45
Hill, Bertie (Kilby), 93-94
Hill, Oscar Albert, 94
hire, hiring, 14, 45, 49-50, 136
homeplace, homestead, 23, 32, 45, 49
Honesty, Arthur, 100
Honesty, Ella May (Reynolds), 99-100
hostility, 6, 77, 105, 115
housekeeper, 102, 118
housework, 99, 102
Hughes River, 4, 9, 64
human being, xviii, 6, 8, 12, 32, 115, 136
humane, humanely, 79, 136
humanity, xix, 7, 40, 42, 48, 135
Hurley, Armstead, 116
identity, xvii, xviii, xix, 6, 12, 14, 26, 29, 40-42, 49, 56-58, 60, 62, 64, 66, 68-70, 88, 101, 125-126, 129-130, 133, 137
immigrant, 104, 120
independence, 27, 57, 83, 94, 122
infant, 17, 42, 55
infantry, 34, 119
influence, 83, 105

informant, 62, 125, 138
infraction, 46, 51, 53, 65, 114
injustice, 7, 97
intestate, 28, 38, 50
inventory, 10, 15, 17-19, 29, 41, 43
Isaac (enslaved by James Hawkins), 15
Johnson, Elizabeth [Lacy/Lizzie] (Kilby), 114, 117-118
Johnson, Thomas, 118
judgment, 28, 72-73, 134-135
Julia. *See* Juliet Ann
Juliet Ann, xvii, 4-7, 13, 18, 26, 29-33, 35, 38-42, 44-45, 47-51, 53-69, 72-73, 78, 82-85, 87-89, 97-98, 102-104, 113-114, 121-122, 125-134, 136-138. *See also* Milton, Juliet
Kilby, Adeline, 13, 32, 48-49, 78
Kilby, Albert Chesterfield, 13, 30-32, 48-49, 53, 55, 78
Kilby, Alice, 59, 62
Kilby, Aronia, 107
Kilby, Bertie. *See* Hill, Bertie
Kilby, Bessie. *See* Mayers, Bessie
Kilby, Bettie [Elizabeth/Betsy] (daughter of Juliet), 63, 67, 84-85, 101-103, 125-126, 131, 138. *See also* Carr, Bettie
Kilby, Catherline (Thomas), 96
Kilby, Charles William [Simon], 50-51, 69, 97. *See also* Kilby, Simon
Kilby, Cora Blanche. *See* Wilson, Cora Blanche
Kilby, Elizabeth (Jackson), 119
Kilby, Elizabeth [Lacy/Lizzie]. *See* Johnson, Elizabeth

216　INDEX

Kilby, Flora Bernice. *See* Walker, Flora Bernice
Kilby, Geo [George/Georgianna], 137
Kilby, Gladys (Gassaway), 119
Kilby, Hamilton Burgess, 13, 34, 48-51, 53, 55, 69, 78
Kilby, Henry William, 117, 119-120
Kilby, Hope Louise, 119
Kilby, Hubert Reid, 93, 95-96
Kilby, James Franklin, 13, 23, 32, 34, 39, 49-53, 55, 69, 78, 131
Kilby, James Henry, 119-120
Kilby, James Jr., 115, 117, 119-120
Kilby, James Oscar, 93, 96
Kilby, James (son of Juliet), xxi, 5, 38-39, 60, 62, 66, 72, 76, 84-85, 93, 96, 101, 113-122, 125-127
Kilby, James (White, son of John, father of Thomas), 10-12, 127-129
Kilby, John Henry, 93, 96-97
Kilby, John (son of James and Mary), 117, 119
Kilby, John (son of Juliet), 5, 32, 38-39, 46, 53, 60, 62, 66, 72, 76, 84-85, 100-101, 103-107, 110-112, 114, 125-127, 131, 133, 137
Kilby, John (White, father of James, grandfather of Thomas), 10-12, 128-129
Kilby, Joseph Mortimer, 6, 13, 30-34, 38-39, 48-49, 53, 55, 69, 78, 104, 113, 131
Kilby, Joseph (White, son of James), 11, 127

Kilby, Julia Belle. *See* Parrish, Julia Belle
Kilby, Lawrence, 119-120
Kilby, Lena Pauline. *See* Vieira, Lena Pauline
Kilby, Leroy (White, son of James), xviii, 11-12, 20, 127
Kilby, Louisa, 13, 48-49, 66, 78
Kilby, Louise (Levin), 120
Kilby, Lucretia, 51
Kilby, Lucy Frances "Fannie" (Wallace), 69, 90-92, 97-99, 102, 111, 137-138
Kilby, Lucy (Sparks), 10, 12
Kilby, Madelene Alberta, 117
Kilby, Malinda Green (Frye), 95-96
Kilby, Malinda (Hawkins), xvii, xviii, 5-6, 9, 13-14, 16-18, 21-23, 25, 27-35, 37-38, 41-43, 45-56, 58, 69, 78, 97-98, 104, 126, 131, 134-138
Kilby, Margaret (Hudson), 51
Kilby, Martha Ann, 13, 48, 78. *See also* Wright, Martha Ann "Mattie"
Kilby, Mary Eliza (Richardson), 114-122
Kilby, Mary Ella (Smith), 96-97
Kilby, Missouri, 13, 48-49, 78
Kilby, Ophelia. *See* Washington, Ophelia
Kilby, Pattie Malinda, 110
Kilby, Richard, 117, 119-120
Kilby, Richard Jr., 119-120
Kilby, Robert, 102
Kilby, Sarah (daughter of Juliet), 5, 39, 62, 66, 72, 76, 83-85,

98-99, 101, 111. *See also*
   Reynolds, Sarah (Kilby)
Kilby, Simon, 5, 32-33, 38-39, 51,
   53, 56, 60-62, 66-69, 72-74, 76,
   83-94, 96-97, 99, 101-102, 111,
   114, 125-133, 137-138
Kilby, Thomas L., 13, 51,
   53, 55, 78
Kilby, Thomas (White, son of
   James), xviii, 5-6, 10-14, 16-17,
   19-23, 25, 27-33, 38, 41-46,
   48-50, 58, 78, 93, 97, 127-129,
   131, 134-135
Kilby, Thompson Albert, 11
Kilby, Tula (Richards) Henry, 119
Kilby, Violet (Green), 119
Kilby, Virenda, 46
Kilby v. Thornhill, 38
Kilby, Walter, 117, 119-120
Ku Klux Klan (KKK), 74-75, 86
laborer, 11-12, 73, 84, 94, 104,
   114-118
land acreage, 8, 12, 20, 23, 28,
   30, 94, 96
landowner, 9-10, 12, 24, 29, 53, 61,
   63, 68, 78, 84, 89-90, 92, 94, 96
laundress, 102, 110, 118
Lawrenceville, 106
lawsuit, 31, 38, 41, 69
ledger, 11, 13-14, 47, 49
legacy, xviii, xix, 79, 96, 101, 122,
   135-136
Levin, Louise. *See* Kilby, Louise
Lewis, Rev. A., 98, 114
Libes, Joyce Colleen, 51-52, 134
literacy, 8, 90-91
Litwack, Leon, 57-58, 84

livestock: unspecified livestock,
   11-12, 17-18, 21, 28-29, 34-35,
   55, 78, 89; cattle, 5, 8, 10, 33, 55;
   hogs, 5, 8, 10; horses, 4, 10, 55,
   117; sheep, 8, 10, 33
Lord Fairfax. *See* Thomas Lord
   Fairfax
love/loving, xvii, 17, 42, 84, 87, 97,
   110, 112, 121-122, 126, 136
lumber, 20, 32, 94
Madison County Eagle, 87, 97
Marble House, 117
Mary (enslaved by James
   Hawkins), 15-16, 44
Masons, Stone Mill Lodge of,
   121-122
maturity, 6, 18, 43, 69, 71
Mayers, Bessie (Kilby), 117
membership, 47, 52, 64-65, 73, 96
merchant, 68, 89-90
migrate, 104-105, 115
Miles, David, 105
Miles, Patsy, 105
Miles, Sarah, 112
Miles, Virginia Frances, 105-107,
   110-112
military, 5, 33-34, 57, 72, 119-120
Milton, Juliet, 66-67
minister, 10, 74, 110
misconduct, 53
Mitchell, Mary Niall, 72
mitochondrial DNA
   (mtDNA), 132
mtDNA. *See*
   mitochondrial DNA
Muddy Run, 12, 21, 30, 34
Native Virginia, The, 74

Nazareth Baptist Church, 74, 94, 96-97
Nazareth Baptist Church Cemetery, 96-97
Newport, 115-118, 120-122
Newport Mercury, 121
New Salem Baptist Church, 45-46, 52, 64
newspapers, 33, 37, 68, 74-77, 90, 100, 105, 110-111, 116, 121
Nigeria, 132
Oakwood Cemetery, 103
occupation, 33, 51, 53, 98, 105, 116
Odd Fellows. *See* Grand United Order of Odd Fellows
opportunity, 38, 40, 44, 57, 73, 87, 92, 104, 114-115, 118, 129
oppression, 76, 85, 89, 92, 121, 136
orphan, 72
over*seer*, 51, 53, 92, 98, 126
Parrish, Julia Belle (Kilby), 100, 107, 111-112
Parrish, Zebedee, 107
partus sequitur ventrem, 113
pastor, 38, 46, 64, 73, 92, 110
paternity, 45, 91, 125-129, 131
"patterolls" [patrols], 33
Pennsylvania Railroad, 119-120
Pittsburgh, 100, 104-106, 108-112
plaintiff, 31, 38-39
plantation, 10-14, 17, 22-23, 25, 32, 36, 38-39, 42-44, 49, 52, 55, 61, 71, 78, 98, 112
planter, 5, 10, 12, 71-72, 92, 115
porter. *See* Pullman porter
power, xviii, xx, 4, 39, 44-45, 57, 72, 83, 92, 134, 136
prejudice, xvii, 40, 76, 89, 117

presentism, 135
privilege, xvii, xx, 3-4, 10, 40, 87-88, 134-135
probate, 10, 15, 18, 43
profession, 96, 110
Pullman porter, 119-120
punishment, 65, 76, 114, 137
Rachel (enslaved by James Hawkins), 15-16
racial discrimination, 85, 121
Ragged Mountain, 3
rape, 44, 67, 137
rations, 36, 72
Reconstruction, 60, 72-73, 92, 112
recruiter, 115-116
relief, 23, 29, 72, 136
resistance, 5, 26
respect, xix, 11, 64, 68, 98, 112, 117, 122, 126
Reynolds, Ella. *See* Honesty, Ella May
Reynolds, Horace, 98
Reynolds, James, 98-99
Reynolds, Jane, 98
Reynolds, Sarah (Kilby), 98-100, 111. *See also* Kilby, Sarah
Richardson, James, 121
Richardson, Lena, 115
Richardson, Mary Eliza. *See* Kilby, Mary Eliza
Richmond Road, 21, 34, 45
rights, 38-39, 43, 48, 50, 78, 94, 134
Rudasilla, Jacob, 16
Saint Stephen CME Church, 100
sale, transfer, or pledging of property: human property,

14-18, 28-30, 38, 42-43, 46-47, 49-51, 136; personal property, 14-18, 28-29, 42-43, 49, 136
Sarah (mother of Juliet Ann), 13, 15-16, 18, 23, 26, 28, 30, 41-48, 50, 97-98, 129-132, 138
school, 72-73, 76, 84, 86, 100, 104, 114, 118, 121
Schoolhouse Blizzard, 78
Scott, John, 46
secrets, xix, 24, 37, 56, 91
Selective Service Act of 1917, 119
separation, 17, 39, 48, 136
servitude, xix, 73
sexton, 90
sexual abuse, sexual assault, rape, 43-45, 67, 126, 137
Shadow and Act, 58
sharecropping, 89
Sheffield Avenue, 118, 120-121
Shiloh Baptist Church, 116, 122
singer, 111
skills, 71, 83, 89, 91, 117
slave schedule, 11, 48, 53-54
Smith, Mary Ella. *See* Kilby, Mary Ella
Sperryville Pike, 34
spiritual (belief), 45, 63-64, 73, 110
Stailing, Louisa, 66
Stokes, Keith, 115
Stonehouse Mountain, 12, 30, 34
Stringfellow, Mary, 46-48
Strother, Eveline, 114
Strother, Mary Eliza. *See* Kilby, Mary Eliza
struggles, struggling, xvii, 6, 28, 77, 79, 85, 92, 121, 138

surnames, 56-64, 66, 68-69, 114, 126-127, 133
taxable property, 11, 14, 43, 45, 47, 49, 55
tax books, 11-12
taxes, 11, 29, 45, 55
teamster, 105
Thomas, Catherline. *See* Kilby, Catherline
Thomas Lord Fairfax, 10
Thompson, Rev. A. Paul, 65
Thornhill, Bluford, 5, 16, 34-37, 39, 44, 56-61, 63-64, 66-67, 72-73, 78, 84-85, 88-90, 101-102, 104, 114
Thornhill, Lucy (Hawkins), 34-37, 64
Thornhill, Malinda (Hawkins) Kilby, 5-6, 37-39, 59-61, 63-64, 72-73, 77-79, 84, 87-90, 101-102, 104, 114, 134
Thornton, Francis, 63
Thornton's Gap Turnpike, 21, 34
timber, 4, 12, 30, 35
tobacco, 36
troops, 33-34, 36
trusts. *See* deeds
USS Arizona, 120
victim, 13, 48, 76, 135-136
Vieira, George, 118, 120
Vieira, George Jr., 120
Vieira, Lena Pauline (Kilby), 115, 117-118, 120
Walden, John, 60
Walker, Flora Bernice (Kilby), 107, 110-112
Walker, Frances Bernice, 107
Walker, Jane, 60-61, 98, 115, 137

Walker [Kilby], Elizabeth, 11, 60, 63, 67-68. *See also* Kilby, Bettie (daughter of Juliet)
Walker [Kilby], James, 60. *See also* Kilby, James (son of Juliet Ann)
Walker [Kilby], John, 60. *See also* Kilby, John (son of Juliet Ann)
Walker [Kilby], Sarah, 60. *See also* Kilby, Sarah (daughter of Juliet Ann)
Walker, Lewis, 60-62, 84, 94, 96, 115
Walker, Lindsay, 60, 115-116
Walker, Robert Monroe, 107
Walker, Sarah, 60
Wallace, Annie, 33
Wallace, Lucy Frances, 69, 90-92. *See also* Kilby, Lucy Frances "Fannie" (Wallace)
Wallace, Martha (Parks), 90-92
Wallace, Walker, 90, 92, 94
Washington, Major, 95
Washington, Ophelia (Kilby), 93-95
wealth, 5, 8-9, 11-12, 30, 44, 79, 134
weather conditions: breezes, 3, 20; chilly, 3; hail, 36; hot sun, 30; rain, 105; snow/blizzard, 36, 78; storm, 36, 76
Wiginton, Juliet, 66
Wilkerson, Isabel, 115
Wilson, Cora Blanche (Kilby), 102-103
Wilson, Lindsay Edward, 103
World War I, 107, 110, 119-120
World War II, 120
worship, 63, 65-66, 121
Wright, Martha Ann "Mattie" (Kilby), 93-94. *See also* Kilby, Martha Ann
Wright, Sim, 94, 132, 137
Y-chromosome, 127-129
Y-DNA, 127-129, 132
yeoman, 10

About the Author

Timothy Kilby is a fifth-generation direct descendant of James Kilby (c. 1740–1829) of Culpeper County, Virginia, the ancestor in common with the lineal descendants of Juliet Ann, the enslaved woman biographed in this book.

Tim grew up in the village of Sperryville, Rappahannock County, Virginia, not far from the homesteads of his forefathers. He went on to earn a baccalaureate from Virginia Tech and a master's degree from Rochester Institute of Technology. Tim had careers in education, art, and information technology before retiring in 2014. His interest in family history began at an early age, but only in the last decade did he devote research into the people and events recounted in this narrative.

Colophon

This book was designed and composed in its entirety by the author. The body text is set in Bembo typeface, chapter headings in Rockwell, and captions and subheadings in Alegreya Sans.